CAPE TOWN

THE MINI ROUGH GUIDE

D0913623

There are more than one hundred and fifty
Rough Guide travel, phrasebook, and music titles,
covering destinations from Amsterdam to Zimbabwe,
languages from Czech to Thai, and music from
World to Opera and Jazz

Forthcoming titles include

Argentina • Croatia • Ecuador
Southeast Asia

Rough Guides on the Internet

www.roughguides.com

Rough Guide Credits

Text editor: Helena Smith
Series editor: Mark Ellingham
Typesetting: Robert Evers
Cartography: Ed Wright

Publishing Information

This first edition published August 2000 by
Rough Guides Ltd, 62–70 Shorts Gardens, London WC2H 9AB

Distributed by the Penguin Group:

Penguin Books Ltd, 27 Wrights Lane, London W8 5TZ
Penguin Putnam, Inc. 375 Hudson Street, New York, NY 10014, USA
Penguin Books Australia Ltd, 487 Maroondah Highway,
PO Box 257, Ringwood, Victoria 3134, Australia
Penguin Books Canada Ltd, 10 Alcorn Avenue,
Toronto, Ontario, Canada M4V 1E4
Penguin Books (NZ) Ltd, 182–190 Wairau Road,
Auckland 10, New Zealand

Typeset in Bembo and Helvetica to an original design by Henry Iles.
Printed in Spain by Graphy Cems.

© Tony Pinchuck and Barbara McCrea 2000
368pp includes index
A catalogue record for this book is available from the British Library.
ISBN 1-85828-548-8

CAPE TOWN

THE MINI ROUGH GUIDE

**by Tony Pinchuck
and Barbara McCrea**

**with contributions by
Carlos Amato**

ROUGH
GUIDES

We set out to do something different when the first Rough Guide was published in 1982. Mark Ellingham, just out of university, was travelling in Greece. He brought along the popular guides of the day, but found they were all lacking in some way. They were either strong on ruins and museums but went on for pages without mentioning a beach or taverna. Or they were so conscious of the need to save money that they lost sight of Greece's cultural and historical significance. Also, none of the books told him anything about Greece's contemporary life – its politics, its culture, its people, and how they lived.

So with no job in prospect, Mark decided to write his own guidebook, one which aimed to provide practical information that was second to none, detailing the best beaches and the hottest clubs and restaurants, while also giving hard-hitting accounts of every sight, both famous and obscure, and providing up-to-the-minute information on contemporary culture. It was a guide that encouraged independent travellers to find the best of Greece, and was a great success, getting shortlisted for the Thomas Cook travel guide award, and encouraging Mark, along with three friends, to expand the series.

The Rough Guide list grew rapidly and the letters flooded in, indicating a much broader readership than had been anticipated, but one which uniformly appreciated the Rough Guide mix of practical detail and humour, irreverence and enthusiasm. Things haven't changed. The same four friends who began the series are still the caretakers of the Rough Guide mission today: to provide the most reliable, up-to-date and entertaining information to independent-minded travellers of all ages, on all budgets.

We now publish more than 150 titles and have offices in London and New York. The travel guides are written and researched by a dedicated team of more than 100 authors, based in Britain, Europe, the USA and Australia. We have also created a unique series of phrasebooks to accompany the travel series, along with an acclaimed series of music guides, and a best-selling pocket guide to the Internet and World Wide Web. We also publish comprehensive travel information on our Web site: **www.roughguides.com**

Help Us Update

We've gone to a lot of effort to ensure that this first edition of *The Rough Guide to Cape Town* is as up to date and accurate as possible. However, if you feel there are places we've underrated or over-praised, or find we've missed something good or covered something which has now gone, then please write: suggestions, comments or corrections are much appreciated.

We'll credit all contributions, and send a copy of the next edition (or any other Rough Guide if you prefer) for the best letters. Please mark letters: "Rough Guide Cape Town Update" and send to:

Rough Guides, 62–70 Shorts Gardens, London WC2H 9AB, or
Rough Guides, 4th Floor, 345 Hudson St, New York, NY 10014.

Or send email to: mail@roughguides.co.uk
Online updates about this book can be found on
Rough Guides' Web site (see opposite)

Acknowledgements

Thanks at the Rough Guides to our wonderful editor, Helena Smith, who piloted the book around the Cape Peninsula and kept us on course with her unfailingly perceptive comments. In the Eastern Cape, thanks to our mothers Lily Pinchuck and Pat McCrea for meals, beds and childminding services. In Cape Town, thanks to Ida Cooper for her inside knowledge; Carlos Amato for his lively coverage of music, clubs, books and other fun stuff; Ian Donald for fixing our coverage of sport; Dave Pinchuck for answering endless questions about the Cape Flats; Patch Pinnock for providing foundations; Sheryl Ozinsky and staff at Cape Town Tourism for their friendly help; and Gabriel Pinchuck for his excellent research into beaches, playgrounds, noisy cars, the local dogs and cafés that serve foamy milk.

The editor would like to thank Jo Mead in editorial; Robert Evers for typesetting; Ed Wright for the maps; Louise Boulton for the cover; Susannah Wight for proofreading; and Judith Bamber for the index.

The Authors

Tony Pinchuck launched his travels hitching around South Africa when he was fifteen. At university he studied African politics, and also drew political cartoon strips, several of which were banned by the apartheid government, after which he left for the UK. He lived in London for eighteen years, earning a living as a designer, cartoonist, editor and writer, and has published articles on southern Africa, as well as ten books, including *Mandela for Beginners*, *The Rough Guide to South Africa* and *The Rough Guide to Zimbabwe*. His latest project has been an experiment in travelling with a child, using his young son, Gabriel, as a guinea pig. He now lives in Kalk Bay, Cape Town.

Barbara McCrea was born in Zimbabwe and went to university in South Africa, going on to teach African literature at the University of Durban-Westville for two years, before going to London in 1983. Driven by homesickness, she wrote *The Rough Guide to Zimbabwe* with Tony Pinchuck, before tackling even lengthier travels for the South Africa and Cape Town guides. Besides writing and travelling between South Africa and London, she works as a movement education teacher, and looks after three-year-old Gabriel in Kalk Bay, Cape Town, where she lives.

CONTENTS

Contents

Introduction

Cape Town's setting, on the Cape Peninsula, is simply stunning. A rugged tail of land washed by two seaboards and dominated by iconic **Table Mountain**, the peninsula culminates dramatically at the **Cape of Good Hope Nature Reserve** and the sea-pounded cliffs of **Cape Point**. To really get to grips with Cape Town you need to spend time outdoors: if walking up Table Mountain sounds like hard work, you can always take the cable car – or catch the train down the False Bay coast to claim a piece of the 150km of sandy beach that fringes the peninsula. Inland, there are terrific opportunities for hiking and picnicking in the many gardens and forests.

The heart of the city is an attractive collage of Georgian, Cape Dutch and Victorian architecture, built on the foundations of the **slave society** that occupied it for the first half of its 350-year existence. Eyed by the Portuguese, Dutch and English in their turn, it became the place where Europe, Asia and Africa met – in markets, alleyways and mosques. Today the **city centre** is as much of a cultural melting pot as ever, where coloured families from the Cape Flats do their shopping, young whites hang out in hip coffee bars, Muslims pray, street kids loiter on corners, buskers play to passing crowds and Africans converge from across the continent to hawk crafts.

While it's the legislative capital of South Africa, Cape Town is the least "African" city in the country: less than a quarter of its population are black Africans. The city's unique feature is the Creolized **coloured culture**, which evolved from the interaction between Europeans and slaves from East Africa and the Far East. Mosques in the Bo-Kaap quarter, adjacent to the city centre, add spice to the colonial streetscape; **Cape cuisine** combines local ingredients with Eastern flavours; and **Cape jazz** is heard in the coloured townships of the Cape Flats as well as city-centre clubs. Over fifty percent of Capetonians are **coloured**, while about 27 percent are **white**, descended mainly from Dutch and British settlers. To complicate matters, language fails to line up conveniently with ethnicity, and **Afrikaans**, the city's most widely spoken language, is used by a large proportion of coloureds and many whites. The city's minority African population predominantly speak **Xhosa**, one of South Africa's nine African languages, but **English** is the effective lingua franca of the city, and will get you by 99 percent of the time. For more on coloured culture, and the complex dynamics of race in Cape Town, see p.317.

With its cultural variety, high standards of accommodation, smart restaurants, slick clubs, laid-back cafés and vibrant gay scene, Cape Town offers a truly cosmopolitan experience. Most visitors see areas that were classified under apartheid as "white" and still remain relatively safe and salubrious: radiating out from the city centre, the largely affluent suburbs cling to the slopes of Table Mountain or perch at the edge of the peninsula's two coasts. But for most Capetonians, exiled to the crowded **townships** and **shantytowns** on the **Cape Flats**, the harsh reality is one of sky-high murder rates, taxi wars, racketeering and gang fights. These areas, to the east of the city, should only be visited on a guided tour.

A stone's throw from the centre, the **V & A Waterfront**

is Cape Town's most popular spot for shopping, eating and drinking in a highly picturesque setting among the piers and quays of a working harbour; from here catamarans cut across Table Bay to **Robben Island**, the notorious site of Nelson Mandela's incarceration. The rocky shore west of the Waterfront is occupied by the gritty inner-city suburbs of **Green Point** and **Sea Point**, whose main drag is lined with some of the peninsula's oldest and best restaurants, while their back streets are crammed with backpacker lodges, B&Bs and hotels. Equally good for accommodation, but leafy and salubrious in comparison, the **City Bowl suburbs** gaze down across the central business district on the matchbox ships in Duncan Dock.

South from Seapoint, a coastal road traces the chilly **Atlantic seaboard** past some of Cape Town's most expensive suburbs and spectacular beaches at Clifton, Camps Bay and Bakoven. South of Hout Bay, the road merges with the precipitous **Chapman's Peak Drive**, ten dramatically snaking kilometres of Victorian engineering carved into the western cliffsides of the Table Mountain massif, high above the crashing waves. Across Table Mountain, along its eastern foot, the middle-class **southern suburbs** stretch down the peninsula as far as Muizenberg. Adjacent to Newlands and Bishop's Court, the exceptionally beautiful **Kirstenbosch National Botanical Gardens** creep up the lower slopes, as do the **Constantia Winelands** a little further south. The Metrorail line, the only viable public transport down the length of the peninsula, cuts through the southern suburbs and continues along the **False Bay seaboard**, passing through villagey **Kalk Bay**, with its intact harbour and working fishing community, and **Fish Hoek**, which has the best bathing beach along the eastern peninsula; trains terminate at the beautiful historic settlement of **Simon's Town**.

An hour's drive east of the Cape Flats into the Western

Cape interior are the beautiful **Winelands**, where you'll find elegant examples of Cape Dutch architecture, and can sample wonderful wines and excellent restaurants. Heading south along the coast you follow one of the most picturesque routes out of Cape Town to reach Hermanus, the largest settlement on the **Whale Coast**, and a fabulous spot for shore-based whale-watching.

When to visit

Cape Town and the Western Cape coastal belt have a **Mediterranean climate** (contrary to expectations, it's not tropical) and the warm dryish summers are balanced by cool wet winters. Cape Town is a windy city and it can gust throughout the year; although seasons are reasonably well defined, it has a notoriously changeable climate. Come prepared for hot days in winter and cold snaps in summer: pack at least one short-sleeved garment during the cooler months and a jumper and jacket whatever time of year you come.

For sun and swimming, the best time to come is from **October to mid-December** and **mid-January to**

The Cape Doctor

The **southeaster**, the cool summer wind that blows in across False Bay, forms a major obsession for Capetonians. Its fickle moods can singlehandedly determine what kind of day you're going to have, and when it gusts at over 60kph you won't want to be outdoors, let alone on the beach. Conversely, its gentler incarnation as the so-called **Cape Doctor** brings welcome relief on humid summer days, and lays the famous cloudy tablecloth on top of Table Mountain.

Cape Town's climate

	°F		°C		Rainfall	
	Average daily		Average daily		Average monthly	
	MAX	MIN	MAX	MIN	IN	MM
Jan	79	60	26	16	0.6	15
Feb	80	60	27	16	0.7	17
March	78	58	25	14	0.8	20
April	73	53	23	12	1.6	41
May	69	49	20	9	2.7	69
June	65	46	18	8	3.7	93
July	64	45	18	7	3.2	82
Aug	64	46	18	8	3.0	77
Sept	67	48	19	9	1.6	40
Oct	70	51	21	11	1.2	30
Nov	74	56	24	13	0.6	14
Dec	77	59	25	15	0.7	17

Easter, when it's light till well into the evening and there's an average of ten hours of sunshine a day. During the Christmas month (mid-December to mid-January), Cape Town becomes congested as the nation takes its annual sea-side holiday. On the other hand this is major party time: the annual minstrel carnival and the Mother City Queer Project, a gay extravaganza, are staged during the festive season, while the Summer Sunset Concert season in Kirstenbosch National Botanical Gardens also starts its four-month run in December.

Despite its shorter daylight hours, the **autumn** period, from April to mid-May, has a lot going for it: the south-easter (see box) has dropped but air temperatures remain pleasantly warm and the light is sharp and bright. For similar reasons the **spring** month of September can be very agreeable, with the added attraction that following the winter rains the peninsula tends to be at its greenest, with much of the fynbos (see p.98) in flower. Although spells of heavy rain occur in **winter** (June and July), it tends to be relatively mild, with temperatures rarely falling below 6°C. Glorious sunny days with crisp blue skies are common, and you won't see bare wintry trees either: indigenous vegetation is evergreen and gardens continue to flower. It's in July that the first migrating whales begin to appear along the Cape Peninsula – they stay till the end of November.

BASICS

Getting there from Britain and Ireland

Frequent **direct flights** (11hr 30min) connect London Heathrow with Cape Town; South African Airways (SAA), British Airways (BA) and Virgin Atlantic all cover this route. However, more flights go to **Johannesburg**, the country's principal gateway and the busiest hub in Africa: domestic connections between the two cities are excellent. There are no direct flights from UK airports other than Heathrow.

You can also often pick up competitive deals on flights with European airlines (including KLM, Lufthansa and Swissair) or African carriers (Air Zimbabwe and Air Namibia amongst others) which entail **stopovers** in their national hubs. On such flights you'll often be allowed to break your journey at little or no extra cost – an attractive option if you want to take a breather on the long-haul route and take in another city. There are no direct flights **from Ireland** to Cape Town or Johannesburg; you need to change in London or, for example, Amsterdam, if you're flying with KLM.

Fares and flights

Most of the discount and specialist travel agents listed below can quote fares on scheduled flights. Check out the ads in the travel pages of the weekend newspapers, London's listings magazine *Time Out*, *Teletext* and *Ceefax* for special deals and the latest prices. Web sites, where available, are listed below – it's worth checking out these sites for **"online specials"** available via Internet auctions. It's invariably cheaper to buy tickets through agents (see opposite) than through airlines themselves.

High season differs slightly from airline to airline, but the most expensive time to travel to Cape Town is always mid-December to mid-January, Easter and mid-July to September, coinciding with European peak holiday periods. The medium-priced **shoulder seasons** run from mid-January to March, June to mid-July and October to mid-December, while the **low season** takes in April and May. It's always worth enquiring when the seasons begin and end as changing your departure date by a day can make a real difference to the price. Discounted return fares to Cape Town can start as low as £400 for a direct flight. Another option is a **round-the-world** (RTW) ticket: an RTW including Cape Town will start at around £800 for a one-year open ticket.

Airlines and flight agents

Air France UK ℡020/8742 6600; Ireland ℡01/844 5633; *www.airfrance.fr*

Air Namibia UK ℡01293/596654; *www.airnamibia.co.na*

Air Zimbabwe UK ℡020/7491 0009; *www.airzim.co.zw*

Alitalia UK ℡020/7602 7111; Ireland ℡01/677 5171; *www.alitalia.co.uk*

British Airways UK ℡0345/222111; BA doesn't have a Dublin office, so for reservations from Eire, call ℡0141/222 2345; *www.british-airways.com*

Iberia Airlines UK ℡020/7830 0011; ℡01/677 9846; *www.iberia.com*

KLM Royal Dutch Airlines UK ℡0990/750900; Northern Ireland ℡0990/074074; *www.klm.nl*
Lufthansa German Airlines UK ℡0345/737747; Ireland ℡01/844 5544; *www.lufthansa.co.uk*
Olympic Airways UK ℡020/7409 3400; Ireland ℡01/608 0090; *www.olympic-airways.gr*
Sabena UK ℡0345/581291; Ireland ℡01/844 5454; *www.sabena.com*
South African Airways UK ℡020/7312 5000; *www.saa.co.za*
Swissair UK ℡020/7434 7300; Ireland ℡01/677 8173; *www.swissair.co.uk*
Virgin Atlantic Airways, UK ℡01293/747747; Ireland ℡01/873 3388; *www.virginatlantic.com*

Flight agents
Bridge the World UK ℡020/7209 9494; *www.b-t-w.co.uk*
Council Travel UK ℡020/7437 7767; *www.ciee.org*
Expedia UK *www.expedia.co.uk*
Flightbookers UK ℡020/7757 2444; ℡01293/568300; *www.ebookers.net*
The London Flight Centre UK ℡020/7244 6411; 020/7727 4290 or 020/8748 6777
North South Travel UK ℡01245/492882
STA Travel UK ℡020/7361 6262; *www.statravel.co.uk*
Trailfinders UK ℡020/7938 3366; Ireland ℡01/677 7888; *www.trailfinders.com*
Travel Bag, Southern Africa enquiries, UK ℡020/7287 5535
The Travel Bug UK ℡020/7835 2000; *www.travel-bug.co.uk*
Travel Cuts UK ℡020/7255 2082; *www.travelcuts.co.uk*
Twohigs Dublin ℡01/677 2666
Usit Campus UK ℡020/7730 8111; Ireland ℡01/602 1700; *www.usitcampusco.uk*
World Travel Centre Ireland ℡01/671 7155

GETTING THERE FROM BRITAIN AND IRELAND

Package tours and exchanges

If time is short and you're keen on seeing the major sights, you might want to join a **package tour**. You can pick up five-day/six-night guided tours of Cape Town for around £400 (excluding meals and flights). Virgin Holidays offers a pick-and-mix range of **self-drive packages** that includes seven-night two-centre packages; their Cape Town and Durban option starts at £1200 (excluding flights) and you'll pay an extra £300 if you combine Cape Town with Vic Falls instead of with Durban.

Tour operators

Africa Travel Centre ©020/7387 1211; *www.africatravel.co.uk*
Grenadier Safaris ©01206/549585; *james@grenadir.demon. co.uk*
Kuoni Worldwide ©01306/743000; *www.kuoni.co.uk*
Rainbow Tours ©020/7226 1004; *rainbow@gn.apc.org*
Thomas Cook Holidays ©01733/418650; *www.tch. thomascook.com*
Virgin Holidays ©01293/617181; *www.virginholidays.co.uk/sa*
Worldwide Journeys and Expeditions ©020/7381 8638

Getting there from the US and Canada

From North America, the only **direct flights** to Cape Town are with South African Airways (SAA), which flies from Atlanta, its US hub, a journey that takes just under fourteen hours. SAA's alliance partner, Delta Air, provides connections with 134 US cities. SAA also has direct flights from New York to Johannesburg, with convenient onward connections to Cape Town.

However, direct flights are limited in number, most travellers get from North America to Cape Town **via Europe**, changing planes there. Daily flights are operated by British Airways and Virgin Atlantic Airways via London; Sabena via Brussels; Air France via Paris; KLM/Northwest via Amsterdam; and Swissair via Zurich. Check the waiting time between connecting flights to avoid a long layover. There are no direct flights to South Africa **from Canada**; Canadians fly via the US or Europe.

Fares and flights

Keep an eye out for **special offers** but, barring these, the cheapest of the airlines' published fares is usually an **Apex** ticket, which will carry certain restrictions. You have to book – and pay – at least 21 days before departure and spend a minimum of seven days abroad (maximum stay three months) and you tend to get penalized if you change your schedule.

Many airlines offer youth or student fares to **under–26s**; a passport or driving licence are sufficient proof of age. These tickets are subject to availability and can have eccentric booking conditions. It's worth remembering that most cheap return fares involve spending at least one Saturday night away and that many will only give a percentage refund if you need to cancel or alter your journey, so check the restrictions carefully before buying.

You can normally cut costs further by going through a **specialist flight agent**: either a consolidator, who buys up blocks of tickets from the airlines and sells them at a discount; or a discount agent, who in addition to dealing with discounted flights may also offer special student and youth-fares and other travel-related services, such as insurance, car rental and tours. See p.251 for a list of agents.

Airlines in the US and Canada

Air France US ✆1-800/237-2747; Canada ✆1-800/667-2747; *www.airfrance.com*

British Airways US ✆1-800/247-9297; Canada ✆1-800/668-1059; *www.british-airways.com*

Delta US ✆1-800/241-4141; *www.delta-air.com*

Northwest/KLM US ✆1-800/374-7747; Canada ✆1-800/361-5073; *www.klm.com*

Sabena ✆1-800/955-2000; *www.sabena-usa.com*

South African Airways ✆1-800/722-9675; *www.saa-usa.com*

Swissair US ✆1-800/221-4750; Canada ✆1-800/267-9477; *www.swissair.com*

Virgin Atlantic Airways ✆1-800/862-8621; *www.virginatlantic.com*

Fares for travel from North America to South Africa are highest between mid-June and mid-September, and early December to mid-January. The rest of the year is low season (most airlines have no shoulder season). Sample standard Apex fares to Cape Town in low season start at around $1150 from Atlanta and New York, while you'll pay in the region of $1500 from Los Angeles.

Discount agents and consolidators

Air Brokers International US ✆1-800/883-3273 or 415/397-1383; *www.airbrokers.com*

Council Travel US ✆1-800/226-8624, 888/COUNCIL or 212/822-2700; *www.ciee.com*

Educational Travel Center US ✆1-800/747-5551 or 608/256-5551; *www.edtrav.com*

Expedia US *www.expedia.com*

High Adventure Travel US ✆1-800/350-0612 or 415/912-5600; *www.highadv.com*

Now Voyager US ✆212/431-1616; *www.nowvoyagertravel.com*

STA Travel US ✆1-800/777-0112 or 212/627-3111; *www. sta-travel.com*

Travel Cuts ✆1-800/667-2887 or 416/979-2406; *www. travelcuts.com*

Travelocity *www.travelocity.com*

Package tours

As well as being convenient, package tours can throw open specialist activities that would otherwise be difficult to co-ordinate. One option is an eleven-day trip with Backroads, which includes exploration of the Cape Peninsula and Winelands on foot as well as big game adventures in northern South Africa: it costs from around US$4700.

Tour operators

Abercrombie and Kent ✆1-800/323-7308; *www.abercrombiekent.com*
Adventure Center ✆1-800/227-8747; *www.adventure-center.com*
Adventures Abroad ✆1-800/665-3998; *www.adventures-abroad.com*
AfricaTours ✆1-800/235-3692; *www.africasafaris.com*
Backroads ✆1-800/462-2848; *www.backroads.com*
Goway Travel ✆1-800/387 8850; *www.goway.com*
International Gay and Lesbian Travel Association ✆1-800/448-8550; *www.iglta.com*
Safaricenter ✆1-800/223-6046; *www.safaricenter.com*
Saga Holidays ✆1-800/343-0273; *www.sagaholidays.com*

Getting there from Australia and New Zealand

South Africa is an expensive destination for travellers from Australia and New Zealand. A ticket to Europe with a stopover in South Africa, or even a round-the-world

(RTW) ticket, generally represents better value than a straightforward return.

There are no nonstop flights to Cape Town from Australia or New Zealand, but there are **direct flights** to Johannesburg from both the eastern states and Western Australia, with good onward connections to Cape Town. From **New Zealand** you fly via Sydney to Johannesburg. South African Airways (SAA) and Qantas have direct flights along this route; some of the Asian airlines (Air Lanka, Malaysia Airlines, Singapore Airlines and Thai Airways) tend to be less expensive, but their routings often entail more stopovers.

Fares and flights

Whatever kind of ticket you're after, your first call should be to one of the specialist flight agents listed on p.12; staff can fill you in on all the latest **fares** and special offers. All the fares quoted are for travel during low or shoulder seasons; flying at peak times (primarily mid-May to Aug and Dec to mid-Jan) can add substantially to these prices. The best return fares you're likely to find are around A\$1900 from the eastern states and A\$1650 from Western Australia. From New Zealand, fares start at NZ\$2200. If you plan to visit Cape Town en route to **Europe**, you can expect to pay in the region of A\$2300/NZ\$2700.

Round-the-world tickets (RTW) that take in South Africa are worth considering. Possible itineraries include: starting from either Melbourne, Sydney or Brisbane, flying to Johannesburg, then travelling overland to Cape Town, before flying to London, and taking in Amsterdam, New York and San Francisco on the way back home (fromA\$2250); or, starting from Perth, flying to Denpasar, Casablanca, Istanbul, Nairobi, then down to Cape Town and Johannesburg on the return leg to Perth (from A\$2200).

GETTING THERE FROM AUSTRALIA & NEW ZEALAND

From New Zealand, you could fly from Auckland to Sydney, Bangkok and London, returning via Cape Town, Johannesburg and Perth to Auckland. Fares for this route start at NZ$2800.

Airlines and flight agents

Air New Zealand Sydney ℂ13 2476; Auckland ℂ09/357 3000; www.airnz.com

British Airways Sydney ℂ02/8904 8800; Auckland ℂ09/356 8690; www.british-airways.com

Malaysia Airlines Sydney ℂ13 2627; Auckland ℂ09/373 2741 or toll-free ℂ0800/657 472; www.malaysiaairlines.com.au

Qantas Sydney ℂ13 1211; Auckland ℂ09/357 8900 or ℂ0800/808 767; www.qantas.com.au

Singapore Airlines Sydney ℂ13 1011; Auckland ℂ09/303 2129; www.singaporeair.com

South African Airways Sydney ℂ02/9223 4402; saairways.com.au

Thai Airways ℂ1300/651 960; Auckland ℂ09/377 3886; www.thaiair.com

Flight agents

Africa Travel Centre Sydney ℂ02/9267 3048 or 1800/622 984; Auckland ℂ09/520 2000

Anywhere Travel Sydney ℂ02/9663 0411

Budget Travel Auckland ℂ09/366 0061 or ℂ0800/808 040

Destinations Unlimited Auckland ℂ09/373 4033

Flight Centres Australia ℂ13 1600; New Zealand ℂ09/309 6171

STA Travel Australia, nearest branch ℂ13 1776; New Zealand ℂ09/309 0458; www.statravelaus.com.au

Thomas Cook Australia ℂ1800/063 913; New Zealand ℂ09/379 3924; thomascook.com.au

Package tours

Package holidays from Australia and New Zealand to South Africa tend to be either expensive or of the extended overland variety, although airlines are beginning to put together bargain fly-drive options as demand increases. Drive Away Holidays offers flights with SAA to Cape Town including ten days' car rental from Sydney, Melbourne, Brisbane and Adelaide for around A\$2300 and around A\$2100 from Perth. You can also buy off-the-peg tours, which you can add on to your independent holiday: Contiki offers a three-day "Cape Town Jaunt," which takes in the city highlights and the Winelands, starting at A\$400.

Tour operators

Abercrombie and Kent ©09/358 4200; *www.aandktours.com*
Contiki Holidays ©02/9511 2200; *www.contiki.com*
Drive Away Holidays ©1300/363 500; *www.driveaway.com.au*
Encounter ©03/9670 1123 or 1800/654 152

GETTING THERE FROM AUSTRALIA & NEW ZEALAND

Visas and red tape

EU nationals, as well as those of the US, Canada, Australia and New Zealand, need only a valid **passport** to stay for up to three months in South Africa. All visitors need a valid **return ticket**; if you try to enter South Africa without one, you may be required to deposit the equivalent of your fare home with customs (the money will be refunded to you after you have left the country). Visitors may also have to prove that they have sufficient funds to cover their stay.

For longer stays, **extensions** (around R270) may be granted in the Aliens Control Section at the Department of Home Affairs (56 Barrack St ✆021/462 4970), where you will be quizzed about your intentions and your funds. Rampant unemployment means that your chances of finding work in South Africa are slim, but if you are offered a job you'll need to apply for a **work permit** through a South African diplomatic mission in your home country – a slow and cumbersome process.

At present, the per person **duty free** allowance in South Africa is two litres of wine and one litre of spirits, 400 cigarettes and fifty cigars and 250g of tobacco.

Money, costs and banks

Cape Town is the most expensive city in South Africa, but visitors coming from Europe, North America or Australasia will still find it generally cheaper than home. Backpackers staying in hostels, eating cheap meals or self-catering and using trains, buses or minibus taxis can come out on R120 per person a day. Staying in an en-suite room in a good B&B or guest house, eating at moderate restaurants, using a couple of taxis a day and paying for the odd tour or museum expect to pay around R400 per person a day. For R800 per person a day you can stay at a top class hotel, eat at the best restaurants and rent a car.

For the most current exchange rates, consult the useful currency converter Web site: www.xe.net/currency

---

Currency

South Africa's currency is the **rand** (R), divided into 100 cents. Notes come in R10, R20, R50, R100 and R200 denominations and there are coins for R1, R2 and R5 as well as 1c, 2c, 5c, 10c, 20c and 50c. At the time of writing, the **exchange rate** was around R10 to the pound sterling, R6 to the US dollar and R4 to the Australian dollar.

Travellers' cheques, credit cards and ATMs

Travellers' cheques are the safest way to carry your funds into South Africa, as they can be replaced if lost or stolen. Travellers' cheques in US dollars, pounds sterling, Australian dollars and most other major currencies can be changed at banks, bureaux de change and hotels. See p.250 for Amex office.

Credit cards come in very handy for hotel bookings and for paying for more mainstream and upmarket tourist facilities, and they are essential for car rental. Visa and Mastercard are the cards most commonly used in Cape Town, while American Express is not widely accepted. Visa, Mastercard, Cirrus-Maestro and Plus as well as a number of other international ATM cards (check with your bank before departing) can be used to withdraw money at **automatic teller machines** (ATMs), open 24 hours a day. When the ATM prompts you for the type of account you have, press "transmission".

Banks and exchange

Most **banks** have foreign currency counters and there are branches in the city centre, the V&A Waterfront and at most of the suburban shopping malls. You'll also find bureaux de change in the major tourist areas of town, which often operate extended hours. Outside banking hours some hotels will change money, although you can expect to pay a fairly hefty commission. You can also change money at branches of American Express and Rennies Travel.

Opening hours and holidays

The working day starts and finishes early in South Africa: most **shops** and **businesses** open on weekdays from 8.30am until 4.30pm or 5pm; on Saturdays many shops close for the day at lunchtime and are closed all day on Sunday. However these patterns have been changing fast with the collapse of apartheid, and you'll find a growing number of retailers that remain open on Sundays and as late as 9pm every night; this applies particularly to the larger malls and shopping centres (see p.192).

Banking hours are Monday to Friday 9am to 3.30pm, and Saturday 9am to 11am, while some **bureaux de change** stay open until 7pm. **Post offices** are open 8.30am to 4.30pm on weekdays and Saturdays 8am to 11.30am, and **government departments** weekdays from 8am until 4pm.

Holidays

School holidays in South Africa can disrupt your plans, especially if you want to stay in cheaper accommodation (self-catering, cheaper B&Bs and so on), all of which are likely to be booked solid. If you do travel to Cape Town over the school holidays, book your accommodation well in advance.

The longest and busiest holiday period is **Christmas** (summer), which for schools stretches roughly from mid-December to mid-January; this is also when accommodation prices peak. Flights and train berths can be hard to get from December 16 to January 2, when many businesses and offices close for their annual break. You should book your flights – long-haul and domestic – as early as six months in advance for the Christmas period. The provinces stagger their school holidays but, as a general rule, the school holidays cover the following periods: Easter, March 20–April 15; winter, June 20–July 21; and spring, Sept 19–Oct 7.

Public holidays

New Year's Day January 1	**Youth Day** June 16
Human Rights Day March 21	**National Women's Day** August 9
Good Friday	**Heritage Day** September 24
Easter Sunday	**Day of Reconciliation** December 16
Easter Monday	
Freedom Day April 27	**Christmas Day** December 25
Workers' Day May 1	**Day of Goodwill** December 26

Trouble and the police

Despite horror stories of sky-high **crime** rates, most people visit Cape Town without incident. This is not to minimize the problem – crime is probably the most serious difficulty facing South Africa. However, **safety** in central Cape Town has greatly improved over the past few years as a result of the deployment of a force of privately funded tourist police and the installation of 24-hour surveillance cameras. The greatest proportion of violent crime takes place in the poorer areas – predominantly townships.

Police

Generally, **police** presence is almost non-existent, and the police have a rather poor image. It's best simply to be reasonably cautious, relying on your own resources. This is exactly what many middle-class people now do, by subscribing to the services of armed, private security firms to protect their property. Protecting property and "**security**" are major national obsessions, and it's difficult to imagine what many middle-class South Africans would discuss at their dinner parties if the problem disappeared. The other obvious manifestation of this obsession is the huge number of alarms, bars, high walls and electronically controlled gates you'll find, not just in the suburbs, but even in less deprived areas of some townships.

In the unlikely event of your being robbed, don't expect too much crime-cracking enthusiasm from the police (and don't expect to get your property back), but you will need to report the incident to the police, who should give you a case reference for insurance purposes. A crime must be reported in the district in which it occurs and you should phone before trawling out to confirm which the correct police station is. Charge offices are listed in the Provincial Government section at the end of the White Pages telephone directory, under "Police Service (SA)".

Guns and muggings

Guns, both licensed and illicit, are an everyday part of life, routinely and openly carried by police – and some citizens. In many high streets you'll spot firearm shops rubbing shoulders with places selling clothes or books, and you'll

Safety tips

Although you should take care in Cape Town, don't allow paranoia to mar your stay. Be aware that you are more exposed in some places, such as the Cape Flats townships, than others, for example the V&A Waterfront or Kirstenbosch National Botanical Gardens, and act accordingly. If in doubt, ask for advice at Cape Town Tourism's office or at your accommodation.

In general
• Try not to look like a tourist
• Dress down: don't wear jewellery and expensive watches
• Don't carry a camera or video openly
• Remain calm and co-operative if you are mugged

On foot
• Grasp bags firmly under your arm
• Don't carry excessive sums of money on you
• Don't put your wallet in your back trouser pocket

- Don't leave valuables exposed (on a seat or the ground) while having a meal or drink
- Be aware of what people in the street around you are doing – especially groups

After dark
- Use taxis rather than public transport
- Avoid wandering around alone in the city centre – especially off the main drags

On the road
- Lock car doors
- Keep rear windows sufficiently rolled up to keep out opportunistic hands
- Never leave anything worth stealing in view when your car is unattended; take items indoors or lock them in the boot

At cash machines
Automatic teller machines (ATMs) are favourite hunting grounds for conmen and ATM scams are a part of South African life. Don't get drawn into any interaction at an ATM, no matter how well-spoken, friendly or distressed the other person appears. You can avoid trouble by following the pointers below.

- Never help anyone who claims to be having problem with a cash machine – tell them to contact the bank
- Never accept help from strangers if you have a problem at a cash machine
- Don't allow people to crowd you while withdrawing money – if in doubt, go to another machine
- Never allow anyone to see you punch in your personal identification number (PIN)
- If your card gets swallowed, report it without delay

TROUBLE AND THE POLICE

come across notices asking you to deposit your weapon before entering the premises. If you fall victim to a **mugging**, you should take very seriously the usual advice not to resist. The chances of being mugged can be greatly minimized by using common sense and following a few simple rules (see box).

THE GUIDE

Introducing the city

Cape Town's reputation as one of the world's most beautiful cities lies in its physical setting on the Cape Peninsula, a fifty-kilometre promontory that curls south from Table Bay. Generally, when people talk about Cape Town, they mean the whole peninsula, not just the central business district and its surrounding suburbs, a fact that perplexes tourists used to visiting the centre of cities to find their essence.

By far the most striking – and famous – feature of South Africa's legislative capital is **Table Mountain**, frequently mantled by clouds. More than a scenic backdrop, Table Mountain is the solid core of Cape Town, dividing the city into distinct zones, with public gardens, wilderness, forests, hiking routes, vineyards and desirable residential areas trailing down its lower slopes. Standing on the tabletop, you can look north for a giddy view of the **city centre**, its **Waterfront** and docks dotted with ships. Looking west, beyond the mountainous Twelve Apostles, the drop is sheer and your eye will sweep across Africa's priciest real estate, clinging to the slopes along the chilly but spectacularly beautiful **Atlantic seaboard**. To the south, the mountainsides are forested, several historic vineyards and the marvellous Kirstenbosch National Botanical Gardens creeping up the lower slopes. Beyond the oak-lined suburbs of

Newlands and Constantia lies the warmer **False Bay seaboard**, which curves around before fading off to **Cape Point**. Finally, furthest away from the mountain, relegated to the grim industrial east, are the extensive coloured **townships** and black **ghettos**, hidden in winter under the smoky pall of coal fires – a stark introduction to Cape Town as you approach from the airport.

The telephone code for Cape town is ☎021.

Arrival

One of the world's great moments of **arrival** is cruising into Table Bay on a luxury liner. For most, however, the approach is much less picturesque – indeed, it can be something of a shock. Whether you come in by air or road, there's small chance of avoiding the grey, industrial sprawl and the miles of squatter camps that line the N2 into town.

By air

Cape Town International Airport is on the Cape Flats, 22km east of the city centre. Intercape (☎934 0802), located at the domestic terminal, operates an hourly **scheduled service** that goes to Cape Town central train station (8.30am–6.30pm; R30). Intercape's free courtesy bus provides transfers to the domestic terminal; their office is upstairs in the international terminal. Their door-to-door service will go anywhere on the Peninsula as far east as Stellenbosch and costs R80–150 per person, subject to distance and the number of people in the group.

A cheaper door-to-door option is the 24-hour **Backpackers Airport Shuttle**, based at Extreme Sports, 220 Long St, in the city centre (bookings 8am–10pm; ℂ426 0294 or 083/528 2690, *extremesports@worldonline. co.za*); their minibus takes passengers from the airport to anywhere in the city centre, City Bowl or Sea Point. The service operates in response to demand, which means you'll either need to prebook or call from the airport and wait up to 45 minutes for them to arrive. Between 7am and 7pm it costs R40 per person and reduces to R25 each if there are four or more passengers; at other times you'll pay R30–60. Metered **taxis** rank in reasonable numbers outside both terminals and cost about R100 for the trip into the city. Inside the terminals, you'll find the desks of the major **car rental** firms (see p.251). There are no trains from the airport.

A **bureau de change** is open to coincide with international arrivals, but exchange rates are better at banks in the city. The **Cape Town Metropolitan Tourism** desk (daily 7am–5pm) will book accommodation for you. Both services are located in the international terminal.

By bus and train

Greyhound, Intercape and Translux intercity **buses** and mainline **trains** from other provinces all terminate in the centre of town around the interlinked central complex that also includes the **Golden Acre** shopping mall, at the junction of Strand and Adderley streets. The Golden Acre shopping complex can be a confusing place, but if you use public transport at all, you're bound to find yourself here at some stage of your stay. Everything you need for your next move is within two or three blocks. There's a **left-luggage** facility at the train station (Mon 8am–7pm, Tues–Thurs 8am–4pm, Fri 6am–6pm, Sat & Sun 8am–3pm; ℂ449 2611).

BY BUS AND TRAIN

Information

Your first port of call for information should be the welcoming **Cape Town Tourism** office, at the corner of Burg and Castle streets (May–Aug Mon–Fri 8am–5pm, Sat 8.30am–1pm, Sun 9am–1pm; Sept–April Mon–Fri 8am–6pm, Sat 8.30am–1pm, Sun 9am–1pm; ✆426 4260, fax 426 4266, *info@cape-town.org*), a five-minute walk two blocks northwest of the station. It operates a comprehensive accommodation booking service, has a swanky coffee shop, a book and gift shop, a cybercafé, lots of brochures and very cheap city maps, and also conducts city-centre walking tours.

A couple of alternative sources of information that are especially good for backpackers lie within easy walking distance of the station. Closest of the two is **Purple Turtle**, First Floor, Purple Turtle Building, at the corner of Long and Shortmarket streets, a wacky hangout that consists of a backpackers' travel agency (where you'll get good independent advice on lodges and tours), a friendly cybercafé and a collection of hip shops selling records and clothes. **One World Travellers' Space**, 309 Long St (Mon–Fri 9am–5pm; ✆ & fax 423 0777, *oneworld@mweb.co.za*), makes bookings for tours and is also a place where you'll get sympathetic advice on all backpacker-related matters. Services include baggage storage (same hours as office), a travellers' notice board and mail-holding facilities.

The best sources for weekly **events listings** are the *Top of the Times* supplement in Friday's *Cape Times*, and the *Good Weekend* pullout in the *Saturday Argus*, while the *Mail & Guardian*, which comes out on Fridays, injects some attitude into its reviews and listings supplement. *Cape Review*, a monthly listings magazine with a passing resemblance to London's *Time Out*, gives a broad range

Cape Town on the Internet

Cape Town 2004 *www.ct2004.com*
Web site of Cape Town's failed 2004 Olympic bid, but still up and running, with live Webcams pointing at city highlights and 360-degree navigable panoramas.

Cape Town Tourism *www.cape-town.org*
Cape Town Tourism's official site, crammed with information on accommodation, transport and other practicalities.

Independent Online *www.iol.co.za*
South African news from the country's biggest newspaper group, sister to the London *Independent*, with links to the *Cape Argus*, Cape Town's afternoon daily.

ZA@PLAY *www.mg.co.za/mg/art/artmenu.htm*
Comprehensive listings of what's on in South Africa's major cities, including daily updates on exhibitions, film, theatre and gigs.

Q-online *www.q.co.za*
The definitive South African gay website, with information on clubs and nightlife as well as useful contacts.

of information on food, wine, gay venues, nightlife and sporting events.

Maps

The inexpensive **maps** available from Cape Town Tourism are adequate for the centre and surrounding areas, but if you're planning to explore beyond the confines of the city centre, you'll need to invest in a detailed

street atlas, found at most bookshops, including the ubiquitous CNA chain. MapStudio's *A to Z Streetmap* is the cheapest and is adequate for the centre and most of the suburbs, although it doesn't cover Simon's Town. Most comprehensive of the lot is MapStudio's *Cape Town Street Guide*, which covers the entire Cape Peninsula as well as the Winelands towns of Paarl, Stellenbosch and Somerset West in detail.

Cape Town's best bookshops are listed on pp.198–9.

Getting around

Municipal public transport in Cape Town is poor and getting worse. Most middle-class Capetonians have never used it, preferring to get around in private cars, while the less well off who can't afford this luxury rely principally on the limited Metro Rail **train system** and the unco-ordinated network of privately operated **minibuses** (usually called "taxis"). For visitors, the most useful municipal services are the Metro Rail train line that cuts through the southern suburbs then along the False Bay coast, and the **bus service** connecting the five-kilometre strip that includes the city centre, Waterfront and Sea Point.

Central Cape Town is compact enough to walk around, but much of what you'll want to see is spread along the considerable length of the Peninsula, so to make the most of your visit you'll need to get to grips with either shuttle buses, metered taxis, rental vehicles or organized tours.

Taking municipal buses, minibus taxis or trains
after dark is not recommended; use one of the
metered taxi or shuttle services listed on p.33.

Buses

The only frequent and reliable **bus** services are those serving the Waterfront and Sea Point; buses also go down the
Atlantic seaboard to Camps Bay and Hout Bay. Don't,
however, attempt to catch a bus to the southern suburbs:
the train is much quicker and more efficient. All the principal terminals are around Adderley Street and Golden Acre
(see box on p.32).

   Tickets are sold on buses by the driver, and if you're
planning on using them frequently, consider buying a **Ten-
Ride Clip Card**, which from the city costs around R20 to
Sea Point, and around R30 to Camps Bay. Valid for fourteen days, the card will save you around 25 percent on the
price of individual tickets. For **timetables**, enquire at the
Golden Arrow **information booth** (toll-free ℂ0801/21
2111) at the Grand Parade central bus terminal. It's always
advisable to check bus times and points of departure at the
booth, as these can change inexplicably.

Taxi services

Metered taxis, regulated by the Cape Town Municipality,
don't cruise up and down looking for fares; you'll need to
go to the taxi ranks around town, including the Waterfront,
the train station and Greenmarket Square. Alternatively, you
can phone to be picked up: Marine Taxi Hire (ℂ434 0434)
is the most reliable company. Taxis must have the driver's
name and identification clearly on display and the meter

Bus information

City bus terminals

Adderley Street, outside OK Bazaars supermarket: buses to Sea Point, Hout Bay and southern suburbs.

Cape Town Station, Adderley Street: buses to Waterfront.

Golden Acre Bus Terminus, outside Golden Acre Shopping Centre in Adderley Street: buses to Table Mountain, Camps Bay and Table Bay.

Grand Parade, on Strand Street behind the train station: the main bus station, where all other services depart from.

Useful bus services

Note that the buses aren't numbered; you identify them from the destination on the front.

City to:

Hout Bay: Golden Acre–Lower Plein St–Darling Rd–Adderley St–Green Point, Main Rd–Sea Point–Camps Bay, Victoria Road–Hout Bay Beach–Hout Bay Harbour. Mon–Fri 4 hourly to Sea Point & 14 daily to Hout Bay, Sat 3 hourly to Sea Point & 6 daily to Hout Bay, Sun 3 daily to Hout Bay.

Kloofnek, for Lower Cable Station (circular). Note: it's an uphill walk of over a kilometre from the Kloofnek Terminus to the Cable Station: Golden Acre–Adderley St–Wale St–Buitengragt St–New Church St–Kloofnek Rd–Kloofnek Terminus. Mon–Fri 1–2 hourly, Sat hourly.

Sea Point (direct): Golden Acre–Mouille Point–Main Road Sea Point. Mon–Sat at least 13 daily.

Waterfront: Cape Town Station–Riebeeck St–Buitengragt St–Waterfront. Mon–Fri every 10min, Sun every 15min.

V&A Waterfront to:
City: V&A Waterfront–Cape Town Station. Mon–Sat every 10min, Sun every 15min.
Sea Point: V&A Waterfront–Mouille Point–Green Point–Three Anchor Bay–Beach Road Sea Point. Daily every 20min.

clearly visible. Fares work out at around R10 per kilometre, which is expensive compared with other forms of transport, but worth it at night when metered taxis are the safest way of getting around.

The term "taxi" is ambiguous in Cape Town
as elsewhere in South Africa: it's used to refer to
conventional metered cars, jam-packed minibuses
and their more upmarket cousins, rikkis.

Minibus taxis

Minibus taxis are cheap, frequent and bomb up and down the main routes at tearaway speeds. As well as crazed driving, be prepared for the pickpockets who work the taxi ranks. Minibus taxis can be hailed from the street or boarded at the central taxi rank, adjacent to the train station. Once you've boarded, pay the *guardjie* (assistant), who sits near the driver. Fares should be under R4 for most trips.

Shuttle buses

A growth area in Cape Town are **shuttle buses**, which are physically indistinguishable from minibus taxis, the difference being that they have to be booked, and they can pick you up from your accommodation. Generally they are minibuses, which in some cases run to a schedule or alternatively are chartered. They tend to be cheaper than metered

MINIBUS TAXIS, SHUTTLE BUSES

taxis but are more expensive than minibus taxis. One of the most useful services, at the time of writing, is a scheduled one being run for the summer on an experimental basis by Linomtha Shuttles (©934 2170) in co-operation with Cape Town Tourism. It goes from the Cape Town Tourism office to: Lower Cable Station (hourly Mon–Sat 9am–4pm; R15); Kirstenbosch National Botanical Gardens (Mon–Sat 9.30am, 12.30pm & 2.30pm; R50); and Ratanga Junction (hourly Mon–Sat 9am–2pm; R50).

Reliable operators you can charter include: Sun Tours & Shuttle (©696 0596, 697 0488 or 083/270 5617, *suntours@ iafrica.com*), which offers a 24-hour service between any two points on the Peninsula including the city to the airport (R100 for the first two, then R30 per additional passenger); and the similarly priced Boogey Bus (©082/495 5698), which specializes in taking passengers to clubs, including those in the Cape Flats.

Rikkis

Rikkis are more visitor-friendly versions of minibus taxis, carrying not more than eight passengers, and aimed principally at tourists. They are small open-backed vehicles, which you need to book by telephone. In Cape Town, rikkis (7am–7pm; ©423 4888 or 423 4892) are restricted to the City Bowl, the Waterfront and the Atlantic seaboard as far as Camps Bay – they don't go into the suburbs. Fares are kept down by picking up and dropping off passengers along the way (R6–15). Rikkis also operate mini-tours to destinations that include Cape Point and Stellenbosch, for which they charge R60–80 an hour for a whole vehicle.

Trains

Cape Town's **train** service (timetable information ©0800/

65 6463), is a relatively reliable if slightly rundown urban line that runs from Cape Town central station, through the southern suburbs and all the way down to Simon's Town. Highly recommended as an outing in its own right, and undoubtedly one of the great urban train journeys of the world, it reaches the False Bay coast at Muizenberg and continues south, sometimes so spectacularly close to the ocean that you can feel the spray and peer into rock pools.

Trains run overground, and there are no signposts to the stations on the streets, so if you're staying in the southern suburbs ask for directions at your accommodation; otherwise look at a map or ask around to find the stations. Tickets must be bought at the station before boarding. You're best off in the reasonably priced first-class carriages; curiously, there's no second class, and third class is not recommended. A first-class single from Cape Town to Muizenberg works out at a little under R7. Suburban trains tend to run approximately to the **timetable**, with departures from the central station to the southern suburbs as far as Retreat leaving roughly every ten minutes at peak times (Mon–Fri 5.30–8am & 3.30–6pm); every twenty minutes as far as Fish Hoek; and every forty minutes to Simon's Town. Services are thinner over weekends: Saturdays every forty minutes (5.10am–2.10pm); and Sundays every hour (7.30–11.30am & 3.30–7.30pm).

Three other lines run east from Cape Town to Strand (through Bellville) and to the outlying towns of **Stellenbosch** and **Paarl**; apart from undertaking these journeys, they aren't recommended as they run through the Flats, and some sections can be risky.

The main stations on the Cape Town–Simon's Town Metro Rail line are shown on map 2.

Driving

Cape Town has good roads and several fast **freeways** that can whisk you across town in next to no time, except at peak hours (7–9am & 4–5.30pm). Take care approaching: the on-ramps frequently feed directly into the fast lane (and Capetonians have no compunction in exceeding the 100kph freeway and 120kph highway speed limits). The obvious landmarks of Table Mountain and the two seaboards make orientation straightforward, particularly south of the centre, and there are some wonderful journeys, the most notable being Chapman's Peak Drive (see p.120), a narrow winding cliff-edge route with the Atlantic breaking hundreds of metres below.

Foreign **licences** are valid in South Africa for up to six months provided they are printed in English. If you don't have an English-language licence, you'll need to get an International Driving Permit before arriving (available from national motoring organizations). When driving, keep your licence and passport on you at all times.

In this former British colony, driving is on the **left-hand side**, and **speed limits** range from 60kph in built up areas to a maximum of 120kph on highways. Note that traffic lights are called **robots** in South Africa. Roundabouts are rare, instead you'll find **four-way stops**, where the rule is that the person who got there first leaves first, and you are not expected to give way to the right.

Road safety

South Africa has among the world's worst **road accident statistics** – the result of recklessness, drunk driving and defective and overloaded vehicles. Keep your distance from cars in front, as pile-ups are common. On national and provincial roads, watch out for **overtaking traffic** coming towards you; overtakers frequently assume you'll pull into the hard shoulder to get out of their way and drivers coming up from behind will also expect you to temporarily drive in the hard shoulder while they overtake. This is perfectly legal, and dangerous, especially in a country where it is common for pedestrians and animals to walk along the hard shoulder.

An unwritten rule of the road on the Peninsula is that **minibus taxis** have the right of way. Don't mess with them: their vehicles are bigger than yours, they carry handguns (turf wars between taxi drivers are a feature of the city) and will often run red lights – as will many Capetonians. Don't assume green means safe: approach cautiously, even on green.

A number of places around the Cape Peninsula have both Afrikaans and English names (Cape Town itself is known to Afrikaners as Kaapstad). Road signs tend to alternate between the two, making it worth familiarizing yourself with both versions if you're driving; see glossary of Afrikaans signs on p.341.

Vehicle rental

Given Cape Town's scant public transport, renting a vehicle is the only convenient way of exploring the Cape Peninsula and it needn't break the bank: there are dozens of competing **car rental** companies to choose from (see p.251). To find out who's currently operating and to get the best deal, either pick up one of the brochures at the Cape Town Tourism office (see p.28) or look in the Yellow Pages telephone directory. For one-way rental (to drive down the Garden Route and fly out of Port Elizabeth, for example), you'll have to rely on one of the bigger and pricier nationwide companies (see p.251).

For **motorbike rental**, Le Cap Motorcycle Hire, 3 Carisbrook St (℃423 0823), can provide all the necessary

Tours

Guided tours enable you to orientate yourself quickly and get to the highlights in a hurry, and a growing number of smaller companies offer niche cultural tours. Among these, the most popular are **townships tours**, which can safely get you around the African and coloured areas that were created under apartheid. Apart from this, a number of other outfits, listed below, can help you scratch beneath Cape Town's surface.

City centre and Peninsula sights

City Walking Tour (©426 4260). Operated by Cape Town Tourism (Mon–Fri 10am & 2pm, Sat 10am), this departs from their visitor centre, on the corner of Burg and Castle streets. The roughly two-hour strolls don't go into any of the sites, but are good for orientation. R50.

Day Trippers (©531 3274, *trippers@iafrica.co.za*). Cycling from Scarborough into the Cape of Good Hope Nature Reserve with hikes down to Cape Point, as well as tours to the usual sights such as the Winelands. R185.

Hylton Ross Tours (©511 1784, fax 511 2401). Cover all the popular sights along the Cape Peninsula and also have scheduled guided day tours to Hermanus (Wed & Sun), which cost R260.

Intercape (©419 8888). Standard tours of the main Peninsula attractions – Cape Point, the city centre, Kirstenbosch Gardens, the penguins at Boulders and so on. Full day R240.

Mother City Tours (©448 3817, fax 448 3844). Half- and full-day tours of the city, Cape Point, Table Mountain and the Winelands. Half day from R160, full day R240. They run whale-watching trips in season (Tue & Fri; R260).

Stumble Inn For budget tours based in Stellenbosch, talk to *Stumble Inn* backpacker hostel (you don't have to be a guest; see p.285), which goes to two or three wineries in a day.

Topless Tours (℡418 5888). Two-hour open-top double-decker buses that follow a fixed route around the main central sights with a running commentary. You can hop on and off throughout the day (departures hourly 9.40am–2.40pm). The tour starts at Vaughan Johnson's Wine Shop on the Waterfront and includes the City Hall, the Castle of Good Hope, District Six, Parliament, the South African Museum, Kloofnek, Signal Hill and Camps Bay. R35.

Cultural and township tours

AfriCultural Tours (℡423 3321). Comprehensive look at Cape Town's "other side", not just the townships, but also a "Slave Route" tour, a tour of San rock art sites and visits to traditional music makers, dancers and artists. For a chance to experience the upbeat side of Cape Flats nightlife, join their "Vibey Jazz" tour. From R50.

Grassroute Tours (℡424 8480, *grassrout@iafrica.com*). An imaginative alternative take on the traditional tour packages includes their "Culture of the Winelands" trip, which visits wineries that have given land to their workers and have progressive labour practices, and a "Culture of Cape Fishermen" tour in which you join Kalk Bay fishermen for the day as part of the crew on their boat. They also do walking tours of the Bo-Kaap, including the *kramats* (Muslim shrines), and the African and coloured townships. Half day R160, full day R280–320.

Muse-Art Journeys (℡919 9168, 082/921 1126). Exciting portfolio of cultural tours, including music outings that take in two or three nightclubs, some in the townships; a craft route that visits township craftworkers who recycle materials; a graffiti tour that looks at murals in Mitchell's Plain; and visits to ancient rock art sites. Half day R160, full day R280–300.

Our Pride (℡082/446 7974). Highly recommended interactive tours, where you get to meet the people of the Bo-Kaap, District Six as well as the African townships and squatter

Continues overleaf

Tours (continued)

camps. They also do jazz outings in which you go to two clubs, and a "Township by Night" trip, which includes supper at a township restaurant and a visit to a shebeen. R160.

Slave Tours (©448 5359, *abank@uwc.ac.za*). Walking tours of central Cape Town, led by University of the Western Cape history lecturer, Andrew Bank, one of the leading experts on slavery. Among the slave sites visited during the hour outing are the castle, the place of execution, the Old Slave Tree, the Gardens and the Slave Lodge. R60.

Western Cape Action Tours (©461 1371). Led by former Umkhonto weSizwe (ANC armed wing) activists from Cape Town, tours focus on the fight against apartheid and the post-apartheid scene. Visitors go to the townships, see sites of political resistance, as well as visiting a traditional healer, housing projects and township markets, where they are encouraged to make face-to-face contact with residents. Half day R180, full day R300.

gear and they rent out bikes (from R180 daily, plus 70c/km) as well as automatic scooters (R120 daily). Helmets are compulsory.

One of the most popular, and hair-raising, road routes for cyclists is along the narrow hairpins of Chapman's Peak Drive (see p.120), which offer great views of the Altantic. There are also a number of dedicated mountain-biking routes in the peninsula's nature reserves. See p.224 for rental outlets.

The city centre

ape Town's city centre is the oldest urban area in Southern Africa and is the most historically intense district in the country. Its has a stunning physical setting, dominated by the omnipresent Table Mountain to the southwest and the pounding Atlantic marking the northeast. While the prime attractions lie elsewhere, the city centre has some interesting museums, and its streets still pulse with the cultural fusion that has been Cape Town's hallmark since its founding in 1652.

**The area covered in this chapter
is shown on colour map 4.**

Adderley Street, connecting the main train station in the north to St George's Cathedral in the south, is the obvious orientation axis and one (with the harbour at one end and Table Mountain rearing up from the other) you'd struggle to lose your way on.

South of Adderley Street, where it takes a sharp right into Wale Street, you'll find the symbolic heart of Cape Town (and arguably South Africa), with the **Houses of Parliament**, museums, historic buildings, archives and De Tuynhuys, the Western Cape office of the President, arranged around the **Gardens**. Adderley Street continues as the oak-lined pedestrianized **Government Avenue**, which cuts through the Gardens and terminates at Orange Street, the hectic route to the southern suburbs that marks the boundary between the city centre and the salubrious inner-city suburbs of Gardens, Tamboerskloof, Oranjezicht and Vredehoek.

West of Adderley Street is the closest South Africa gets to a European quarter – a tight network of streets with cafés, buskers, bookstores, street stalls and antique shops congregating around the pedestrianized **St George's Mall** and **Greenmarket Square**. Parallel to St George's Mall, **Long Street**, the quintessential Cape Town thoroughfare, is lined with colonial Victorian buildings that house pubs, bistros, nightclubs, backpacker lodges, bookshops and antique dealers, whose wrought-iron balconies afford glimpses of Table Mountain and the sea. The **Bo-Kaap**, or Muslim quarter, three blocks further west across Buitengracht (which means the Outer Canal, but is actually a street), exudes a piquant contrast to this, with its minarets, spice shops and cafés selling curried snacks.

East of Adderley Street, and close to each other near Cape Town station, lie three historically loaded sites. The oldest building in South Africa, the **Castle of Good Hope** is an indelible symbol of Europe's colonization of South Africa, a process whose death knell was struck from nearby **City Hall**, the attractive Edwardian building from which Nelson Mandela made his first speech after being released. Southeast of the castle lie the poignantly desolate remains of **District Six**, the coloured inner-city suburb that was razed in the name of apartheid.

Strand Street marks the edge of Cape Town's original beachfront (though you'd never guess it today); all urban development on the **Foreshore** to its north stands on reclaimed land, where there's little to see apart from **Duncan Dock**, where tankers and large passenger ships drop anchor.

Six of the best: central museums

Cape Town has some of the most important **museums** in South Africa, but on the whole they're seriously underfunded and you shouldn't expect the levels of sophistication found in Europe or North America. With a couple of exceptions, most notably the world-class Aquarium (see p.83) and the exhibition in the Holocaust Centre (see below), you'll encounter inconsistent quality, but usually enough of interest to justify the generally cheap entrance fees. Top of the agenda are:

Bo-Kaap Museum (p.66). Located in the historical Muslim quarter, it provides insights into the culture of the area.

Castle of Good Hope (p.68). South Africa's oldest colonial building, with a fine collection of seventeenth- to nineteenth-century domestic objects used at the Cape.

Holocaust Exhibition (p.58). Worth visiting for its brilliant design alone, but it's also the only display in Africa that deals with the Holocaust.

Slave Lodge (p.46). The best place to find out about the city's cultural history, including its slave heritage.

South African Museum (p.58). Recommended for its good ethnographic coverage and its whale well, dominated by a massive whale skeleton.

South African National Gallery (p.54). One of the most important showcases of contemporary South African art.

ADDERLEY STREET

Map 4, D2–4. Cape Town station.

Adderley Street, once lined with centuries' worth of handsome buildings, still merits a stroll today for what grand architecture remains. The attractive streetscape has been blemished by large 1960s shopping centres and office blocks, but just minutes away from its crowded malls, among the streets and alleys around Greenmarket Square, you can still find some human scale and historic texture.

Adderley Street was formerly the Heerengracht (Gentlemen's Canal): a waterway that ran from the Company's Gardens down to the sea. Low-walled channels, ditches, bridges and sluices once ran through Cape Town and earned it the name Little Amsterdam. However, during the nineteenth century the canals were buried underground, and in 1850 Heerengracht was renamed Adderley Street (see box on p.45). There's little evidence of the canals today, except in name – one section of the street is still called Heerengracht and a parallel street to its west is called Buitengracht (sometimes spelled Buitengragt), meaning the Outer Canal. Apart from the **Slave Lodge**, **Groote Kerk** and **St George's Cathedral**, all at the southwest end of the street, the only notable building is the **First National Bank**, completed in 1913, which was the last South African building designed by Sir Herbert Baker. Inside the banking hall, a solid timber circular writing desk, its original inkwells still in place, resembles an altar to capital.

The Groote Kerk

Map 4, D4. Daily 9.30am–4.30pm; free.

Sometimes described as "Cape Gothic" in style, the **Groote Kerk** (Great Church), diagonally opposite the First National Bank in Adderley Street, is essentially a Classical building with Gothic and Egyptian elements. The soaring space created by its vast vaulted ceiling and the magnificent **pulpit**, a masterpiece by sculptor Anton Anreith and carpenter Jan Jacob Graaff, are worth stepping inside for. Supported on a pair of sculpted lions with gaping jaws, the pulpit was carved by Anreith when his first proposal,

The naming of Adderley Street

Although the Dutch used Robben Island (see p.85) as a political prison, the South African mainland only narrowly escaped becoming a second Australia, a **penal colony** where British felons and enemies of the state could be dumped. By the 1840s, "respectable Australians" were lobbying for a ban on the transportation of criminals to the Antipodes, and the British authorities responded by trying to divert convicts to the Cape.

In 1848, the *Neptune* set sail for Cape Town with a cargo of 282 prisoners, where the news of its departure was met with outrage. Five thousand citizens gathered on the Grand Parade the following year to hear prominent liberals denounce the British government, an event depicted in *The Great Meeting of the People at the Commercial Exchange* by Johan Marthinus Carstens Schonegevel, which hangs in the Rust-en-Vreugd Museum (see p.52). When the ship docked in September 1849, governor Sir Harry Smith forbade any criminal from landing, while, back in London, politician **Charles Adderley** successfully addressed the House of Commons in support of the Cape colonists. In February 1850, the *Neptune* set off for Tasmania, and grateful Capetonians renamed the city's main thoroughfare **Adderley Street**.

featuring Faith, Hope and Charity, was rejected by the church council for being "too Popish".

Designed and built between 1836 and 1841 by **Hermann Schutte** (see p.321), a German who became one of the Cape's leading early nineteenth-century architects, the church replaced an earlier Baroque one that had become too small for the swelling ranks of the Dutch Reformed congregation at the Cape. The beautiful freestanding **clock tower** adjacent to the newer building is a remnant of the original church.

The Slave Lodge

Map 4, D4. Mon–Sat 9.30am–4.30pm; R5.

Previously known as the Cultural History Museum, the **Slave Lodge** houses an eclectic collection of antiquities and artefacts from around the world as well as good displays on the Cape, which you won't see elsewhere. The museum was renamed on Heritage Day, September 24, 1998, and is currently in the process of reinventing itself to portray South African social history, especially the bloodstained story of slavery.

For 186 years, more than half its existence as an urban settlement, Cape Town's economic and social structures were built on slavery (see box, p.47), and the Slave Lodge was built in 1679 for the Dutch East India Company to house its human chattels. The Company was the largest single-gle owner of slaves at the Cape; by the 1770s, almost a thousand of them were held at the Lodge. Under Company administration the Lodge also became the Cape Colony's main brothel, its doors thrown open to all comers for an hour each night. Following the British takeover and the auctioning of the slaves, it became the Supreme Court in 1810, and remained so until 1914. From 1914 the building was used as government offices, and in 1966 became a museum.

A couple of small but interesting displays can be found on the ground floor, to the left of the entrance hall. The first deals with **Khoisan hunter-gatherers**, the original inhab-itants of the Cape (and South Africa), focusing on their knowledge of plants and herbs, many of which are still in use today. An adjacent room houses "**186 Years of Slavery**", centred around a model of the lodge as it was 300 years ago. A poignant memorial plaque on one wall lists, by first name only, the slaves who endured the appalling conditions of the fortress-like structure, and a map

Slavery at the Cape

Slavery was officially abolished at the Cape in 1838, but its legacy lives on in South Africa: the country's coloured (mixed race; see p.317) inhabitants, who make up fifty percent of Cape Town's population, are largely descendants of slaves, and some historians argue that apartheid was a successor to slavery. Certainly, domestic service, still widespread throughout South Africa, and certain labour practices such as the "*dop* system" in which workers on some farms are partially paid in rations of cheap plonk, can be directly traced back to slavery.

By the end of the eighteenth century, the almost 26,000-strong slave population of the Cape exceeded that of free burghers. Despite the profound impact this had on the development of social relations in South Africa, until the publication of a number of studies on slavery in the 1980s, it remained one of the most neglected topics of the country's history. There's still a reluctance on the part of most coloureds to embrace their slave origins.

Few if any slaves were captured at the Cape for export, making the colony unique in the African trade. Paradoxically, while people were being captured elsewhere on the continent for export to the Americas, the Cape administration, forbidden by the VOC from enslaving the local indigenous population, had to look further afield. Of the 63,000 slaves who were imported to the Cape before 1808, most came from East Africa, Madagascar, India and Indonesia, representing one of the broadest cultural mixes of any slave society. This diversity initially worked against the establishment of a unified group identity, but eventually led to a Creolized culture that, among other things, played a major role in the development of the Afrikaans language.

on another wall refers to sites in the city centre with slave connections: where they worked, worshipped, were sold, punished and executed.

You pass through a couple of rooms devoted to a smattering of Greek and Roman antiquities to the "**Cape Kaleidoscope**" exhibition, occupying two large galleries – well worth taking in for the crash course it offers on the political and economic development of Southern Africa's first European settlement. Bizarrely, four rooms of artefacts from China, Japan, Tibet and Indonesia, followed by displays of African and Oriental weapons, interrupt the flow before you once again return to galleries relating to Cape Town, which occupy the entire southwest wing. The collection includes some intriguing items: the **padrãos** (stone crosses) left by sixteenth-century Portuguese mariners; engraved **postal stones** that marked the arrival of passing ships at Table Bay; and some historic **postage stamps**. However, the selection may prove a little too random to hold your interest for long.

> **Behind the Slave Lodge, on the traffic island in Spin Street, a simple and inconspicuous plinth marks the site of the Old Slave Tree, under which slaves were auctioned.**

St George's Cathedral

Map 4, C4.

Diagonally opposite the Slave Lodge, at the south end of Adderley Street as it turns into Wale Street, **St George's Cathedral**, built in the early twentieth century, is more interesting for its history than for Herbert Baker's Victorian Gothic design. The previous Anglican church on the same site had been an impressive structure based on the Greek

Revival St Pancras church in London, but was considered too "pagan" for a Christian place of worship, and was pulled down.

It was against the doors of the present St George's that **Desmond Tutu** hammered on September 7, 1986, symbolically demanding to be enthroned as South Africa's first black archbishop. Three years later, he heralded change by leading 30,000 people from the Cathedral to the Grand Parade, where he coined his now famous slogan of multi-racialism, telling the crowd: "We are the rainbow people! We are the new people of South Africa!" The fact that this was the first mass demonstration in the city since 1960 allowed to go ahead without police disruption hinted that the final days of apartheid were at hand.

The walk from the Slave Lodge to Bertram House is sometimes referred to as "Museum Mile" because it provides access to around a dozen significant sites, including the flagship institutions of the National Gallery, the Holocaust Centre, the South African Museum and the Planetarium, covered in detail below.

GOVERNMENT AVENUE AND THE GARDENS

Map 4, D5–7. Cape Town station.

Government Avenue, the pedestrianized southern extension of Adderley Street, is one of the most serene walks in central Cape Town. This oak-lined boulevard runs past the rear of parliament through the Gardens.

Looming on your right as you enter the north end of the avenue, the **South African Library** (Mon–Fri 9am–6pm, Sat 9am–1pm; free) houses one of the country's best collections of antique historical and natural-history books covering Southern Africa. Built with revenue from a tax on wine, it opened in 1822 as one of the first free libraries in the world.

Continuing along Government Avenue from the South African Library, past the rear of parliament, you can peer through an iron gate to see the grand buildings and tended flowerbeds of **De Tuynhuys**, the office (but not residence) of the president. Built in 1700 as the guest house for visiting VOC (Dutch East India Company) dignitaries, the building was subjected to additions and alterations by the Dutch throughout the eighteenth century. Under the governorship of Lord Charles Somerset during the nineteenth-century British occupation, extensive changes were made and the wings, visible from the Gardens, were built, with verandahs covered by elegantly curving awnings typical of the Colonial Regency style. To peer into the gardens of Tuynhuys, stand on the walkway leading up to its locked gates, the ditches to either side of you are all that remain visible of Cape Town's former **canal system**. One party of tourists, during Mandela's presidency, stood amazed here as the great man – who is renowned for his common touch – strolled across the lawns for a friendly chat.

A little further along, the tree-lined walkway opens out into a formal gravel square with ponds and statues, around which are sited Cape Town's most important museums, covered from p.52.

The Gardens

Stretching from here to the South African Museum and Avenue Road, the **Gardens** (aka the Cape Town, Botanical or Company's Gardens) were the initial *raison d'être* for the Dutch settlement at the Cape. Established in 1652 to supply fresh greens to the VOC, whose ships traded between the Netherlands and the East, the Gardens were initially worked by imported slave labour. This proved too expensive, as slaves had to be shipped in, fed and housed, so the Company phased out its own farming and granted land to free burghers, from whom it bought fresh produce (see p.305). At the end of the seventeenth century, the gardens were turned over to botanical horticulture for Cape Town's growing colonial elite, with ponds, lawns, landscaping and a crisscross web of oak-shaded walkways being introduced. Today they are full of local plants, the result of long-standing interest in Cape botany; European scientists have been sailing out since the seventeenth century to classify and name specimens.

Cecil Rhodes certainly thought the gardens a pleasant place to meander – it was during a stroll here that he plotted the invasion of Matabeleland and Mashonaland, both of which became amalgamated into Rhodesia and subsequently Zimbabwe. Rhodes also introduced an army of small, furry colonizers to the gardens: North American grey squirrels. There's a statue of Rhodes here, as well as an unexceptional outdoor **café**.

THE HOUSES OF PARLIAMENT

Map 4, D5. Tours Mon–Fri 11am & 2pm ©403 2537 or 403 2201; free. Cape Town station.

South Africa's **Houses of Parliament** back onto Government Avenue, with their entrance on Parliament Street. Not one building but a complex of interlinking ones, the labyrinthine corridors connect hundreds of offices and debating chambers.

One-hour **tours** take in the old and new debating chambers, the library and museum, and should be booked in advance through the Tours Section, which is also the place to contact for day tickets to watch the **debating sessions** – the most interesting of which is question time (Wed 3pm onwards), when you can hear ministers being quizzed by MPs if parliament is sitting. Members of the ANC sit to the right of the speaker, so if you want to see them you should enter the gallery at the rear via the right entrance; minority parties sit opposite. You're most unlikely to see the President, who is not a member of parliament and rarely attends sittings. When he does, for the opening of parliament or for visits by foreign leaders, seats are invariably already snapped up.

Completed in 1885, the original building is in imposing Victorian Neoclassical style, and first served as the legislative assembly of the Cape Colony. After the Boer republics and British colonies amalgamated in 1910, it became the parliament of the **Union of South Africa**. This is the old parliament, where more than seven decades of repressive legislation, including apartheid laws, were passed. It's also where **Hendrik Verwoerd**, the arch-theorist of apartheid, met his bloody end, not at the hand of a political activist, but stabbed to death by a parliamentary messenger who committed the act because, as he told police, "a tapeworm ordered me to do it." Due to his mental state the assassin escaped the gallows to outlive apartheid – albeit in an institution. Verwoerd's portrait, depicting him as a man of vision and gravitas, once hung over the main entrance to the dining room; in 1996 it was removed, ostensibly for "cleaning", along with paintings of generations of white parliamentarians. The new chamber was built in 1983 as part of the **tricameral parliament**, P.W. Botha's attempt to avert majority rule by trying to co-opt Indians and coloureds – but in their own separate debating chambers (see p.314). This chamber has become the **National Assembly**, where you can watch sessions of parliament (see above).

RUST-EN-VREUGD

Map 4, E5. Mon–Sat 9am–4pm; R3. Cape Town station.

The most beautiful of Cape Town's house museums,

Rust-en-Vreugd, a couple of blocks east of the Gardens at 78 Buitenkant St, was once surrounded by countryside, but now stands along a congested route that brushes past the edge of the central business district.

Designed by architect **Louis Michel Thibault** and sculptor **Anton Anreith**, the two-storey facade features a pair of stacked balconies, the lower one forming a stunning portico fronted by four Corinthian columns carved from teak. Framed by teak pilasters, the front door is a real work of art, rated by architectural historian de Bosdari as "certainly the finest door at the Cape". Above the door, the fanlight is executed in elaborate Baroque style.

The house was built in 1778 for **Willem Cornelis Boers**, the colony's Fiscal (a powerful position akin to the police chief, public prosecutor and collector of taxes rolled into one), who was forced to resign in the 1780s following allegations of wheeler-dealing and extortion. Under the British occupation, it was the residence of **Lord Charles Somerset** during his governorship (1814–1826).

Inside, the William Fehr Collection of **artworks on paper** occupies two ground-floor rooms and includes illustrations by important documentarists such as **Thomas Baines**, who is represented by hand-coloured lithographs and a series of watercolours recording a nineteenth-century expedition up Table Mountain. **Thomas Bowler**, another prolific recorder of Cape scenes, painted his stunning landscape of Cape Point from the sea in 1864, showing dolphins frolicking in the foreground.

A tranquil escape from the busy street, the **garden** is a reconstruction of the original eighteenth-century semi-formal one, laid out with herbaceous hedges, gravel walkways and a lawn with a gazebo, the property being defined by a boundary of bay trees.

RUST-EN-VREUGD

You can park inside the grounds of Rust-en-Vreugd, which is fortunate given the jammed roadsides of Buitenkant and the surrounding streets; to do so, temporarily leave your car in front of the museum while you ask at reception to be let in through the gates.

THE SOUTH AFRICAN NATIONAL GALLERY

Map 4, D6. Tues–Sun 10am–5pm; free. Cape Town station.

Not far from the southern end of Government Avenue, on the corner of tiny Gallery Lane, is the **South African National Gallery**, which contains a fine permanent collection of contemporary South African art.

As the number of items far exceeds the capacity of its exhibition space, displays regularly change, but one of the few pieces almost invariably on display is **Jane Alexander**'s powerfully ghoulish plaster, bone and horn sculpture, *The Butcher Boys* (1985–6), created at the height of apartheid repression. It features three life-size figures with distorted faces that exude a chilling passivity, expressing the artist's interest in the way violence is conveyed through the human figure. Alexander's work is representative of "**resistance art**", which exploded in the 1980s, broadly as a response to the growing repression of apartheid. Resistance art, produced by committed people from all ethnic groups, was inspired by the idea that artists had a responsibility to engage politically; it spanned a wide range of subject matter, styles and media. **Paul Stopforth**'s powerful graphite-and-wax triptych, *The Interrogators* (1979), featuring larger-than-lifesize portraits of three notorious security policemen, is a work of monumental hyper-realism.

Many other artists, unsurprisingly for a culturally diverse

country, aren't easily categorized; while works have tended to borrow from Western traditions, their themes and execution are uniquely South African. The late **John Muafangelo** employed Biblical imagery in works such as *The Pregnant Maria* (undated), producing highly stylized, almost naive black-and-white linocuts, while in *Challenges Facing the New South Africa* (1990), **Willie Bester** used paint and found shanty-town objects to depict the melting pot of the Cape Town squatter camps.

Since the 1990s, and especially in the post-apartheid period, the gallery has engaged in a process of redefining what constitutes contemporary **indigenous art** and has embarked on an acquisitions policy that "acknowledges and celebrates the expressive cultures of the African continent, particularly its southern regions". Material that would previously have been treated as ethnographic, such as a major **bead collection** as well as carvings and **craft objects**, is now finding a place alongside oil paintings and sculptures.

In the vicinity of the Gardens, the best place for snacks and refreshments is the National Gallery's café (opening hours same as gallery), which serves light lunches, coffees and cakes; there's also a small shop selling art books, postcards, artwork and crafts.

THE SOUTH AFRICAN JEWISH MUSEUM AND THE GREAT SYNAGOGUE

Map 4, D7. Mon–Thurs & Sun 10am–5pm, Fri 10am–1pm; R25. Cape Town station.

Partially housed in South Africa's first synagogue, built in 1863, the **South African Jewish Museum** at 84 Hatfield St, to the south of the National Gallery, is one of Cape

Town's most ambitious permanent exhibitions. It tells the story of South African Jewry from its beginnings 150 years ago to the present – a narrative which starts in the Old Synagogue from which visitors cross, via a gangplank, to the upper level of a new two-storey building, symbolically re-enacting the arrival by boat of the first Jewish immigrants at Table Bay harbour in the 1840s. Employing multimedia interactive displays, models and Judaica artefacts, the exhibition follows three threads: "**Memories**", looking at the roots and experiences of the immigrants; "**Reality**", covering their integration into South Africa; and "**Dreams**", examining a diversity of views about the role of Jews in South Africa, their relationship to Israel and their position in the world. Other displays examine anti-Semitism, apartheid and the Jews who opposed it, as well as Nelson Mandela's relationship with the Jewish community.

Drawing parallels between Judaism and the ritual practices and beliefs of South Africa's other communities, the "**Culture among Cultures**" display covers topics such as birth, marriage, circumcision and death. The **basement level** houses a walk-through reconstruction of a Lithuanian *shtetl* or village (most South African Jews have their nineteenth-century roots in Lithuania), as well as the **Discovery Centre**, an interactive computer with a genealogy bank, a searchable database on Jewish life and culture and a "glimpse into Israel". A restaurant, shop and an auditorium are also housed in the museum.

The Great Synagogue

Map 4, D7.

One of Cape Town's outstanding religious buildings, the **Great Synagogue**, adjacent to the Jewish Museum, faces onto the oak-lined walkways of the Gardens. Designed by

Judaism in South Africa

Today there are around twenty thousand Jews in Cape Town, the majority descended from **Eastern European refugees** who fled discrimination and pogroms during the late nineteenth and early twentieth centuries.

Since 1795, when the occupying British introduced freedom of worship at the Cape, Jews in South Africa have faced few legal impediments. However, there have been instances of semi-official anti-Semitism during the twentieth century, the most notable being in the policy of the Nationalist Party while in opposition during the 1940s. Before World War II, elements in the party came under the influence of Nazi ideology, which was being poured into South Africa by the German foreign and propaganda offices, and began to attribute all the ills facing Afrikanderdom to a "British-Jewish capitalist" conspiracy. In 1941, the party adopted and touted a policy of ending Jewish immigration and even repatriating "undesirable immigrants", as well as placing stronger controls over naturalization and the introduction of a "vocational permit" system to protect "the original white population against unfair competition". Ironically, on the eve of taking power in 1947, the party of apartheid turned its back on anti-Semitism: one of its first acts after winning the 1948 election was to recognize the newly created state of Israel, with which it maintained links until it relinquished power in 1994.

Scottish architects, it was completed in 1905 and features an impressive dome and two soaring towers after the style of central European Baroque churches. To see the arched interior and the alcove decorated with gilt mosaics, you need to ask at the Holocaust Centre (see below), and may be asked to provide some form of identification.

THE CAPE TOWN HOLOCAUST CENTRE

Map 4, D7. Mon–Thurs & Sun 10am–5pm, Fri 10am–1pm; free.
Cape Town station.

Opened in 1999, the **Holocaust Exhibition** constitutes one of the most moving and brilliantly executed museums in Cape Town. Housed upstairs in the Holocaust Centre, which lies just west of the National Gallery and the Jewish Museum in Hatfield Street, the centre resonates sharply in a country that only recently emerged from an era of racial oppression – a connection that the exhibition makes explicitly. A densely layered narrative is related through text, photographs, artefacts (such as a concentration camp uniform), film clips, soundtracks, multimedia and interactive video, while the design uses modulated lighting, cobblestones reminiscent of the ghettos and pieces of barbed wire and railway track to evoke the death camps.

Exhibits trace the history of anti-Semitism in Europe, culminating with Nazism and the Final Solution; they also look at South Africa's Greyshirts, who were motivated by Nazi propaganda during the 1930s and were later absorbed into the National Party. There are accounts of heroism, often tragic, including acts of resistance by Jews, and a touch screen portrays many individuals in Europe who risked their lives to protect or rescue the victims of Nazism. To conclude, a twenty-minute video tells the story of survivors who eventually settled in Cape Town.

THE SOUTH AFRICAN MUSEUM AND PLANETARIUM

Map 4, D7. Daily 10am–5pm; museum R5, planetarium R7, combined R10. Cape Town station.

The nation's premier museum of natural history and human sciences, the **South African Museum**, west of Government Avenue and across the Gardens from the

National Gallery at 25 Queen Victoria St, has cultural and wildlife displays that will satisfy both adults and kids (see p.233).

Downstairs, the **ethnographic galleries** are stunning and include casts of San hunter-gatherers, whose culture has now virtually died out in South Africa, and superb dioramas depicting nineteenth-century San life. There are very good displays on the traditional arts and crafts of several African groups, some exceptional examples of rock art (entire chunks of caves sitting in the display cases), and casts of stone birds found at Great Zimbabwe, across South Africa's border. Upstairs, the **natural history galleries** display mounted mammals, dioramas featuring prehistoric Karoo reptiles, a slightly old-fashioned but appealing dinosaur display, and Table Mountain flora and fauna. The highlight is the four-storey "**whale well**", in which a collection of beautiful marine mammal skeletons hang like massive mobiles, accompanied by the eerie strains of their song. Free one-hour screenings of natural-history films take place in the museum's **T.H. Barry Auditorium** (Wed 1pm, Sat & Sun 1, 2 & 3pm).

The display at the attached **Planetarium** (shows Mon–Fri 1pm, Sat & Sun noon, 1pm & 2.30pm, Tues also at 8pm) depicts the southern sky in all its glory. In addition, a changing programme of exhibits covers topics such as San sky myths, as well as special shows for kids. Leaflets at the museum provide a list of forthcoming attractions and you can buy a monthly chart of the current night sky, which is especially handy if you're staying outside the city.

THE SOUTH AFRICAN MUSEUM AND PLANETARIUM

The BP Mindspaces exhibition at the museum has ten computers with Internet access for R5 per half-hour – the cheapest surfing in town.

BERTRAM HOUSE

Map 4, D7. Tues–Sat 9.30am–4.30pm; R3. Cape Town station.

At the top (southernmost) end of Government Avenue, you'll come upon **Bertram House**, whose beautiful two-storey brick facade looks out across a fragrant herb garden. Built in the 1840s, the museum is significant as the only surviving brick Georgian-style house in Cape Town, and displays typical furniture and objects of a well-to-do colonial British family in the early half of the nineteenth century.

The site was bought in 1839 by John Barker, an attorney from Yorkshire who came to the Cape in 1823. He named the house after his wife, Ann Bertram Findlay, who died in 1838, and it is believed that he was responsible for building it. Declared a National Monument in 1962, Bertram House was extensively restored to its current state between 1983 and 1984. Imported face brick and Welsh slate were used to recreate the original facade, while the interior walls were redecorated in their earlier dark green and ochre, based on the evidence of paint scrapings. Reception rooms are decorated in the Regency style, while the porcelain is predominantly nineteenth-century English, although there are also some very fine Chinese pieces.

For more on Cape architecture, see p.320.

AROUND ST GEORGE'S MALL

Map 4, C4. Cape Town station.

A block southwest of Adderley Street, **St George's Mall**, a pedestrianized road, runs from Thibault Square, near the railway station, terminating at Wale Street. It's a less hectic route between the station and the Company's Gardens than parallel Adderley Street, while coffee shops, snack bars, street traders, buskers, dancers, drummers, choirs and painters add a certain buzz.

Church Street (which crosses the mall towards its southern end) and the surrounding area abound with antique dealers, and on the pedestrianized section at its northeastern end you'll find an informal antique market. Prices are competitive and you may pick up unusual jewellery, bric-a-brac, Africana and old sheet music.

Nearby **Greenmarket Square**, surrounded by Art Deco buildings, is worth at least a little exploration to soak up the vaguely European atmosphere, with cobbled streets, coffee shops and grand buildings. As its name implies, the square started as a vegetable market, though it spent many ignominious years as a car park. Human life has returned and it's now a flea market, selling crafts and jewellery.

The Old Town House

Map 4, C4. Feb–Dec daily 10am–5pm; ✆424 6367; R3.

On the western side of Greenmarket Square are the solid limewashed walls and small shuttered windows of the **Old Town House**, entered from Longmarket Street. Built in 1755, this charming example of Cape Dutch architecture with its fine interior has seen duty as a guard house, a police station and Cape Town's city hall, and these days houses the **Michaelis Collection** of seventeenth-century Dutch and Flemish paintings.

Referred to as the Dutch "Golden Age", the seventeenth century was one of great prosperity for the Netherlands, during which it threw off the yoke of its Spanish colonizers and sailed forth to establish colonies of its own in the East Indies, and of course at the Cape. The wealth that trade brought to the Netherlands stimulated the development of the arts, with paintings reflecting the values and experience of Dutch Calvinists. A notable example is **Frans Hals'** *Portrait of a*

AROUND ST GEORGE'S MALL

Woman, hanging in the upstairs gallery. Executed in shades of brown, relieved only by the merest hint of red, it reflects the Calvinist aversion to ostentation. The sitter for the picture, completed in 1644, would have been a contemporary of the settlers who arrived at the Cape some eight years later. Less dour and showing off the wealth of a middle-class family is the beautiful *Couple with Two Children in a Park*, painted by **Dirck Dirckz Santvoort** in the late 1630s, in which the artist displays a remarkable facility for portraying sensuous fabrics, which glow with reflected light; you can almost feel the texture of the lace trimming.

Other paintings, most of them quite sombre, depict mythological scenes, church interiors, still lifes, landscapes and seascapes, the last being very close to the seventeenth-century Dutch heart, often illustrating vessels belonging to the Dutch East India Company or the drama of rough seas encountered by trade ships. A tiny **print room** on the ground floor has a small selection of works by Daumier, Gillray and Cruikshank, as well as one of **Goya**'s most famous works, *El Sueno de la Razan Produce Monstruos* (The Sleep of Reason Produces Monsters).

Small visiting exhibitions also find space here, and good evening classical concerts are a regular thing. You can pick up the Town House's quarterly newsletter, which lists forthcoming events, or watch the press (*The Good Weekend* entertainment supplement in *Saturday Argus* being a good source). Tickets are available at the door immediately prior to the event.

> In the eighteenth century, the portico of the Town House was known as the "slaves' portico" because in rainy weather slaves would take refuge and, according to a commentator who visited the Cape in 1805, "talk over the hardships of life in slavery".

LONG STREET

Map 4, C2–6. Cape Town station.

Parallel to Adderley Street and one block northwest of Greenmarket Square, **Long Street** aptly runs the full length of the city centre and continues as lively Kloof Street, which cuts through the City Bowl suburbs to Kloofnek, a junction that splays out to the Lower Cable Station, Sea Point, the Atlantic seaboard and Signal Hill. The buzzing artery itself is still a touch seedy but fast becoming trendy, and is one of Cape Town's most fascinatingly diverse thoroughfares – a great place for some leisurely exploration, with views of Table Mountain, Signal Hill and Lion's Head, as well as glimpses of the sea.

When it was first settled by Muslims some three hundred years ago, Long Street marked Cape Town's boundary; by the 1960s it had become a sleazy alley of drinking holes and whorehouses. Miraculously it's all still here, but with a whiff of gentrification. Mosques still coexist with bottle stores, brothels above old-fashioned locksmiths, pawnbrokers alongside porn shops. Gun shops sit next to delicatessens, wonderful antique dealers, craft shops and cafés. Several excellent second-hand bookshops feature, and more **backpacker lodges** per square metre than on any other street in Cape Town with, in their wake, a growing number of student travel agencies, cheap car-rental outfits and adventure-activity outlets.

For details on Long Street accommodation
see p.140, and for eating see p.182.

The Palm Tree Mosque

Map 4, C5.

An unmistakable landmark at number 185, along the upper

reaches of Long Street, the **Palm Tree Mosque** (not open to the public) is fronted by a lone palm tree, its fronds caressing the upper storey. Significant as the only surviving eighteenth-century house in a street that was once full of them, it was erected in 1780 by Carel Lodewijk Schot as a private dwelling. The house was bought in 1807 by Frans van Bengal, a member of the local Muslim community, and a freed slave, Jan van Boughies, who became its imam, turning the upper floor into a mosque, which it remains, and the lower into his living quarters.

The Pan African Market

Map 4, C4. Mon–Fri 9.30am–5pm, Sat & Sun 9.30am–3.30pm.
One of Cape Town's most intriguing places for African crafts is also one of the easiest to miss. The inconspicuous frontage of the **Pan African Market** at 76 Long St belies the three-floor warren of passageways and rooms, which burst at the hinges with traders selling vast quantities of art and artefacts from all over the continent. Hidden amongst less inspiring offerings you'll find terrific masks from West Africa, brass leopards from Benin as well as textiles, contemporary South African art, CDs, musical instruments, leathersmiths, tailors, hair braiders and a drum instructor.

The South African Missionary Meeting-House Museum

Map 4, C3. Mon–Fri 9am–4pm; free.
Towards the harbour end of Long Street at no.40, the **South African Missionary Meeting-House Museum** is an exceptional building with one of the most beautiful frontages in Cape Town. Broken into three bays by four slender Corinthian pilasters surmounted by a gabled pediment, its facade gives the remarkable appearance of being

all window. Inside, an impressive Neoclassical timber **pulpit** perches high above the congregation on a pair of columns, framing an inlaid image of an angel in flight. Completed in 1804 by the South African Missionary Society, it was the first missionary church in the country, where slaves were taught literacy and instructed in Christianity.

The Society itself was founded in 1799 by Reverend Vos in alarmed response to the fact that many slave owners were neglecting the religious education of their slaves. Owners believed that, once baptized, their slaves' emancipation became obligatory – a misunderstanding of the law, which merely stated that Christian slaves couldn't be sold. Vos, himself a slave owner, saw proselytization to the bonded as a Christian duty and even successfully campaigned to end the prohibition against selling Christian slaves, which he believed was "a great obstacle in this country to the progress of Christianity", because it encouraged owners to avoid baptizing their human chattels.

An interesting permanent set of display boards covers the work of the early missionaries and mission stations through-out the Western Cape.

THE BO-KAAP

Map 4, B3–6. Cape Town station.

Minutes from parliament on the slopes of Signal Hill, the **Bo-Kaap** is one of Cape Town's oldest and most attractive residential areas, brightly painted nineteenth-century Dutch and Georgian terraces concealing a network of alleyways that are the arteries of the **Muslim community**. The Bo-Kaap harbours its own strong identity, made all the more unique by the destruction of District Six, with which it had much in common. A particular dialect of Afrikaans is spoken here, although it is steadily being eroded by English, which has a higher social status and lacks the associations with apartheid.

Bo-Kaap residents are descended from dissidents and slaves imported here by the Dutch in the sixteenth and seventeenth centuries. They became known collectively as "**Cape Malays**", a term you'll still hear, even though it's a misnomer: fewer than one percent of slaves actually came from Malaysia; most originated from East Africa, India, Madagascar and Sri Lanka.

The Bo-Kaap is most easily reached by foot along Wale Street, which trails up from the south end of Adderley Street and across Buitengracht to become the district's main drag.

....

The Bo-Kaap's charming facades and quiet cobbled streets give it a deceptively quaint feel; apart from Wale Street and the Museum, this is not a good place to wander alone. The safest way to get under the skin of the area is on one of the several tours that take in the museum and walk you around the district, the best (and cheapest) of these being the two-hour walk run by Bo-Kaap Guided Tours (bookings on ©422 1554; R35), operated by residents of the area.

....

The Bo-Kaap Museum

Map 4, A4. Mon–Sat 9.30am–4.30pm; R3.

A good place to find out about the Muslim quarter is the **Bo-Kaap Museum**, 71 Wale St, near the Buitengracht end. The museum consists mainly of the house and effects of Abu Bakr Effendi, a religious leader brought out from Turkey by the British authorities in 1862 as a mediator between feuding Muslim factions. He stayed and became an important member of the community, started an Arabic school and wrote a book in the local vernacular – possibly the first book to be published in what can be recognized as Afrikaans. Exhibits also explore a local brand of Islam, which has its own unique traditions and nearly two dozen *kramats* (shrines) dotted about the peninsula.

Architecturally, the museum is typical of the modest single-storey houses of the Bo-Kaap, employing a raised *stoep* (verandah) to accommodate the extreme slope of the site. Like many of the earlier buildings, some of which date as far back as the 1780s, it has sash windows, a fanlight above the door, a flat roof and a decorative wavy parapet.

The Auwal Mosque

Map 4, A5.
One block south of the museum, on Dorp Street, is the **Auwal**, South Africa's first official mosque, founded in 1797 by the highly influential Imam Abdullah ibn Qadi Abd al-Salam (commonly known as Tuan Guru or Master Teacher), a Moluccan prince and Muslim activist who was exiled to Robben Island in 1780 for opposing Dutch rule in the Indies. While on the island he transcribed the Koran from memory and wrote several important Islamic commentaries, which provided a basis for the religion at the Cape for almost a century. On being released in 1792, he began offering religious instruction from his house in Dorp Street, before founding the Auwul nearby.

The Auwal Mosque can only be visited as part of an organized Bo-Kaap **tour** (see p.66). Ten more mosques in the Bo-Kaap, whose minarets give spice to the quarter's skyline, now serve its 10,000 residents.

CITY HALL AND THE GRAND PARADE

Map 4, E3–4. Cape Town station.
Built in 1905 in an Italian Renaissance style, the **City Hall**, south of the station on the corner of Parade and Darling streets, is typical of the British colonial town halls erected

throughout the Empire in the late nineteenth and early twentieth centuries. One of the most photogenic buildings in Cape Town, it presents a pleasingly self-confident Edwardian facade dominated by a huge clock tower, with the unparalleled backdrop of Table Mountain.

As well as being frequently snapped, the hall can probably also claim to be the most televised South African building: **Nelson Mandela** stood on its balcony on a sweltering February day in 1990 to give his first public speech in decades, an audience of 100,000 supporters having waited for hours on the **Grand Parade**, across Darling Street, for their hero to arrive from Victor Vester Prison.

Usually the Parade is a desolate square, in the shadow of the station, but it livens up on Wednesdays and Saturdays when it becomes the site of a non-touristy flea market where you can buy spicy foods and an array of bits and pieces, including secondhand clothes.

....

Stand on the Grand Parade to snap the City Hall, and you'll not only capture the building and Table Mountain, you'll get the foreground of palm trees on the north side of Darling Street: a classic Cape Town image.

....

THE CASTLE OF GOOD HOPE

Map 4, F3–G3. Daily 9am–4pm; R7.50, free tours daily at 11am, noon & 2pm. Cape Town station.

From the outside, South Africa's oldest building looks a trifle desolate due its position behind the train station and city bus terminal, between busy Strand and Darling streets. Nevertheless, the **Castle of Good Hope** is well worth the entrance fee, having enjoyed a meticulous ten-year restoration that has returned the decor to the British Regency style introduced in 1798. Built in accordance with seventeenth-century European principles of fortification, the castle has strong bastions from which it could be protected by cross fire. Finished in 1679, complete with the essentials of a moat and torture chamber, it replaced van Riebeeck's earlier mud-and-timber fort, which stood on the site of the Grand Parade. For 150 years, until the early nineteenth century, the castle was the symbolic heart of the Cape administration, and the centre of the city's social and economic life.

Inside, there's a strong sense of order in the castle's pentagonal plan, though ironically there was nothing ordered about its construction, which lasted over thirteen years, with work constantly coming to a standstill either because of labour shortages or insufficient materials, and being regularly revived by the outbreak of various wars in Europe. The original seaward entrance had to be moved to its present landward-facing position because the spring tide sometimes came crashing in – a remarkable thought given that due to land reclamation it's now almost a kilometre inland.

The current **entrance gate** displays the coat of arms of the United Netherlands and those of the six Dutch cities in which the VOC Chambers were situated; the bell, cast in 1697 by Claude Fremy in Amsterdam, was used variously as an alarm signal and a summons to residents to receive pronouncements, and still hangs from its original wooden beams in the tower above the entrance. Inside the walls, the **courtyard** is sliced in half by a defensive twelve-metre-high defensive structure or *kat*, from which cannons could be fired. Providing entry to the *kat*, the exquisite ceremonial **Kat Balcony** from which ordinances were pronounced is flanked by two shallow curving staircases, its portico supported on six fluted ionic columns carved out of solid teak.

Free tours are useful for orientation around the castle and include the prison cells and dungeons, with centuries-old graffiti painstakingly carved on their walls. The castle is also home to the Defence Force's Western Province Command, and you may catch a glimpse of armed soldiers marching in and stepping across the elegant courtyard, Table Mountain peeking over the west wall.

The William Fehr Collection

Elaborately carved double doors at the rear of the castle's Kat Balcony open onto four interleading rooms that were the heart of VOC government at the Cape and now house the bulk of the excellent **William Fehr Collection**, one of the country's most important exhibits of decorative arts. The contents, acquired by businessman William Fehr from the 1920s, were sold and donated to the government in the 1950s and 1960s and continue to be displayed informally as Fehr preferred, instead of being arranged thematically.

Galleries are filled with items found in middle-class Cape households from the seventeenth to nineteenth centuries, with some fine examples of elegantly simple **Cape furniture** from the eighteenth century. Early colonial views of Table Bay appear in a number of **paintings**, including one by Aernot Smit that shows the castle in the seventeenth century, right on the shoreline. Among the fascinating items of antique oriental **ceramics** are a blue-and-white Japanese porcelain plate from around 1660, displaying the VOC monogram, and a beautiful polychrome plate from China dating to about 1750, which depicts a fleet of Company ships in Table Bay against the backdrop of a very oriental-looking Table Mountain.

There's a very tranquil tea shop in the castle courtyard, where you can sit outdoors under umbrellas, enjoy the Cape Dutch architecture and catch a view of Table Mountain.

District Six

The apocalyptic sound was complete when the first buildings toppled. They fell down, the facades, the inside walls, in clouds of dust that in the end were just a single cloud . . . of resentment.
Coloured poet Adam Small, recalling the destruction of District Six

South of the castle, in the shadow of Devil's Peak, is a vacant lot shown on maps as the suburb of Zonnebloem. Before being torn apart by the apartheid regime during the Sixties and Seventies, it was **District Six**, an impoverished but lively community of 55,000 people, predominantly coloured. Once known as the soul of Cape Town, this inner-city slum harboured a rich cultural life in its narrow alleys and crowded tenements. Along the cobbled streets, hawkers rubbed shoulders with prostitutes, gangsters, drunks and gamblers, while craftsmen plied their trade in small workshops. After its demise, the district became mythologized as a rich place of the South African imagination, inspiring novels, poems, jazz and the blockbuster musical *District Six*.

In 1966, P.W. Botha (then Minister of Community Development – a title that carries a measure of Orwellian irony) declared District Six a **White Group Area**, meaning that Africans, Indians and coloureds were prohibited from living there. The bulldozers moved in, taking fifteen years to drive its presence from the skyline, leaving only mosques and churches.

In the wake of the demolition gangs, international and domestic outcry was so great that the area was never developed, apart from a few luxury town houses on its fringes and the hefty Cape Technikon, a college that now occupies nearly a quarter of the former suburb. After years of negotiation, the original residents are being allowed to move back under a scheme to develop low-cost housing in the district.

THE DISTRICT SIX MUSEUM

Map 4, F4; Mon–Sat 10am–4.30pm; donation. Cape Town station.

Located on the corner of Barrack and Buitenkant streets, the **District Six Museum** is a memorial to the vibrant down-at-heel inner-city suburb (see box on p.71) that stood southeast of here until it was erased from the map under apartheid. The museum occupies the former **Central Methodist Mission Church**, which offered solidarity and ministry to the victims of forced removals right up to the 1980s, and was a venue for anti-apartheid gatherings. Today the church houses a collection of documentary photographs, a huge map of District Six as it was before the bulldozers moved in occupies most of the floor, and there's an almost complete collection of original street signs retrieved at the time of demolition.

As a living installation, intended as much for residents as tourists, it invites visitors to jot down comments, memories or reflections – which are as powerfully evocative as the exhibit itself – on any part of the display. There are few places in Cape Town that speak more eloquently of the effect of apartheid on the day-to-day lives of ordinary people.

STRAND STREET AND THE LOWER CITY CENTRE

Map 4, A1–3, B1–3 & C1–3. Cape Town station.

A major artery from the N2 freeway to the central business district, **Strand Street** neatly separates the more respectable Upper from the aptly named Lower city centre. Between the mid-eighteenth and mid-nineteenth centuries, Strand Street, because of its proximity to the shore, was one of the most fashionable streets in Cape Town, a fact that's now only discernible from the couple of quietly elegant National Monuments left standing amid the roar of traffic:

the **Evangelical Lutheran Church** and **Koopmans-De Wet House**.

For centuries, the **Lower City Centre** has been a marginal area between Cape Town and the sea, and stretches north of Strand Street to the shore, taking in the still-functional **Duncan Dock**. In the mid-nineteenth century, the city's middle classes viewed this seedy but vibrant quarter with a mixture of alarm and excitement – a tension that remains today.

Lower Long Street divides the area just inland from the docklands into two. To the east is the Foreshore, an ugly post-World War II wasteland of grey corporate architecture, among which is the **Nico Theatre Centre**, Cape Town's prestige arts complex. To the west, in sharp contrast, is the city's densely packed clubbing and pubbing locality.

Evangelical Lutheran Church Complex

Map 4, B3. Mon, Wed & Fri 9am–noon; free.

At the corner of Buitengracht, which marks the eastern boundary of the Bo-Kaap, and Strand Street, the **Evangelical Lutheran Church** now stands dwarfed by office blocks, but was once a Cape Town skyscraper, its spire towering over a one- and two-storey roofscape. Converted by **Anton Anreith** in 1785 from a barn, its facade includes Classical details such as a broken pediment perforated by the clock tower, as well as Gothic ones, such as the pointy arched windows. Inside, the magnificent **pulpit**, supported on two life-size Herculean figures, is one of Anton Anreith's masterpieces; the white swan perching on top of the canopy is a symbol of Lutheranism.

The establishment of a Lutheran church in Cape Town struck a significant blow against the extreme **religious intolerance** that pervaded under VOC rule. Prior to 1771, when permission was granted to Lutherans to establish their own congregation, not only was Protestantism the only form of worship allowed, but the Dutch Reformed Church held an absolute monopoly over saving people's souls. The Lutheran Church's congregation was dominated by Germans, who at the time constituted 28 percent of the colony's free burgher population.

Koopmans-De Wet House

Map 4, C3. Tues–Sat 9.30am–4.30pm; R3.

Sandwiched between two office blocks, **Koopmans-De Wet House**, 35 Strand St, is an outstanding eighteenth-century pedimented Neoclassical town house and museum, accommodating a very fine collection of antique furniture and rare porcelain. An inexpensive **guide** booklet gives interesting contextual background to the house and its history, while a separate brochure describes items in the collection: both are available at the entrance.

The building's **facade** has been attributed to Louis Thibault and Anton Anreith, but there's no proof of this. Whoever was responsible, the house represents a fine synthesis of Dutch elements – sash windows and large entrance doors – with the demands of local conditions, including the front *stoep* (verandah) punctuated at each end by a plastered masonry seat. Huge rooms, lofty ceilings and shuttered windows also take account of high summer temperatures.

The earliest sections of the house were built in 1701 by **Reyner Smedinga**, a well-to-do goldsmith who imported the building materials from Holland. The house changed hands more than a dozen times over the following two centuries, with minor additions made in the 1760s and a second storey added between 1774 and 1790. In 1806 it came into the hands of the de Wet family, eventually becoming the home of **Marie Koopmans-De Wet**

(1834–1906), a prominent figure on the Cape social and political circuit.

> The lantern in the fanlight of the entrance
> of Koopmans-De Wet House was a compulsory
> feature of all Cape town houses in the eighteenth
> and early nineteenth centuries, its purpose to
> shine light onto the street and thus hinder
> slaves from gathering at night to plot.

West of Lower Long Street: clubland

Map 4, A–B2.

As long as the docks have existed, there's been life after dark west of Lower Long Street, particularly along **Waterkant Street** and at the northern ends of **Bree** and **Loop streets**, where they intersect Waterkant. Frequented by sailors, dockers and sex workers, Cape Town's red-light district used to be a hard-drinking, drugged-up, apartheid-free zone where some of the city's best jazz was played and raids by the police were a regular part of the scene. These days, with a high density of **nightclubs** and **pubs**, the area has become the best place in Cape Town to club-crawl – one of the few where you're guaranteed action seven nights a week.

> For Lower City Centre club details,
> see "Clubs, Pubs and Live Music" on p.212.

The Foreshore

Map 4, E–G1.

The Foreshore, an area of reclaimed land north of Strand Street stretching to the docks and east of Lower Long Street, is a clumsy post-war development which was intended to transform Cape Town's harbour into a symbolic gateway to Africa, but instead turned out as a series of large concrete boxes surrounded by acres of windswept tarmac parking lots.

Heerengracht, a truncated two-lane carriageway running from Adderley Street to the harbour and punctuated at either end by massive roundabouts, each solemnly guarded by statues of Jan Van Riebeeck and Bartholomeu Dias, was meant to be the ceremonial axis through this grand scheme, joining the city to the sea. But the road never quite makes it to the water, coming to a disappointing standstill at the dock perimeter fence before bearing east under the dismal shadow of the N1 and N2 flyovers.

Cape Town's major performance venue is the **Nico Theatre Centre**, on DF Malan Street just east of Heerengracht. Incorporating the large Main Theatre, it also houses the small Arena Theatre and an opera house. Currently making attempts to throw off the burden of a long association with the apartheid establishment, the theatre is branching out into Afrocentric productions.

For more about the Nico Theatre Centre, see "Theatre and Cinema" on p.208.

Duncan Dock

Map 3, F2–F3.

North of the Foreshore, **Duncan Dock** is Cape Town's working harbour and presents a forbidding industrial landscape of large ships and towering cranes, cut off from the city by an enormous perimeter fence. Work started on the dock in 1938, swallowing the city beachfronts at Woodstock and Paarden Island to cater for the growing supertanker traffic that was outstripping the capacity of the

Victoria and Alfred Basins (see p.79). It's a fabulous place to take moody photographs of gigantic hulks against Table Mountain, but you won't want to linger here alone.

The Waterfront and Robben Island

The Victoria and Alfred Waterfront (known simply as the Waterfront), adjoining the west of Duncan Dock, is Cape Town's original Victorian harbour and now the most popular attraction on the peninsula. After two decades of stagnation it began to be redeveloped at the beginning of the 1990s, and has become the city's central shopping area, its most fashionable eating and drinking venue, the site of an excellent aquarium and the embarkation point for trips to Robben Island. Period buildings, imitation Victorian shopping malls, piers with waterside walkways and a functioning harbour complement the wide range of restaurants, outdoor cafés, pubs, clubs, cinemas, museums and outdoor entertainment, with magnificent Table Mountain rising beyond.

The Waterfront has drawn fire, though, partly because it is quite literally cut off from the rest of the city, by a security fence. Also, some feel it presents a sanitized, Anglo-Saxon version of history, with little acknowledgement of the thousands of slaves, press-ganged sailors, impoverished fishermen and prostitutes who made the place work and created its real historical atmosphere.

Controversy here is nothing new – arguments raged throughout the first half of the nineteenth century over the need for a proper dock. The Cape was often known as the **Cape of Storms** because of its vicious weather, which left Table Bay littered with wrecks. Many makeshift attempts were made, including the construction of a lighthouse in 1823, and work was begun on a jetty at the bottom of Bree Street in 1832. Clamour for a harbour grew with the expansion of sea traffic arriving at the Cape in the 1850s, and reached its peak in 1860, when the Lloyds insurance company refused the risk of covering ships dropping anchor in Table Bay.

The British colonial government eventually conceded and, on a suitably stormy September day in 1860, at a huge ceremony, the teenage Prince Alfred tipped the first batch of stones into Table Bay to begin the **Breakwater**, the westernmost arm of the harbour, which was subsequently completed with convict labour. In 1869, the dock – consisting of two main basins – was completed, and the sea was allowed to pour in.

Thirty-two information boards are arranged around the Waterfront to create an excellent self-guided historical tour that starts at the visitor centre, where you can buy an illustrated booklet covering the same route.

THE VICTORIA AND ALFRED BASINS

Map 5, E1–4 & F1–4. Waterfront shuttle bus.

Victoria Basin, the smaller **Alfred Basin** to its west, and the **Marina** beyond, create the Waterfront's geography of piers and quays, with most of the activity concentrated around the northwest side. The **Waterfront Visitor**

Centre, set back from the Victoria Basin on Dock Road (©418 2369, *info@waterfront.co.za*), provides maps and bookings for tours and taxis.

North of the visitor centre, the outdoor action centres around **Market Square** and the **Agfa Amphitheatre**, where you can sometimes catch free rock or jazz performances and occasionally hear the Cape Town Symphony Orchestra (details from the visitor centre). The shopping focus of the Waterfront is **Victoria Wharf**, an enormous flashy mall on two levels, extending along Quays Five and Six northeast of the amphitheatre. Inside the mall, you could be in any large city in the world, but the restaurants and cafés with outdoor seating on the mall's east side have fabulous views of Table Mountain across the busy harbour. On the west side of Victoria Wharf, the rather contrived **Red Shed Craft Workshop** (Mon–Sat 9am–9pm, Sun 10am–9pm) brings together craft workers such as glass blowers, leatherworkers, township artists and jewellery makers under one huge roof.

Head west from Market Square (away from the water) and you'll find yourself on Dock Road; 100m north along here is the **Imax Cinema** (information ©419 7365, booking via Computicket ©918 8970, tickets at the door) at the BMW Pavilion on the corner of Portswood Road. It shows nature documentaries on topics such as African elephants, the Grand Canyon and the Amazon.

Adjacent to the visitor centre is one of Cape Town's best wine shops, Vaughan Johnson's (see p.203) and, to the west, the **Telkom Exploratorium** (see p.234) in Union Castle Building, a small hands-on science museum that's a winner with kids. West of here along the Alfred Basin's North Quay, **Alfred Mall Shopping Centre** is a complex of fifteen touristy curio shops, boutiques and restaurants. West again is the **South African Maritime Museum** (daily 9am–5pm; R7), which is only worth visiting if you have a specialist

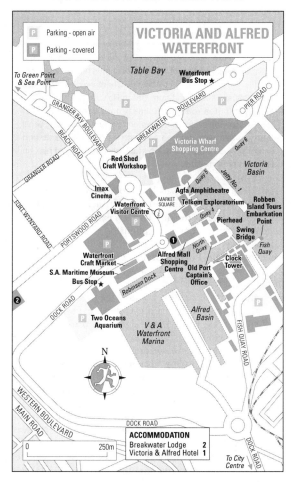

Waterfront transport

The Waterfront is one of the easiest points to reach in Cape Town by **public transport**. Waterfront shuttle buses leave from outside the train station in Adderley Street every ten minutes (daily 6.30am–10pm) and from Beach Road in Sea Point every twenty minutes (daily 6.30am–10pm), and terminate at Breakwater Boulevard on the Waterfront. Arriving by **car**, you'll find yourself well catered for, with several car parks and garages. If you want to leave by **taxi**, head for the taxi rank on Breakwater Boulevard.

interest and want to see its large collection of model ships. It's better to keep going west for a further 200m and conserve your energies for the **Two Oceans Aquarium** (see opposite), which is quite exceptional.

East of the Alfred Shopping Mall, the Pierhead is dominated by the **Old Port Captain's Office**, a gabled Arts and Crafts building erected in 1904, with an imposing presence that reflected its status as the nerve centre of the harbour in the early twentieth century. It is now the headquarters of the Victoria and Alfred Waterfront Company. From the Pierhead you can use the swing bridge to cross to **Fish Quay** and the Robben Island Tours Embarkation Point (see p.85). As its name suggests, the swing bridge pivots to allow ships to pass through the narrow channel that connects the Victoria and Alfred basins. Rising up from Fish Quay, the **Clock Tower** (not open to the public) is Cape Town's finest architectural folly. Built as the original Port Captain's office in 1882, this strange-looking octagonal structure with gothic windows consists of three stacked rooms with a stairwell running through its core. The mirror room on the second floor enabled the Port Captain to survey all the activities of the harbour without leaving his office.

Restaurants, cafés, pubs and takeaway joints by the score are dotted around the Waterfront, many of them along the quayside. Recommendations for eating are given on p.182, and for nightlife on p.215.

TWO OCEANS AQUARIUM

Map 5, 4E. Daily 9.30am–6pm; adults R34, children R18. Waterfront shuttle bus.

An unquestionable Waterfront highlight, the **Two Oceans Aquarium** on Dock Road at the Marina's North Wharf showcases the Cape's unique marine environment, where the warm waters of the Indian Ocean and the cold Atlantic mingle. It's all great fun, with lots of appeal for adults and kids, and is a major reason to visit the Waterfront.

Although you're not obliged to follow it, a designed route takes in the nine major galleries in sequence, starting on the **Ground Floor** with the **Indian Ocean**, where you'll see tank after tank of psychedelic fish. One of the most beautiful displays is of scores of small gossamer-like jellyfish floating gently in their ultra-violet cylindrical tank like parachutists. To its rear, the **Diversity Hall**, as its name implies, contains an astonishing variety of strange marine creatures, including giant spider crabs, octopuses, sea horses and the deadly devil firefish, whose lacey beauty disguises lethal spines. Also on the ground floor, the **Agfa Auditorium** shows videos on South Africa's marine life and related topics (such as underwater photography).

The **Basement** houses the **Alpha Activity Centre**, another good place to keep the kids occupied, with free organized activities such as puppet shows and face painting, and computers, which allow youngsters to explore marine ecology. The Centre is combined with the **Diving Animals** display, where you can watch a group of resident Cape fur seals frolicking under water.

The **Top Floor**, reached via a ramp, accommodates the **Story of Water**, which, in glorious reconstruction, traces the course of a river from its mouth, through a salt marsh and lagoon, to its source. Not to everyone's taste, it features a small colony of African penguins (which you can see in their natural state at Boulders; see p.131), while captive sea birds fly about the rafters. In the **Kelp Forest** in an adjacent gallery, a dense jungle of giant seaweed sways hypnotically with the rhythmic surge of the water; you can sit in the small amphitheatre and gaze at beautiful shoals of silvery fish shimmering through sunlit sea. From here a ramp takes you in a gentle downward spiral through the **Predators** exhibit, for many visitors the most compelling attraction of all. A massive tank, open to the ocean, houses some large resident ragged-toothed sharks, which glide past as you walk through a glass underwater tunnel; other species confined here include rays and giant turtles. The ramp brings you back to the ground floor and the chilling **Fangs** room. Walking through a highly theatrical reconstruction of a sunken wreck, with smoke, laser beams and spooky fish, you enter a space full of tanks containing a collection of the toothiest, deadliest and most monstrous eels and sea serpents in the world.

An **aquarium shop**, off the entrance foyer, with its plastic sharks, fluffy dolphins and souvenirs, can't help seeming slightly banal, but you'll also find some interesting natural history books, CDs and videos.

....

In the Touch Pool, adjacent to the Diversity Hall, you can get your hands wet stroking crabs, starfish and prickly sea urchins.

....

ROBBEN ISLAND

Map 1, B1–2. Inclusive ferry fare and island entry fee R100. Waterfront bus then Robben Island ferry; hourly ferry departures 8am–4pm daily.

A deeply atmospheric place, only a few kilometres from the commerce of the Waterfront, **Robben Island** is suffused by a meditative, otherwordly silence. This key site of South Africa's liberation struggle was intended to silence apartheid's domestic critics, but instead became an international focus for opposition to the regime. A flat and windswept island – which for nearly two decades was "home" to Nelson Mandela – it measures six square kilometres and is sparsely vegetated by low scrub. In December 1999 the entire island was declared a **UN World Heritage Site**.

The only way to get to Robben Island is from the Waterfront on one of the **tours** run by the Department of Arts and Culture. Tickets are sold at the **Clock Tower terminal**, which is also the embarkation point, and is reached across a swing bridge connecting the Pierhead to Fish Quay. It's worth opting for the longer visit, which includes time to explore the island on your own (4hr 30min inclusive of sailing time), since there's a lot to see and Robben Island is no place to rush around.

The island

Catamarans to the island take thirty minutes. On arrival at the tiny Murray's Bay harbour, you can start off with a **bus tour** around the island or, alternatively, a **tour of the prison**.

The bus tour gives a strong sense of the island's windswept, strangely forlorn environment, and stops off at several historical landmarks, the first of which is the **kramat**, a beautiful shrine built in memory of Tuan Guru, a

Muslim cleric from present-day Indonesia who was imprisoned here by the Dutch in the eighteenth century. On his release, he helped to establish Islam among slaves in Cape Town, where it has flourished ever since. You will also pass a **leper graveyard** and **church** designed by Sir Herbert Baker, both of which are quiet reminders that the island was a place of exile for leprosy sufferers in the early twentieth century.

Robert Sobukwe's house is a place that seems to echo with loneliness, and is perhaps the most affecting relic of incarceration on the island. It was here that Sobukwe, leader of the Pan Africanist Congress (a radical offshoot of the ANC; see p.313) was held in solitary confinement for nine years. He was initially sentenced to three years, but was regarded as so dangerous by the authorities that they passed a special law – the "Sobukwe Clause" – to keep him on Robben Island for a further six years. No other political prisoners were allowed to speak to him, but on seeing him they gestured solidarity with another son of the soil by letting sand trickle through their fingers. After his release in 1969, Sobukwe was restricted to Kimberley under house arrest, until his death from cancer in 1978.

Another stopoff is the **lime quarry** where Nelson Mandela and his fellow inmates spent countless hours of hard labour. The soft, pale stone is extremely bright under the summer sun, as a result of which Mandela and others have in later years suffered eye disorders. As the years passed, the lime quarry became a place of furtive study among the prisoners, with the help of sympathetic wardens.

The bus tour also takes in a stretch of coast dotted with shipwrecks and abundant seabirds, including the elegant **Egyptian sacred ibis**. You may also spot some of a recently expanded population of **antelope**: springbok, eland and bontebok.

The Maximum Security Prison

The **Maximum Security Prison**, a forbidding complex of unadorned H-blocks on the edge the of the island, is introduced with the **Footsteps of Mandela** tour through the famous **B-Section**; you'll be guided by a former inmate, after which you're free to wander. B-Section is a small compound full of tiny rooms that has become legendary in South African history; initially a place of defeat for the resistance movement, it ironically came to incubate and concentrate the energies of liberation. **Mandela's cell** is marked with fine understatement, but the rest have been left locked and empty. It is a fascinating challenge to the imagination of the free.

In the nearby **A-Section**, the "Cell Stories" exhibition skilfully suggests the sparseness of prison life; the tiny isolation cells contain personal artefacts loaned by former prisoners (including a functional saxophone made of found objects), plus quotations, recordings and photographs. There is a powerful minimalism to this exhibit; take your time, and let the recent past envelop you.

Towards the end of the 1980s, cameras were sneaked onto the island, and inmates took snapshots of each other, which have been enlarged to almost life size and mounted as the **Smuggled Camera Exhibition** in the D-Section communal cells. The jovial demeanour of the prisoners indicates their knowledge that the end was conceivably within sight; moreover, the warm cameraderie that evidently connects them suggests how people endured so many years of captivity. Another good option during the prison visit is the **Living Legacy** tour in F-Section, in which ex-political prisoner guides describe their lives here and answer your questions.

"We serve with pride"

Nelson Mandela may have been the most famous Robben Island prisoner, but he certainly wasn't the first. Established in the seventeeth century, it was a place of banishment for those who offended the political order – first for the **Dutch**, later the **British** and most recently the **Afrikaner Nationalists**. The island's first prisoner was the Strandloper leader **Autshumato**, who became an emissary of the British. After the Dutch settlement was established, he was jailed on the island in 1658 by Jan van Riebeeck. The rest of the seventeenth century saw a succession of East Indies political prisoners and Muslim holy men exiled here for opposing Dutch colonial rule (the latter going on to establish Islam at the Cape).

During the nineteenth century, the **British** used Robben Island as a dumping ground for deserters, criminals and political prisoners. Captured **Xhosa leaders** who defied the Empire during the Frontier Wars of the early to mid-nineteenth centuries were transported by sea from the Eastern to the Western Cape to be imprisoned, and many ended up on Robben Island. In 1846, the island's brief was extended to include a whole range of the **socially marginalized**, and criminals and political detainees were joined by vagrants, prostitutes, lunatics and the chronically ill – all endured a regime of brutality and maltreatment, even in hospital. In the 1890s, a leper colony was established alongside the social outcasts. The mentally ill were removed in 1921, and the lepers in 1930. During World War II, the **Defence Force** took over the island to set up defensive guns against a feared Axis invasion, which never came.

Robben Island's greatest era of notoriety began in 1961, when it was taken over by the **Prisons Department**. Prisoners arriving at the island prison were greeted by a slogan on the gate that read: "Welcome to Robben Island: We Serve with

Pride." By 1963, when Nelson Mandela arrived, it had become a maximum security prison, and all the warders – and none of the prisoners – were white; prisoners were only allowed to send and receive one letter every six months, and common-law and political prisoners were housed together, until 1971, when they were separated in an attempt to further isolate the politicals. Harsh conditions, including routine beatings and forced hard labour, were exacerbated by geography; there's nothing but sea between the island and the South Pole, with icy winds blowing in from across the Atlantic, and inmates were made to wear shorts and flimsy jerseys. Like every other prisoner, Mandela slept on a thin mat on the floor (until 1973, when he was given a bed because he was ill), and was kept in a solitary confinement cell measuring two metres square for sixteen hours a day.

The prisoners found ways of **protesting**, using hunger strikes and other means such as legal action and go-slows, and won improved conditions over the years. The island also became a university behind bars, where people of different political views and generations communed; it was not unknown for prisoners to give academic help to their warders. The last political prisoners were released from Robben Island in 1991, and the remaining common-law prisoners were transferred to the mainland in 1996. On January 1, 1997, control of Robben Island was transferred from the Department of Correctional Services to the Department of the Arts, Culture, Science and Technology, which established it as a museum.

Robben Island became the central focus of South Africa's **millennium celebrations**. Two hours before midnight, Mandela, President Mbeki and six former political prisoners walked to Mandela's former cell, where the 81-year old liberation hero handed a lighted candle to his successor. "It symbolizes that the freedom flame can never be put down by anybody," Mandela said. "There are good men and women around that will always keep it alight."

"WE SERVE WITH PRIDE"

The southern suburbs

The bulk of Cape Town's residential sprawl extends east into South Africa's interior away from Table Mountain and the city centre. It's here that the southern suburbs, the formerly whites-only residential areas, cut a swath from town, down the east side of Table Mountain, ending just before Muizenberg on the False Bay coast. Most of the peninsula's suburban attractions are concentrated here, including the best malls and cinemas.

From anywhere in the southern suburbs you can see Table Mountain rising above Cape Town. The area offers some quick escapes from the city heat into forests, gardens and **vineyards**, all hugging the eastern slopes of the mountain, and its extension, the Constantiaberg.

Adjacent to the southern suburbs and separated from them by the M5 freeway, the **Cape Flats** tail off to the east in a nondescript conglomeration of coloured suburbs, African townships and burgeoning shantytowns. This is where most Capetonians live, yet because of its reputation for crime and violence it's the part of the city least explored by tourists. Conducted tours, which are the safest way of getting around, will give you a real insight into the other side of Cape Town.

....

Southern suburbs stations along the Metrorail line, from Cape Town to Simon's Town, are shown on map 2.

....

WOODSTOCK, SALT RIVER AND OBSERVATORY

Map 3, G4–5 & H4–5. Woodstock, Salt River & Observatory stations.

First and oldest of the suburbs as you take an easterly exit from town is **Woodstock**, unleafy and windblown, but redeemed by some nice Victorian buildings, originally occupied by working-class coloureds but now largely yuppified.

To its east, **Salt River** is a harsh, industrial, mainly coloured area, built initially for workers and artisans, while **Observatory**, abutting its Salt River's southern end, is generally regarded as Cape Town's bohemian hub, a reputation fuelled by its proximity to the University of Cape Town in Rondebosch and its large student population. Many of the houses here are student digs, but the narrow Victorian streets are also home to young professionals, hippies and arty types. The refreshingly unrestored peeling arcades on Observatory's Lower Main Road, and the streets off it, have some nice cafés and lively bars, as well as a wholefood store, an African fabrics shop, one of Cape Town's few African restaurants – the *Africa Café* (see p.186), and a couple of antiques emporiums. The huge Groote Schuur Hospital, which overlooks the freeway that sweeps through Observatory, was the site of the world's first heart transplant in 1967.

WOODSTOCK, SALT RIVER AND OBSERVATORY

Observatory is safer after dark than the city centre, making it a good bet for party animals who want their nightlife (see p.216) and accommodation (see p.156) within easy walking distance of one another.

MOWBRAY AND ROSEBANK

Map 3, H6–7. Mowbray & Rosebank stations.

Heading along Station Road, away from the mountain and south of Observatory, is **Mowbray**, originally and gruesomely called Drie Koppen (Three Heads), after the heads of three slaves were impaled there in 1724; its name was changed in the 1840s. In the nineteenth century, this was the home of philologist Willem Bleek, who lived with a group of Khoisan convicts provided by the colonial authorities, so that he could study their languages and world-view. Bleek's pioneering work still forms the basis of much of what we know about traditional Khoisan life.

   Rosebank, to Mowbray's south, has a substantial student community, some resident in the so-called Tampax Towers, the unmistakable circular blocks on Main Road. Just beyond them is the brown-brick **Baxter Theatre**, on the corner of Woolsack and Main roads, one of Cape Town's premier arts complexes (see p.207). Heading west up Woolsack Road, after about 400m the road leads to the back of **Mostert's Mill** (daily 9am–5pm), which incongruously faces onto the busy M3 freeway. A real Dutch-style windmill with sails, built in 1796, it harks back to the days when there were wheat fields here instead of highways.

UCT Irma Stern Museum

Map 3, H7. Tues–Sat 10am–5pm; R5. Rosebank station.

Irma Stern is acknowledged as one of South Africa's pioneering twentieth-century artists, perhaps more for the fact that she brought modern European ideas to the colonies than anything else. The **UCT Irma Stern Museum** on Cecil Road, about 100m from Mostert's Mill, was the artist's home for 38 years until her death in 1966. It's definitely worth a visit to see Stern's collection of Iberian, African, Oriental and ancient artefacts; the whole house, in fact, reflects the artist's fascination with exoticism, starting with her own Gauguinesque paintings of "native types", the fantastic carved doors she brought back from Zanzibar, and the very untypical garden that brings a touch of the tropics to Cape Town with its exuberant bamboo thickets and palm trees.

Born in 1894 in the South African backwater town of Schweitzer-Reneke to German-Jewish parents, Stern studied at Germany's Weimar Academy, against whose conservatism she reacted. She adopted **expressionist distortion** in her paintings, some of which were included in the *Neue Sezession* Exhibition in Berlin in 1918. Stern went on several expeditions into Zanzibar and the Congo in the 1940s and 1950s, where she found the source for her intensely sensuous paintings. One of her most famous works is the much reproduced *The Eternal Child* (1916), a simple but vibrant portrait of a young girl, while *The Wood Carriers* (1951) uses raw ochres, browns and oranges to create an exoticized portrayal of a pair of African women.

Although Stern's work was appreciated in Europe, when she returned to South Africa after World War II, critics claimed that her style was simply a cover for technical incompetence. Indeed, her paintings shocked contemporary South Africa, but the country's art historians now regard her as the central figure of her generation.

MOWBRAY AND ROSEBANK

RONDEBOSCH

Map 3, H7. Rosebank & Rondebosch stations.

South of Rosebank, neighbouring **Rondebosch** is home to the **University of Cape Town** (UCT), handsomely festooned with creepers and sitting grandly on the mountainside, overlooking Main Road and the M3 highway. Of passing interest on the UCT campus is **The Woolsack**, just off Woolsack Road, a "cottage in the woods for poets and artists" designed in 1900 by Sir Herbert Baker for Cecil John Rhodes, who invited **Rudyard Kipling** "to hang up his hat there" whenever he visited the Cape. Taking his friend at his word, Kipling fled the English winter every year from 1900 to 1907, bringing his family to Cape Town and spending five to six months at The Woolsack, where it's said he wrote his famous poem *If*. The house is now occupied by the University's architecture faculty.

Rhodes features big in this neck of the woods; if you continue south from The Woolsack down the M3 (known here as Rhodes Drive), you'll pass **Groote Schuur**, another house built for him. One of Herbert Baker's most celebrated South African buildings, Groote Schuur exemplifies the Cape Dutch Revival style, which combined Cape vernacular elements with ideas from the Arts and Crafts Movement, then current in Baker's native Britain: it established a basis for what became seen as a local architectural idiom. Groote Schuur became the official prime ministerial (then presidential) residence of the Cape, though Nelson Mandela prefered to stay at the adjacent **Genadendal**. Neither building is open to the public.

The Rhodes Memorial

Map 3, H6. Daily dawn to dusk; free. Rosebank station.

North of the Upper Campus of the University of Cape

Town, towards the city, is **Rhodes Memorial**, built to resemble a Greek temple and grandiosely conspicuous against the slopes of Devil's Peak. The monument is reached via a signposted road that spurs northwest off the M3 just as Rhodes Drive becomes the Princess Anne Interchange. On a site chosen by Herbert Baker and Rudyard Kipling, the temple-like structure celebrates Cecil Rhodes' energy with a sculpture of a horse rearing up wildly; the empire builder's bust is planted at the top of a towering set of stairs. These are lined by reclining lions inspired by the Avenue of Sphynxes at Karnak in Egypt, a site greatly admired by Rhodes. Carved in stone beneath the bust, a ponderous inscription by Kipling reads: "The immense and brooding spirit still shall order and control."

Equally eye-catching are the herds of wildebeest and zebra, which nonchalantly graze in the Rhodes Estate on the slopes around the Memorial as cars fly past on the M3. From here you can walk to the King's Blockhouse, formerly a signalling station, to Muizenberg and on to the contour path, which follows the eastern side of the mountain, way above the southern suburbs to Constantia Nek (see "Table Mountain walks" on p.112).

....

The *Rhodes Memorial Restaurant*, a popular and recommended venue for breakfast or lunch with terrific views of Cape Town, is described on p.179.

....

SOUTH OF RONDEBOSCH

Map 2, E3–4. Newlands & Claremont stations.

Continuing **south from Rondebosch** along the M3 (here called the Van der Stel Freeway), or along the more congested Main Road, you pass some of Cape Town's most prestigious suburbs. **Newlands**, almost merging with

Rondebosch, is home to the city's famous rugby and cricket stadiums, while the well-heeled suburb of **Claremont** to its south is becoming an alternative to the city centre and the Waterfront for shopping and entertainment, with two cinema complexes and several malls. Alongside the high-quality shops, hawkers sell clothes, vegetables and herbs; closer to Claremont Station you can buy tasty *boerewors* rolls from women who cook them outdoors on *skottel braais* (gas braziers).

A little further on, **Bishopscourt**, as its name suggests, is home to the Anglican bishop of Cape Town; Archbishop Desmond Tutu lived here when it was a whites-only suburb. Partly because of its prime siting next to Kirstenbosch National Botanical Gardens – some plots have views of both the forested mountainside and the sea – this is one of the most prestigious areas in Cape Town; a number of consuls occupy huge properties behind forbiddingly high walls. Further down the line, **Wynberg** is known for the open-air Maynardville Theatre (see p.207) and quaint little row of shops and eating places.

KIRSTENBOSCH NATIONAL BOTANICAL GARDENS

Map 2, D4. April–Aug 8am–6pm, Sept–March 8am–7pm; R10. Shuttle bus from Cape Town Tourism.

Five kilometres south of Rondebosch, on Rhodes Avenue, are the popular **Kirstenbosch National Botanical Gardens**. The gardens are magnificent, glorying in lush shrubs and exuberant blooms, which trail off into **fynbos**, covering a huge expanse of the rugged eastern slopes and wooded ravines of Table Mountain. The setting is quite breathtaking – this is a great place to have tea and stroll around gazing up the mountain, or to wander onto the paths, which meander steeply to the top.

If you don't have a car and don't want to take an organized tour, the best way to get to Kirstenbosch is on one of
the **buses** operated from Cape Town Tourism by Linomtha
Shuttles (©934 2170; departures during season Mon–Sat
9.30am, 12.30pm & 2.30pm; R50); at other times you'll
have to rely on one of the local taxi services (see p.33). If
you're driving, take the M5, and leave it at the signposted
Rhodes Avenue turn-off. There is no train.

Kirstenbosch is the oldest and largest botanical garden in
South Africa, and was created by **Cecil Rhodes** in 1895
(his camphor and fig trees still flourish). Today, over 22,000
indigenous plants, and a research unit and library, attract
researchers and botanists from all over the world. There's a
nursery selling local plants, while characteristic Cape plants,
found nowhere else in the world, are cultivated on the
slopes. Little signboards and paved paths guide you through
the highlights of the gardens, with trees and plants identi-
fied by tags. One unusual route is the one created for blind
visitors, with labels in braille and an abundance of aromatic
and textured plants.

The cultivated gardens blend seamlessly into the mountainside, as there are no fences cutting off the way to the
top of **Table Mountain**. From here, you can make your
way up the mountain: two popular paths, starting from the
Contour Path above Kirstenbosch, are **Nursery Ravine**
and **Skeleton Gorge** (see p.115).

Kirstenbosch is wonderful for picnics;
if you're in town over the summer, bring a bottle
of Cape fizz to one of the Sunday evening open-air
concerts held in the gardens (see p.248). There's
also a good restaurant with outdoor seating for
breakfasts, lunches, teas and good coffee (see p.179).

KIRSTENBOSCH NATIONAL BOTANICAL GARDENS

Fynbos and the Cape Floral Kingdom

Early Dutch settlers were alarmed by the paucity of good timber on the Cape Peninsula's hillsides, which were covered by nondescript, scrubby bush they described as *fijn bosch* (literally "fine bush") and which is now known by its Afrikaans name **fynbos** (pronounced "fayn-bos"). They set about planting exotics, like the oaks that now shade central Cape Town, and over the ensuing centuries their descendants established pine forests on the sides of Table Mountain in an effort to create a landscape that fulfilled the European idea of the picturesque. It's only relatively recently that Capetonians have come to claim fynbos proudly as part of the peninsula's unique natural heritage.

You'll see fynbos all over Cape Town, and especially on the mountainsides. Remarkable for its astonishing variety of plants, it makes up eighty percent of the vegetation of the **Cape Floral Kingdom**, the smallest and richest of the world's six floral kingdoms; its 8500 species make it one of the global biodiversity hot spots. The Cape Peninsula alone, measuring less than 500 square kilometres, has 2256 plant species (nearly twice as many as Britain, which is 5000 times bigger). While the other five floral kingdoms cover vast areas such as Australia or the northern hemisphere, the entire Cape kingdom stretches across a relatively narrow coastal crescent. And despite the rather unpromising grey-green appearance from afar of the Cape Town mountainsides, if you get into the fynbos at any time of year (although spring and summer are the best times) you'll encounter countless beautiful little flowering shrubs.

The four basic types of fynbos are: **proteas**, South Africa's national flower which you'll see sold in bouquets at the airport if nowhere else; **ericas**, which comprise 600 species of heather (there are just 26 in the rest of the world); **restios**, or reeds; and **geophytes**, including ground orchids and the startling flaming red disas, which flower on Table Mountain in late summer.

CONSTANTIA AND ITS WINELANDS

Map 2, C5 & D4–5.

South of Kirstenbosch lie the elegant suburbs of **Constantia** and the Cape's oldest **winelands**. Luxuriating on the lower slopes of Table Mountain and the Constantiaberg, with tantalizing views of False Bay, the winelands are a thirty-minute drive from the centre off the M3, which runs south to Muizenberg.

The winelands started cultivated life in 1685 as the farm of **Simon van der Stel**, the governor charged with opening up the fledgling Dutch colony to the interior. Thrusting himself wholeheartedly into the task, he selected an enormous tract of the choicest land set against the Constantiaberg, the section of the peninsula just south of Table Mountain. Today, Constantia is Cape Town's oldest and most prestigious residential area, exuding the easy ambience of landed wealth, shaded by oak forests and punctuated with farm stalls, riding schools, designer Cape Dutch-style shopping centres and, of course, the vineyards.

Constantia grapes have been used for winemaking since van der Stel's first ouput in 1705. After his death in 1712, the estate was divided up and sold off as the modern **Groot Constantia**, **Buitenverwachting** and **Klein Constantia** vineyards. All three estates are open to the public and offer tastings – they're definitely worth devoting a few hours to, especially if you aren't heading further afield to the Winelands proper. Smaller in scale than Groot Constantia, Buitenverwachting and Klein Constantia both offer free wine tasting in less regimented conditions than at the bigger estate.

The Cape Winelands proper around the towns of Stellenbosch, Paarl and Franschhoek are covered on pp.276–300.

Getting to the wineries

There is no public **transport** to Constantia, but Groot Constantia features on most organized **tours** of Cape Town or the peninsula; see p.38. To get to the estates **by car**, take the signposted Groot Constantia off-ramp from the M3 onto Ladies Mile Extension, and follow the signs to Groot Constantia. Buitenverwachting and Klein Constantia are on Klein Constantia Road, just off Ladies Mile Extension, and are clearly signposted.

Groot Constantia

Map 2, D5. Museum daily 10am–5pm; R5. Cellar tours (booking essential ✆794 5128): April–Sept 11am & 3pm; Oct–March daily every hour 10am–4pm; R10. Wine tasting: April–Sept daily 10am–4.30pm; Oct–March daily 9am–5.30pm; R12. Grounds free.

The largest Cape Town wine estate and the one most geared to tourists is **Groot Constantia**, a national monument and satellite of the Cultural History Museum. Apart from having beautiful buildings and delightful gardens, it offers enough attractions in its museum, shop, cellar and two restaurants to justify a half-day visit.

Built in 1692, the **manor house**, a quintessential Cape Dutch building, was van der Stel's home, modified at the end of the eighteenth century, possibly by the French architect Thibault. It's thought that the magificent gables were added in the eighteenth or early nineteenth centuries, with an allegorical figure representing Abundance recessed into a niche in the central gable. The interior forms part of the **museum** and is decorated in a style typical of eighteenth- and ninetenth-century Cape landowners, containing interesting Neoclassical as well as Louis XV and XVI furniture and Delft and Chinese ceramics.

If you walk straight through the house and down the ceremonial axis, you'll come to the so-called **cellar** (actually a two-storey building above ground), fronted by a brilliant relief pediment. Attributed to the sculptor Anton Anreith, it depicts a riotous bacchanalia, featuring Ganymede in a scene that symbolizes winemaking. Inside, you can see the collection of wine-related objects dating from antiquity – such as amphoras – to the present.

Booking is essential for tours of the modern production cellar, but if you only want to taste and buy you're free to pop in to the **Bertrams Cellar** tasting room, where you should sample their flagship Governeurs Reserve, a red whose blend varies from vintage to vintage, and their Shiraz Reserve. Their best whites include the Chardonnay Reserve, Sauvignon Blanc and Weisser Riesling.

> The estate's informal and child-friendly
> *Tavern Restaurant* has outdoor seating and
> a kid's playground; the more formal
> *Jonkershuis* is described on p.179.

Buitenverwachting

Map 2, D5. Mon–Fri 9am–5pm, Sat 9am–1pm; free.

Buitenverwachting (roughly pronounced: bay-tin-fur-vuch-ting, with the "ch" as in the Scottish rendition of loch), on Klein Constantia Road, is a bucolic place in the middle of the suburbs, with sheep and cattle grazing in the fields as you approach the main buildings. Ducks, part of the environmentally friendly approach, are used for pest control – feeding on snails that prey on vines – while around the main buildings you might also spot a fine pig, contributing to the beautifully manicured gardens by nibbling at the lawns.

The **architecture** and setting at the foot of the Constantiaberg are as good reasons to come here as are the top-ranking wines. Overlooking the vineyards and backing onto the garden, the homestead was built in 1794 (the 1769 on the gable appears to be wrong) by Arend Brink, and features an unusual gabled pediment broken with an urn motif. Buitenverwachting produces some of South Africa's best **wines**, among them the classy Christine, a claret-style blend, and some excellent whites including their Sauvignon Blanc, Chardonnay and Rhine Riesling.

Despite deep historic roots, the estate is mould-breaking and has for many years provided its workers with some of the best living conditions of any South African farm. Unusual labour practices include the provision of two social workers, weekly visits by a doctor to the farm clinic, and worker involvement in the selection of new staff.

....

This estate excels at food as well as wine and the *Buitenverwachting Restaurant* (see p.186) is consistently rated one of South Africa's top ten. They also do luxury picnic lunches (Mon–Sat 12.30–2.30pm; R55; booking essential ©794 1012 or 794 2122), which you can enjoy under the oaks in their fabulous gardens.

....

Klein Constantia

Map 2, C5. Mon–Fri 9am–5pm, Sat 9am–1pm; free.

Klein Constantia, Klein Constantia Road (just over a kilometre west of Buitenverwachting), has a friendly atmosphere despite its slightly austere Cape Dutch exterior, and produces some fine wines. Something of a cult curiosity is its **Vin de Constance**, the recreation of an eighteenth-century Constantia beverage that was a favourite of Napoleon, Frederick the Great and Bismarck. It's a delicious dessert wine with a hefty price tag attached, packaged in a replica of the original bottle, and makes a novel souvenir. Apart from this, the estate shines through its **white wine** output, producing top-ranking Sauvignon Blanc, Semillon and Rhine Riesling. As well as wine, there's wildlife here: look out for the guinea fowl that roam the estate munching on beetles, and in summer you may see migrant steppe buzzards preying on unsuspecting starlings, which eat the grapes.

TOKAI

Effectively the southern extension of Constantia, forested **Tokai** is an excellent area for leafy recreation away from the centre, with some relaxed and child-friendly places for eating and drinking. To drive to Tokai from the centre of Cape Town, head south along the M3 and exit north onto Ladies Mile Road; continue for 100m before turning south into Spaanschemat River Road, which runs through the suburb.

> You can easily combine Tokai with a trip to the seaside, as the suburb is fifteen minutes' drive from the False Bay seaboard. Because it's protected from the winds, it also makes a good refuge when the southeaster blows.

Tokai Forest

Map 2, C6. Daily dawn to dusk.

Most people come out to Tokai for the well-marked hiking paths and mountain biking trails in the pine plantations of the **Tokai Forest**. You can get there along the M3 or Spaanschemat River Road (which becomes Orpen Road) – then turn west from either into Tokai Road, which leads

TOKAI

straight to the forest. About 1.2km from the M3 or 500m from Spaanschemat River Road, the road first passes through a forested section, equipped with picnic tables, though this isn't the nicest part of the forest or the best place to picnic. Rather keep on till you reach the Arboretum (see below).

A little further along the road from the picnic sites, you'll come to an opening in the forest occupied by **Tokai Manor House** (not open to the public). Designed by Louis Michel Thibault (see p.321) and built around 1795, this National Monument is an elegant gem of Cape Dutch architecture surrounded by trees, and combines the Cape Dutch style with the understated elegance of French Neoclassicism.

A hundred metres to its west lies the entrance to another National Monument, the historic plantation of trees that constitute the **Tokai Arboretum** (daily dusk to dawn; R2 donation), which has a car park and is the best place to begin rambling or have tea and scones at the thatched **café** close to the entrance gate. The arboretum is the work of Joseph Storr Lister, who was a nineteenth-century Conservator of Forests for the Cape Colony. In 1885 he experimented with planting 150 species of trees from temperate countries, with oaks and eucalyptus featuring extensively as well some beautiful California redwoods. Storr discovered that conifers were best suited to the Cape, which is why the plantation to the west of the arboretum, owned by the Safcol timber company, consists mainly of pines.

Several tracks and trails crisscross the arboretum and plantation providing easy walks and mountain biking trails (bring your own bike). There are several longer hikes, including the walk from the entrance gate to **Elephant's Eye Cave** (6km). This can easily be completed in well under three hours, and passes through beautiful moist woodland, before opening into montane fynbos that covers the slopes of the Constantiaberg, eventually leading to the cave, which offers terrific panoramas. Ask for a map and directions at the entrance gate or, if this is unattended, at the adjacent café.

Steenberg Vineyards

Map 2, D6. Tasting and sales: March–Aug Mon–Fri 8.30am–5.30pm; Sept–Feb Mon–Fri 8.30am–5.30pm, Sat 9am–1pm; free.

In a fabulous location at the foot of Steenberg mountain, the **Steenberg Vineyards** comprise a fine Cape Dutch manor house and three other farm buildings, set around large formal garden dating from 1695. This is South Africa's oldest wine estate: the lands were granted by Governor Simon van der Stel to the five-times widowed Catherina Michelse in 1682 and sold on in 1695 to Frederik Roussouw. That year Roussouw erected the first buildings and made the first wine on the estate. After his death, his widow Christina Diemer turned it into a highly profitable business providing hospitality to travellers and provisions to the fleet when the VOC declared Simon's Town its winter port in 1741. It is now one of Cape Town's best country hotels, using the refurbished buildings that were declared a National Monument in 1996. Of their wines, the fine Merlot is the best of their reds and, when it comes to whites, the Sauvignon Blanc and Semillon stand out.

Apart from wines, Steenberg is also known for its elegant country hotel (see p.162). For family refreshments, the Barnyard Farmstall, just outside the winery gate, does excellent coffee and tasty snacks, and has a kids' playground (see p.240).

TOKAI

The Cape Flats

The **Cape Flats** are exactly that: flat, as well as being barren and windswept. This is Cape Town's largest residential area, taking in the coloured districts, African townships and shanty-town squatter camps – you can't miss it as it stretches east away from the former whites-only southern suburbs, the M5 acting as a dividing line. Exclusively inhabited by Africans and coloureds in their own separate areas, the Cape Flats can be both shocking and heartening, their abject poverty coexisting with a spirit of enterprise and stoicism.

Several projects are underway to encourage tourists to visit the townships but, as a high proportion of Cape Town's nearly 2000 annual murders take place here, the recommended way to visit is on one of the **tours** listed on p.38. All the tours recommended in the guide are operated by residents of the Cape Flats or in co-operation with local communities, and emphasize face-to-face encounters with ordinary people. What you see depends on the interests of the tour group, but could include: visits to shebeens, nightclubs and a township restaurant; chats to residents of squatter camps and the Langa hostels; and meetings with traditional healers and music makers, township artists and craftworkers. Some tours also take in "sites of political struggle", where you'll be taken to places where significant events in the fight against apartheid occurred.

African townships were set up as dormitories to provide labour for white Cape Town, not as places to build a life, which is why they had no facilities and no real hub. **Men-only hostels**, another apartheid relic, are at the root of many of the area's social problems. During the 1950s, the government set out a blueprint to turn the tide of Africans flooding into Cape Town. No African was permitted to settle permanently in the

Cape west of a line near the Fish River, the old frontier over 1000km from Cape Town; women were entirely banned from seeking work in the city and men prohibited from bringing their wives to join them. By 1970, there were ten men for every woman in Langa.

In the end, apartheid failed to prevent the influx of work-seekers desperate to come to Cape Town. Where people couldn't find legal accommodation they set up **squatter camps** of makeshift iron, cardboard and plastic sheeting. During the 1970s and 1980s, the government attempted to eradicate these by demolishing them and destroying people's property. But no sooner had the police left than the camps reappeared, and they are now a permanent feature of the Cape Flats. One of the best known of all South Africa's squatter camps is **Crossroads**, whose inhabitants suffered campaigns of harassment that included killings and continuous attempts to bulldoze it out of existence. Through sheer determination – and no little despera-tion – its residents hung on and eventually won the right to stay. Today, the government is making attempts to improve condi-tions in the shantytowns by bringing in running water and sani-tation: facilities are starting to improve, families are moving in and traders are beginning to operate.

Langa is the oldest and most central township, lying just east of the white suburb of Pinelands and north of the N2. In this relentlessly grey and shapeless place, without the tiniest patch of green relief, you'll find women selling sheep and goat heads, alongside township entrepreneurs running state-of-the-art public phone bureaus from inside recycled cargo contain-ers. Middle-class black families live in smart suburban houses while, in the former men-only hostels, as many as three fami-lies share one room.

South of the African ghettos is **Mitchell's Plain**, a coloured area stretching down to the False Bay coast, which you'll skirt
Continues overleaf

THE CAPE FLATS

107

The Cape Flats (continued)

if you take the M5 to Muizenberg. More salubrious than any of the black townships, Mitchell's Plain reflects how lighter skins meant better conditions under apartheid. But for coloureds the forced removals were also tragic, many being summarily forced to vacate family homes because their suburb had been declared a White Group Area. Many families were relocated here when District Six was razed (see p.71), and their communities never fully recovered – one of the symptoms of dislocation are the violent gangs, which have become an everyday part of Mitchell's Plain youth culture.

Table Mountain

The icon that announces Cape Town to seafarers, Table Mountain (1087m), a flat-topped massif with dramatic cliffs and eroded gorges, dominates the northern end of the peninsula. Its north face overlooks the city centre, with the distinct formations of Lion's Head and Signal Hill to the west and Devil's Peak to the east. The west face is made up of a series of gabled formations known as the Twelve Apostles. The southwest towers over Hout Bay, and the eastern face looks down over Cape Town's suburbs.

Table Mountain is a compelling feature in the middle of the city, a wilderness where you'll find wildlife and 1400 species of **flora**. Indigenous mammals include baboons, dassies (hyraxes) and porcupines, while the animals that resemble mountain goats are Himalayan tahrs, descended from specimens introduced by Cecil Rhodes onto his estate, which escaped to flourish on the mountain.

A popular source of recreation for Capetonians, Table Mountain has suffered under the constant pounding of **hikers**, though the damage isn't always obvious – certainly not from the dizzying summit. If you plan on tackling one of the hundreds of walks and climbs on its slopes, go properly prepared (see box); you might also like to consider the services of a guide (see "Sports and outdoor activities" on p.221). One common difficulty is people losing the track

Dassies

The outsized fluffy guinea pigs you'll encounter at the top of Table Mountain are **dassies** or hyraxes (*Procavia capensis*) which, despite their appearance, aren't rodents at all, but the closest living relatives – some way back – of elephants. Their name (pronounced like "dusty" without the "t") is the Afrikaans version of *dasje*, meaning "little badger", given to them by the first Dutch settlers. Dassies are very widely distributed, having thrived in South Africa with the elimination of predators, and hang out in suitably rocky habitat all over the country.

Like reptiles, dassies have poor body control systems and rely on shelter against both hot sunlight and the cold. They wake up sluggish and first thing in the morning seek out rocks where they can catch the early morning sun – this is one of the best times to look out for them. One adult stands sentry against predators and issues a low-pitched warning cry in response to a threat. Dassies live in colonies of a dominant male and eight or more related females and their offspring.

(often due to sudden mist falling) and ending up stranded and lost.

THE CABLE CAR

Map 3, C6–7. Mid-April to mid-Sept R45; mid-Sept to Nov R60; Dec to mid-April R65. Kloof Nek bus, then walk; shuttle bus from Cape Town Tourism; or minibus taxi.

The **cable car** journey up Table Mountain is a Cape Town must: don't go home without doing it. To cope with half a million visitors annually, a state-of-the art Swiss system was installed in 1997; the floor of the fishbowl-shaped car is designed to complete a 360-degree rotation on its way to the top, giving passengers a full panorama. Cars

Table Mountain safety

MAKE SURE YOU . . .
- Don't climb alone
- Inform someone you're going up the mountain, tell them your route, when you're leaving and when you expect to be back
- Leave early enough to give yourself time to complete your route during daylight
- Don't try to descend via an unknown route – if you get lost in poor weather, seek shelter, keep warm and wait for help
- Never leave litter on the mountain
- Never make fires – no cooking (even on portable stoves) is allowed

WEAR . . .
- Good footwear – boots or running shoes are recommended
- A broad-rimmed hat to keep the sun off

TAKE . . .
- A backpack
- A water bottle – allow two litres per person
- Enough food – sandwiches, glucose sweets, nuts, raisins, juice
- A warm jersey
- A waterproof windbreaker
- Sunglasses
- High-factor sunscreen
- Plasters for blisters
- Money for the cable car

leave from the **Lower Cable Station** on Tafelberg Road (daily every 10–20 min: May–Oct 8.30am–6pm; Nov 7.30am–9pm; Dec–April 7.30am–10pm; ©424 5148 or 424 8181).

The trip takes you to the **Upper Cable Station** at the

northeastern end of the Western Table, a height of 1073m. From here you can walk along a circular paved path to get spectacular views of Table Bay on one side and the Atlantic seaboard on the other. An overpriced but pleasant **tea room** has fine views, plus there's a classier bistro and a gift shop.

TABLE MOUNTAIN WALKS

Walking up the mountain will give you a greater sense of achievement than being ferried up by the cable car, but proceed with extreme caution: the **weather** is subject to rapid changes, both in general and in small localized areas, the main hazards being sun, mist and violent winds. Unless you're going with a knowledgeable guide, attempt only the simplest routes as outlined below.

....

The *Approved Paths on Table Mountain* map is published by the **Mountain Club of South Africa**, and available from Cape Union Mart at the Waterfront or Cavendish Square Shopping Centre in Claremont (R15).

....

Signal Hill and Lion's Head

Map 3, C3 & B5. Signal Hill Road to Lion's Head, 2hr; Lion's Head ascent, 2hr.
From the roundabout at the top of Kloof Nek, the junction of Kloof Nek and Tafelberg roads, where you'll find the Kloof Nek bus terminus, a road leads all the way along **Signal Hill** to a car park and lookout with great views over Table Bay, the docks and the city. A cannon was formerly used for sending signals to ships at anchor in the bay, and the Noon Gun, still fired from the viewpoint at the top, sends a thunderous rumble through the Bo-Kaap below.

Halfway along the road is a sacred Islamic *kramat* (shrine), one of several dotted around the Peninsula.

You can also walk up **Lion's Head**, an unstrenuous and popular hike that seems to bring out half of Cape Town every full moon. Heading north from Kloof Nek for about 500m along Signal Hill Road, you'll come to a car park. A jeep track, which becomes a path, leads west from here up the head.

Platteklip Gorge and Maclear's Beacon

Map 2, D3. Tafelberg Road to Platteklip Gorge, 2–3hr.

The first recorded ascent of Table Mountain was by the Portuguese captain, Antonio de Saldanha, in 1503. He wisely chose **Platteklip Gorge**, the gap visible from the central front table (the north side) which, as it turned out, is the most accessible way up. It's a very steep slog though, which takes two to three hours from the foot to the summit, if you're reasonably fit. A short and easy extension will get you to Maclear's Beacon (1086m), the highest point on the mountain. Taking the Platteklip route, you end up at the Upper Cable Station, so you can hop on a car to get back down.

The route starts out at the Lower Cable Station. From here, walk east for 1.5km along Tafelberg Road until you see a high embankment built from stone and maintained with wire netting; just beyond and to the left of a small dam is a sign pointing to Platteklip Gorge. A steep fifteen-minute ascent brings you onto the **upper contour path**. Head east along this for about 25m, then take the path heading up the mountain indicated by a sign reading "Contour Path/Platteklip Gorge". Zigzagging from here onwards, the path is very clear. Once on top, turn right and ascend the last short section onto the **front table**, for a breathtaking view of the city. A sign points the way to the

Upper Cable Station – a fifteen-minute walk along a concrete path, which is usually thronged with visitors.

Maclear's Beacon is about 2km (45min) from the top of the Platteklip Gorge on a path leading eastward, with waymarks – white squares on little yellow footsteps – guiding you all the way. The path crosses the front table with Maclear's Beacon visible at all times. From the top you'll look out over False Bay and the Hottentots Holland Mountains to the east.

The Pipe Track

Map 3, C5–7. Kloof Nek bus terminus; up to 3hr each way.

One of the most rewarding and easiest walks along the mountainside is along the **Pipe Track**, a service road that leads from Kloof Nek along the west flank of Table Mountain. The route begins at some stone steps opposite the Kloof Nek bus terminus, just to the west of the Tafelberg Road turnoff (if you're driving, park on Tafelberg Road). Steps lead up alongside forestry staff houses before the path levels off under some pines. On the level for roughly 7km, the track runs beneath the Twelve Apostles and follows the mountain's contours, offering fantastic views of the Atlantic.

The route intersects several climbs up the mountain. The first, after about 45 minutes, is indicated by a sign to **Blinkwater Ravine** (closed to the public due to rockfalls). A further ten to fifteen minutes brings you to the Kasteelspoort ascent (signposted under gum trees), followed by **Woody Ravine** and the last, roughly 25 minutes after Kasteelspoort, at **Slangolie Ravine**, where the path ends. The rock bed on Slangolie is steep, unstable and to be avoided. Turn back when you see the first of the Woodhead Tunnel danger signs. The Pipe Track isn't a circular route, so you can turn back at any point; the walk takes two to three hours each way.

Skeleton Gorge and Nursery Ravine

Map 2, D4. Skeleton Gorge ascent, 2hr 30min; Nursery Ravine descent, 2hr 30min.

You could make an ascent of Table Mountain via one route and descend down another, ending at the Kirstenbosch National Botanical Gardens' **restaurant** for tea; the entire walk lasts about five hours. Starting at the restaurant, follow the **Skeleton Gorge** signs, which lead you onto the **Contour Path**. At the Contour Path, a plaque indicates that this is **Smuts' Track**, the route favoured by Jan Smuts, the Boer leader, statesman, philosopher, friend to the British, and South African prime minister (1919–1924 and 1939–1948). The plaque marks the start of a broad-stepped climb up Skeleton Gorge, involving wooden and stone steps, wooden ladders and loose boulders. Be prepared for steep ravines and difficult rock climbs, and under no circumstances stray off the path as it's easy to get lost. It requires reasonable fitness, but can take as little as an hour. Skeleton can be an unpleasant way down, especially in the wet season when it gets slippery.

Nursery Ravine is recommended for the descent. At the top of Skeleton Gorge, walk a few metres to your right to a sign indicating Kasteelspoort. It's just 35 minutes from the top of Skeleton along this path to the head of Nursery Ravine; the descent returns you to the 310-metre Contour Path, which leads back to Kirstenbosch.

....

**Kirstenbosch National Botanical Gardens
are covered in detail on p.96.**

....

TABLE MOUNTAIN WALKS

115

The Atlantic seaboard

Table Mountain's steep drop into the ocean along much of the western peninsula forces the generally upmarket suburbs along the Atlantic seaboard to cling dramatically to the slopes. The sea washing the west side of the peninsula can be very chilly, far colder than on the False Bay seaboard, but there's consolation in the dramatic coastal roads, particularly beyond Sea Point. The coast itself consists of a series of bays and white-sand beaches, edged with smoothly sculpted rocks; inland, the series of rocky buttresses known as the Twelve Apostles, gaze down onto the surf. The beaches are ideal for sunbathing or sunset picnics – it's from this side of the Peninsula that you can watch the sun sink into the ocean, creating fiery reflections on the sea.

GREEN POINT AND SEA POINT

Maps 5 & 6. Sea Point & City–Bakoven/Hout Bay buses.

Inland from the Waterfront and stretching for about a kilometre to the west, **Green Point** is one of the suburbs closest to the city centre, with a growing supply of budget accommodation, but little else to recommend it. Green Point's Main Road is notorious as a major hangout for prostitutes and pimps, who are conveniently close here to their gangland turf in the Bo-Kaap.

Continuing southwest along Main Road, Green Point merges with the more fashionable **Sea Point**, a long-established place for great restaurants. Middle-class couples, pram-pushing mothers, street kids and drunks create a blend of respectability and seediness that dissipates as you move into the wealthier suburbs down the Atlantic seaboard.

The closest seaside to the city centre is a block down from Main Road, although it's too rocky for swimming. Halfway along the kilometre-long beach promenade, running alongside Beach Road, you'll catch views of **Graaff's Pool**, an institutionalized and exclusively male nudist spot, while at the westernmost end is the only place in the vicinity to swim, at the spanking-new Olympic-sized **saltwater pool** (daily Easter to Sept 8am–5pm; Oct to Easter 7am–6.45pm), alongside the crashing surf.

Sea Point and Green Point are the closest suburbs to both the city and the sea and are dense with accommodation, which you'll find listed on p.152.

CLIFTON TO SANDY BAY

Map 2. Hout Bay bus.

Suburbia proper begins south of Sea Point at Bantry Bay. Fashionable **Clifton** (C2), on the next cove, is sheltered by Lion's Head: the sea here is good for surfing and safe for swimming, but bone-chillingly cold. Clifton is studded with fabulous seaside apartments and has four wonderful sandy beaches, reached via steep stairways. First Beach (they're all numbered) is colonized by pneumatic athletic types and surfers, so avoid it unless your tan is up to scratch. Second and Third beaches are split between teenagers and thirtysomethings; if in doubt, head for Fourth, which has become the family beach because it has the fewest steps.

A little to the south, **Camps Bay** (C3) suburb climbs the slopes of Table Mountain and is scooped into a small amphitheatre, bounded by the Lion's Head and the Twelve Apostles sections of the Table Mountain range. This, and the high views across the Atlantic, make Camps Bay one of the most desirable places to live in Cape Town. The main drag, Victoria Road, skirts the coast and is packed with trendy restaurants, while the wide sandy beach is accessible by bus and is enjoyed by families of all colours. Lined by a row of palms and with welcome shade for picnics, Camps Bay beach positively throngs around the Christmas and Easter breaks, despite the chilly waters.

There's little development between Camps Bay and **Llandudno** (B4), a wonderful cove 20km from Cape Town along Victoria Road (not served by public transport; the small car park spills over into the suburban streets at peak periods). A steep and narrow road winds down past smart homes to the shore, where the sandy beach is punctuated at either end by magnificent granite boulders and rock formations. This is a good sunbathing spot and a choice one for bring-your-own sundowners.

Isolated **Sandy Bay** (B5), Cape Town's main nudist beach, can only be reached via a twenty-minute walk from Llandudno. In the apartheid days the South African police went to ingenious lengths to trap nudists, but nowadays the beach is relaxed. To get there, take the path from the south end of the Llandudno car park, through fynbos vegetation (see p.98) and across some rocks to the beach. It's a fairly easy walk, but watch out for broken glass – and bring your own food supplies, as there are no facilities of any kind.

HOUT BAY

Map 2, B–C5. City–Bakoven/Hout Bay bus.

Hout Bay is at a convenient junction for the rest of the peninsula and has the highest concentration of places to stay south of Sea Point, including the upmarket, country-style *Hout Bay Manor* (✆ 790 0116; ⑦–⑧). From Cape Town it's a twenty-kilometre trip either along the coast or inland via Constantia.

Although not the quaint fishing village it once was, Hout Bay still has a functioning **harbour** and is the centre of the local crayfish industry. And, despite ugly modern development and a growing shantytown, the natural setting is quite awesome. Next to the harbour and car park, the little **Mariner's Wharf** waterfront development shelters the Seafood Emporium, which has an upstairs restaurant and sells fresh fish – it's a good place to pick up fresh snoek, a Western Cape speciality.

The sea off the long slender beach is no good for swimming – too cold, too close to the harbour and too prone to fish scales floating in its surf – but the beach is perfect for walking. Away from the harbour, the **Hout Bay Museum**, 4 St Andrews Rd (Tues–Sat 10am–12.30pm & 2–4.30pm; R2), offers good exhibits on the Strandloper (Khoisan people who hunted and gathered along the shore) and the local fishing industry.

World of Birds

Map 2, C5. Daily 9am–5pm; R25.

Near the harbour, **World of Birds** on Valley Road is one of the world's biggest bird parks, with huge walk-through aviaries. It's a great chance to see unusual species such as African blue cranes and Australian cassowaries, and there's also a wildlife sanctuary, as well as a children's "touch"

HOUT BAY

farmyard. Alternatively, go down to the estuary near the harbour to see local birds in their natural environment for free; kingfishers and blacksmith plovers are commonly sighted residents.

CHAPMAN'S PEAK DRIVE

Map 2, C6.

Continuing south from Hout Bay, **Chapman's Peak Drive** is a thrilling journey: one of the most beautiful drives in the world. For 10km the road carves into the mountainside on the one side, dropping hundreds of precipitous metres to the ocean on the other. Unceasingly spectacular views take in the breadth of Hout Bay to the 331-metre high Sentinel, which sits on a curved outcrop. **Viewpoints** are provided along the route, but take care in high winds as it can be dangerous, with occasional rockfalls, one of which forced the authorities to close the road for several months at the beginning of 2000.

NOORDHOEK, KOMMETJIE AND SCARBOROUGH

Noordhoek (Map 2, B7), a low-key settlement at the end of the descent from Chapman's Peak Drive, consists of smallholdings in a gentle valley, its long white beach stretching 3km across Chapman's Bay to Kommetjie. The sands are fantastic for walking and horse-riding, but can be whipped up fiercely when the southeaster blows. Swimming is hazardous, though surfers relish the rough waters around the rocks to the north. For refreshment, the only place around here is the excellent *Red Herring* **restaurant** (see p.190), about ten minutes on foot from the car park as you head away from the sea, with fine views from its outdoor deck.

Although it's only a few kilometres south of Noordhoek along the beach, getting to **Kommetjie** by road involves a fifteen-kilometre haul inland up the peninsula spine south along Noordhoek Road, taking a west turn into Kommetjie Road, to descend again. The beach's small basin (*kommetjie*), which is always a few degrees above the surrounding sea temperature, is perfect for swimming. Just to its north, Long Beach is a favourite **surfing** spot used by devotees even during the chilly winter months.

Almost 10km by road from Kommetjie, the developing village of **Scarborough** is the most far-flung suburb along the peninsula. A long wide beach edges temptingly to its south just beyond Schusters River Lagoon – resist the potentially treacherous sea and stick to the lagoon. The *Camel Rock* is a decent place to stop and eat.

**For more about surfing, see
"Sports and outdoor activities" on p.221.**

NOORDHOEK, KOMMETJIE AND SCARBOROUGH

The False Bay seaboard

Flase Bay, on the east coast of the peninsula, is Cape Town's longest-established and most popular seaside development, its waters several degrees warmer than those on the Atlantic seaboard. A series of village-like suburbs, served by the Metro Rail, backs onto the mountains – from Muizenberg down to Simon's Town. The most characterful of these places is Kalk Bay, which has a small working harbour, a string of intriguing shops, some good cafés and the Brass Bell, a great seaside pub-restaurant. Fish Hoek, otherwise drab, has a lovely bathing beach, while Simon's Town, one of South Africa's oldest settlements, is worth taking in as a day-trip and makes a good base for visiting the Cape of Good Hope Nature Reserve and Cape Point. A wilderness area, the reserve is an excellent place to see fynbos as well as Cape wildlife (baboons, seals and antelope species such as the horse-sized bontebok), while, at dramatic Cape Point, cliffs drop to an angry sea.

MUIZENBERG

Map 2, E7. Muizenberg station.

Once South Africa's most fashionable beachfront, today **Muizenberg** has become rather tacky, although plans are in the pipeline to upgrade and restore it. Brightly coloured bathing huts are reminders of a more elegant heyday, when it was visited by the likes of Agatha Christie, who enjoyed riding its waves while holidaying here in the 1920s: "Whenever we could steal time off," she wrote, "we got out our surf boards and went surfing."

Despite the slight air of tawdriness, Muizenberg's gently shelving sandy **beach** is the most popular along the peninsula for swimming – with reason. It's safe, the water tends to be warm and there's good surfing, plus a pavilion complex around the car park featuring tea shops, a waterslide and minigolf. Along the beachfront and Main Road you'll also find shops, cafés and restaurants catering to the seaside trade.

A paved coastal path ribbons along the ocean from Muizenberg to St James (1.5km); it's a perfect way to take in the stupendous views across the bay, and leads conveniently to the Natale Labia Museum (see p.125) for refreshment.

THE HISTORICAL MILE

Map 2, E7–8. Muizenberg & St James stations.
Striking out south from Muizenberg, Main Road and the railway line hug the shore all the way to Simon's Town. A short stretch, starting at Muizenberg station, is known as the **Historical Mile**, dotted with notable buildings and easily explored on foot. **Muizenberg station**, an Edwardian-style edifice completed in 1913, is now a national monument, while further towards Simon's Town is

Whale-watching sites

Cape Town's finest **whale-watching sites** are on the warm False Bay side, but its worth noting that there are more spectacular spotting opportunities east of Cape Town, especially around Hermanus (see p.260). You'll need binoculars to get a decent sighting, and look out for whale signboards, indicating the best places to spend time looking for them. The commonest whales along this section of coast are southern rights (see pp.263–264).

Boyes Drive, running along the mountainside behind Muizenberg and Kalk Bay, provides an outstanding vantage point. To get there by car, head out on the M3 from the city centre to Muizenberg, taking a sharp right into Boyes Drive at Lakeside, from where the road begins to climb, descending finally to join Main Road between Kalk Bay and Fish Hoek. Alternatively, sticking close to the shore along Main Road, the stretch between **Fish Hoek** and **Simon's Town** is recommended, with a particularly nice spot above the rocks at the south end of Fish Hoek Beach, as you head south towards Glencairn. **Boulders Beach** at the southern end of Simon's Town has a whale signboard, and smooth rocky outcrops above the sea to sit on and gaze out over the sea. Even better vantage points are further down the coast between Simon's Town and **Smitswinkel Bay**, where the road goes higher along the mountainside.

Without a car, it's easy enough to go by **train** to Fish Hoek or Simon's Town and whale-spot from the Jager's Walk beach path that runs along the coast from the beachfront restaurant at Fish Hoek to Simon's Town.

Information on exactly where whales have been sighted in the past 24 hours is available from the **Whale Watch Hotline** (toll-free ©0800/22 8222).

the **Posthuys**, a rugged whitewashed and thatched building dating from 1673 and a fine example of the Cape vernacular style.

Natale Labia Museum

Map 2, E7. Tues–Sun 10am–5pm; R3. Muizenberg station.

Most idiosyncratic of the buildings along the historical mile is the **Natale Labia Museum**, 192 Main Rd, completed in 1930 as the residence of the Italian Consul. Built in eighteenth-century Venetian style, it sits incongruously in the Main Road townscape. Inside, heavy lace obscures the magnificent view, but the museum is a satellite of the South African National Gallery and often has strong exhibitions of work from their permanent collection. An excellent **restaurant** serves up breakfasts, light meals and teas in the ersatz-Baroque interior or on the Italianate patio.

Rhodes' Cottage Museum

Map 2, E7. Tues–Sun 10am–1pm & 2–5pm; free. St James station.

The **Rhodes' Cottage Museum**, to the south of the Natale Labia Museum, was the home of Cecil Rhodes, bought by him in 1899; he died at this unassuming little building in 1902 before his grander dwelling, neighbouring Rust en Vrede (closed to the public) could be completed. Rhodes' Cottage paints a distinctly rosy portrait of the man, with photographs and a model of the Big Hole in Kimberley (where Rhodes made his fortune at the diamond diggings). Also on display is a curious diorama of World's View in Zimbabwe's Matopos Hills, where Rhodes lies buried.

THE HISTORICAL MILE

February 1902 was a particularly hot month in Cape Town and Cecil Rhodes, who was asthmatic, was finding it difficult to breath at Groote Schuur, his grand house in Newlands. He asked to be moved to his cottage in Muizenberg, where he could be cooled by the sea breezes. Even Muizenberg became unbearable and Rhodes decided to return to England on March 26 – the day he died.

ST JAMES

St James station.

St James, 2km south of Muizenberg and just one stop away by train, is far more upmarket than its northern neighbour, and its pleasing villagey feel makes it a nice place to hop off the train. The compact beach draws considerable character from its much-photographed Victorian-style bathing huts, whose primary colours catch your eye as you pass by road or rail. The rocky beaches here don't make for great sea swimming, although it's always sheltered from the wind and there's a tidal pool that is safe for toddlers and fun for bathing at high tide, when enormous breakers crash over the sea wall.

KALK BAY

Map 2, D8. Kalk Bay station.

Kalk Bay, one of the most southerly and smallest of Cape Town's suburbs, is a lively **working harbour** with wooden fishing vessels, mountain views and a shopping precinct packed with trendy coffee shops, antique dealers and curiosity shops.

Apart from the larger Hout Bay, Kalk Bay is the only

harbour settlement still worked by coloured fishermen; the suburb somehow managed to slip through the net of the Group Areas Act, making it one of the few places on the peninsula with an intact coloured community. From the small docks you can watch the boats come in, buy fresh fish from stalls on the quayside and, for a few extra rand, have them scaled and gutted while you wait.

Perched on the harbour wall in the station building, pounded by waves, is the popular *Brass Bell* **restaurant** (see p.190), one of Kalk Bay's biggest attractions and one of the few restaurants along the peninsula where you can actually sit by the sea – and enjoy a glass of draught Guinness.

FISH HOEK

Map 2, D8. Fish Hoek station.

In contrast to Kalk Bay, the very white suburb of **Fish Hoek**, to the south, is one of the most conservative along the entire False Bay coast. A local by-law bans the sale of alcohol, boosting the town's image as the dullest retirement village on the Cape. However, it does boast the peninsula's best swimming **beach**, with a long stretch of sand: the Cape Town to Simon's Town train stops just opposite. The surprisingly good *Fish Hoek Galley* **restaurant** (see p.190), located right on the beach, has outside seating.

From in front of the restaurant, picturesque **Jager's Walk** skirts the rocky shoreline above the sea as far as Sunny Cove. The walkway, which continues unpaved for 5km as far as Simon's Town, provides a good vantage point for seeing whales.

SIMON'S TOWN

Map 2, D9. Simon's Town station.

South Africa's principal naval base, **Simon's Town** is the country's third-oldest European settlement, an exceptionally pretty place with a near-perfectly preserved streetscape. It's slightly marred on the ocean side by the **naval dockyard**, but this, and glimpses of naval squaddies parading behind the high walls or strolling to the station in their crisp white uniforms, are what give the town its distinct character.

Trains run from Cape Town roughly every hour during the day. The trip takes an hour, the last twenty minutes from Muizenberg skirting the coast spectacularly close to the shoreline – it's worth it just for the train ride. Trains are met at Simon's Town by rikkis (℡786 2136), which can also be booked to take you on excursions to Boulders or Cape Point. There are no buses to Simon's Town.

Simon's Town accommodation is listed on p.169.

Simon's Town Museum

Map 2, D9. Mon–Fri 9am–4pm, Sat 10am–4pm, Sun 11am–4pm; R2. Simon's Town station.

The **Simon's Town Museum** in Court Road (the first road on your left as you walk south from the station) is in the Old Residency built in 1772 for the Governor of the Dutch East India Company. It also served as the slave quarters (the dungeons are in the basement) and town brothel. The motley collection of artefacts inside includes maritime displays and an inordinate amount on Able Seaman Just Nuisance, a much-celebrated seafaring Great Dane who was adopted as a mascot by the Royal Navy during World War II, and is reputed to have enjoyed the odd pint along with the sailors, whom he would accompany into Cape Town on the train.

SIMON'S TOWN

Shelter from the storm

Founded in 1687 as the winter anchorage of the Dutch East India Company, Simon's Town was modestly named by **Governor Simon van der Stel** after himself. Its most celebrated visitor was Lord Nelson, who convalesced here as a midshipman while returning home from the East in 1776. Nineteen years later, the British sailed into the town and occupied it as a bridgehead for their invasion of Cape Town and the first British occupation of the Cape; after just seven years they left, only to return in 1806. Simon's Town remained a British base until 1957, when it was handed over to South Africa.

There are fleeting hints, such as the odd mosque, that the town's exclusively white appearance doesn't give the whole story. In fact, the first **Muslims** arrived from the East Indies in the early eighteenth century, imported as slaves to build the Dutch naval base. After the British banning of the slave trade in 1808, ships were compelled to disgorge their human cargo at Simon's Town, where one district became known as Black Town. In 1967, when Simon's Town was declared a White Group Area, there were 1200 well-established coloured families descended from these slaves. By 1973 the majority had been **forcibly removed**, because of the Group Areas Act (see p.313), to the desolate township of Ocean View (ironically, one of the few places along the peninsula that hasn't got an ocean view). Their departure made a significant impact, with the town's significant historic buildings being destroyed or allowed to decay.

The building also reputedly still houses the ghost of Eleanor, the fourteen-year old daughter of Earl McCartney, who lived here in the closing years of the eighteenth century. Forbidden by her parents from playing on the sands with the children of coloured fishermen, Eleanor would escape to the beach through a secret tunnel she had discovered. The dankness of the tunnel supposedly gave her pneumonia, from which she tragically died.

South African Naval Museum

Map 2, D9. Daily 10am–4pm; free. Simon's Town station.

At the **South African Naval Museum**, displays – only likely to appeal if you have a special interest in the subject – include the inside of a submarine, the bridge of a ship simulating rocking, and loads of official portraits of South African Navy big guns with double-barrelled names, from 1922 to the present. From the beginning of December to mid-January, the museum operates free one-hour tours (Mon–Fri 10am & 1.30pm) of the Naval Dockyard, leaving from under the palm trees in Jubilee Square.

Jubilee Square and the Marina

Map 2, D9. Simon's Town station.

In the centre of Simon's Town, a little over a kilometre south of the station, is **Jubilee Square**, a palm-shaded car park just off St George's Street, the main drag running through town. Flanked by cafés and shops, its harbour-facing side has a broad walkway with a statue of the ubiquitous Able Seaman Just Nuisance (see p.128). A couple of sets of stairs lead down to the Marina, a modest development of shops and restaurants set right on the waterfront. One of the best reasons to venture onto the quayside is to take a high-speed **catamaran trip** on the *Cape of Good Hope*, which embarks on exhilarating ninety-minute excursions around Cape Point (daily 10am & 2.30pm; R120) and shorter outings to Seal Island (daily noon & 1.15pm; R80). Booking is advisable: contact Tigre Cruises (©786 1045 or 786 1055).

Long and Seaforth beaches

Map 2, D10. Simon's Town station, then rikki taxi.

Long Beach, just north of Simon's Town station, offers no shade and is little used. However, on windless days it can be pleasant for long walks, with views of the Hottentots Holland Mountains, and its tidal pool is safe for bathing. Access is by a number of gaps in a brick wall alongside the main road and about midway along the beach (opposite Hopkirk Way). There are free changing rooms and toilets nearby, as well as fresh water.

One of the best beaches for swimming is at **Seaforth**, adjacent to and east of the Naval Museum, where clear deep waters lap around the rocks. It's calm, protected and safe, but not pretty, being bounded on one side by the looming grey mass of the naval base.

BOULDERS

Map 2, E10. Simon's Town station, then rikki taxi.

Two kilometres from the station towards Cape Point you leave town and come to **Boulders**, the most popular local beach, with a number of places to stay. The area takes its name from the huge rounded rocks that create a cluster of little coves with sandy beaches and clear sea pools.

Boulders Coastal Park

Map 2, E10. Open 24hr; R10 entry fee 8am–5pm. Simon's Town station, then rikki taxi.

The main reason people come to Boulders is for the **African penguins** (formerly known as jackass penguins), in the **Boulders Coastal Park**, a fenced reserve on Boulders Beach. Passing sailors used to prey on the quirky birds and their eggs, but more recently they have fallen victim to vandals, and some locals who consider them pests; they are now under the protective wing of a guard. African penguins usually live on islands off the west side of the South African coast, the Boulders birds forming one of only two mainland colonies in the world. This is also the only place where the endangered species are actually increasing in numbers, and provides a rare opportunity to get a close look at them.

MILLER'S POINT AND SMITSWINKELBAAI

Map 2, E11. Simon's Town station, then rikki taxi.

Almost 5km south of Boulders is the popular and attractive **Miller's Point** resort, which has a number of small sandy beaches and a tidal pool protected from the southeast wind. There's a **campsite** at the caravan park, with great sea views. Along Main Road, the notable *Black Marlin* seafood **restaurant** draws busloads of tourists, while the boulders around the point attract rock agama, black zonure lizards and dassies.

The last place before you get to the Cape of Good Hope Nature Reserve is **Smitswinkelbaai**, a little cove with a small beach, which is safe for swimming but feels the full blast of the southeast wind. It's not accessible by car, as local property owners fiercely guard their privacy. To get there, you must park next to the road and walk down a seemingly endless succession of stairs.

CAPE OF GOOD HOPE NATURE RESERVE

Map 2, C10 & C11–E14. Daily: April–Sept 7am–5pm; Oct–March 7am–6pm; R20; ©780 9100.

The sea and mountain scenery in the **Cape of Good Hope Nature Reserve** are reason enough to travel the 66km from central Cape Town. Most visitors make a bee-line for **Cape Point**, seeing the rest of the reserve through a vehicle window, but walking (see the box on p.135) is the best way to appreciate indigenous **Cape flora**. At first glance the landscape appears rocky and bleak, with short, wind-cropped plants, but the vegetation is surprisingly rich – there are as many plant varieties in this small reserve as in the whole of Britain. Many familiar bright blooms such as geraniums, freesias, gladioli, daisies, lilies and irises are hybrids grown from indigenous Cape plants.

The 78-square-kilometre reserve incorporates the southern-most section of the Cape Peninsula and stretches along some 40km of rocky Atlantic and False Bay coastline which converge at Cape Point. Principally a botanical reserve, it's also packed with herbivorous **game**, including grey rhebok, Cape grysbok, the rare Cape mountain zebra, bontebok, eland, red hartebeest, duiker, dassies and ostriches. Chacma baboons are frequently sighted, while less common species include the Cape fox, caracal and porcupines. Over 150 varieties of **birds** have been recorded here. The west coast extends into the sea as a **marine reserve**: Cape Point is one of the best spots in Cape Town for sighting **whales** and **dolphins**.

Getting there

There is no public transport to the reserve, although you can rent a Simon's Town **rikki** there and back (©786 2136; R65, seats 8 people). To get there **by car**, take the M3 to Muizenberg, continuing on the M4 via Simon's Town to the reserve gates, where you'll be given a good **map** that marks the main driving and walking routes, as well as the tidal pools and other facilities.

Cape Point and around

Map 2, E14.

Most people come to the reserve to see what is frequently

touted as both the southernmost tip of Africa, and the place where the Indian and Atlantic oceans meet at **Cape Point**. In fact, it's the site of neither, but is nevertheless an awesomely dramatic spot, which should on no account be missed. Cape Point sits atop massive sea cliffs with huge views, strong seas, and an even wilder wind, which whips off hats and sunglasses as visitors gaze southwards from the old lighthouse buttress. The continent's real tip is at Cape Agulhas, some 300km southeast of here (see p.269), but Cape Point is a lot easier to get to than Agulhas and a lot more exciting. The usual thing is to come to the Point as part of a round trip, returning via Kommetjie and the scenic Chapman's Peak Drive.

Navigators since the Portuguese in the fifteenth century had to contend with the treacherous rocky promontory when they "rounded the Cape" on their way to the East. Plenty of ships lie submerged off its coast, and at **Olifantsbos** on the west side of Cape Point you can walk to two wrecks: one a US vessel sunk in 1942, and the other a South African coaster, which ran aground in 1965. The **Old Lighthouse**, built in 1860, was too often dangerously shrouded in cloud, failing to keep ships off the rocks, so another was built lower down in 1914, not always successful in averting disasters but still the most powerful light beaming onto the sea from South Africa.

....

Numerous tours take in the peninsula highlights:
Day Trippers (℃531 3274) run fun outings from
Cape Town for R185 (including a picnic lunch),
giving you the option to cycle part of the way.
For general tours that take in the reserve, see p.38.

....

From the Cape Point car park, the famous viewpoint is a short, steep walk, crawling with tourists, up to the old lighthouse. Alternatively, a **funicular** runs to the top, where

Swimming and walking

Several waymarked **walks** lead through the Cape of Good Hope Nature Reserve. If you're planning a big hike it's best to set out early, as shade is rare and the wind can be foul, especially during summer, often increasing in intensity as the day goes on. One of the most straightforward **hiking routes** is the signposted forty-minute trek from the car park at **Cape Point** to the more westerly **Cape of Good Hope**. For exploring the shoreline, a clear path runs down the Atlantic side from Hoek van Bobbejaan; a convenient place to join it is at **Gifkommetjie**, which is signposted off Cape Point Road. From the car park, several sandy tracks drop quite steeply down the slope across rocks, through bushes and milkwood trees to the shore, along which you can walk in either direction. Alternatively, take a copy of the Government Printer's *Cape Town* map (1:50,000) for some more intrepid exploration. Bring water on any walk in the reserve, as there are no reliable fresh sources.

You'll find the **beaches** along signposted sideroads branching out from Cape Point Road, the main route through the reserve, going from the entrance gate to the car park at Cape Point. The sea is too dangerous for swimming, but there are safe tidal pools at the adjacent **Buffels Bay** and **Bordjiesrif**, midway along the east shore. Both have *braai* stands, but more southerly Buffels Bay is the nicer, with big lawned areas and some sheltered spots to have a picnic.

there's a curio shop. The decent *Two Oceans* restaurant at the car park has outdoor seating and huge picture windows taking in the drop to the sea below.

LISTINGS

Accommodation

Finding accommodation in Cape Town isn't always easy, especially in summer; the only way to guarantee the kind of place you want is to book ahead. The greatest concentration of accommodation is around the City Bowl and the adjacent seaside strip as far as Sea Point. The City Bowl, spreading up from the centre to the slopes of Table Mountain, comprises the city centre, Kloof Nek Road, the down-at-heel and lively suburb of Gardens, as well as the desirable inner-city suburbs of Tamboerskloof and Oranjezicht, which are close to the centre, sufficiently elevated to provide sea views and are only ten minutes' drive from the stunning Atlantic coast.

There are a few accommodation **agencies** (see p.249) that may be able to help if you're stuck.

If you don't have your own transport you'll probably want to stay in the city centre or somewhere connected to it by Metro Rail train: either the southern suburbs or the False Bay seaboard. The City Bowl suburb of Gardens is adjacent to the centre and is easily walkable. The only frequent buses are to Green Point and Sea Point.

Accommodation price codes

Accommodation prices vary throughout the year. Rates given are those you can expect to pay per person in a hotel, guest-house or B&B for a double room in summer (October to March). These types of accommodation are usually en suite and include breakfast in the rate. If you're visiting during the Christmas school holidays (Dec to mid-Jan) or Easter, expect a substantial price hike. Self-catering accommodation is usually charged per unit, but for consistency we have given a per per-son rate. There is no seasonal variation for backpacker lodges and the codes given represent the price per person.

① up to R50	④ R150–200	⑦ R300–400
② R50–100	⑤ R200–250	⑧ R400–500
③ R100–150	⑥ R250–300	⑨ over R500

CITY CENTRE

A cluster of backpacker lodges are concentrated on **Long Street** in the city centre, with a couple of others nearby. Most of the other accommodation consists of mid-range to expensive hotels, with the odd B&B and some self-catering cottages in the **Lower City Centre**.

The telephone code for Cape Town is ℗021.

BACKPACKER LODGES

Bob's Backpack
Map 4, C5. 187 Long St ℗ & fax 424 8223. Cape Town station.
Sizeable hostel with a party atmosphere, located on the top two floors of an undistinguished three-storey converted block of

flats above a bar/bistro. Fully refurbished in 1999, its great attraction is that the twelve dorms (sleeping a maximum of six) and half-dozen doubles are each self-contained, with their own kitchens and bathrooms. A good budget self-catering option in the city centre. Dorms ①, doubles ②.

Cat & Moose

Map 4, C6. 305 Long St ℂ & fax 423 7638, *cat&moose@hotmail.com* Cape Town station.

The most stylish of the Long Street lodges, housed in an eighteenth-century building a couple of doors from the steam baths at the south end of the city centre. Timber floors with Turkish-style rugs, exposed beams, earthy reds and ochres as well as some African masks imbue it with a warm ethnic feel. The six dorms, two triples and one double room are arranged around a small leafy courtyard, with a waterfall cascading into a plunge pool. Dorms ①. Doubles and triples ②.

City Slickers

Map 4, A3. Corner 25 Rose and Hout streets ℂ422 2357, fax 422 2355. Cape Town station.

Lively lodge in the Bo-Kaap, five minutes from the city centre, whose roof garden has views to Table Mountain. Train carriage-style rooms have only one twin bunk or double bed in each. There are also a couple of self-contained cottages (sleeping six) a few doors up Hout Street. On the downside, the vicinity isn't safe to wander around at night and cars may be broken into. Bunk rooms ①, doubles and cottages ②.

Lion's Den

Map 4, C6. 255 Long St ℂ423 9003, fax 423 9166, *lionsden@iafrica.com* Cape Town station.

Clean, spacious and friendly establishment in an airy Victorian apartment building converted into a lodge. A buzzing bar makes this a good place for party animals. Visitors can share the lodge with a resident menagerie consisting of an Amazonian parrot, a boa constrictor and three American corn snakes that live in the reception office. Clean but uninspiring rooms: twelve dorms, mostly sleeping four to six people, eight doubles and four singles. Dorms ①, doubles and singles ②.

Long Street Backpackers

Map 4, C5. 209 Long St ✆423 0615, fax 423 1842, *longstbp@mweb.co.za* Cape Town station.
The oldest Long Street backpacker lodge, on the top two floors of an unexceptional three-storey former apartment block arranged around a courtyard. Quieter than some of the other lodges in the vicinity, it's a well-organized, plain but clean place with a laundry, Internet facilities and an arrangement for cheap day membership of the Health and Racquet Club gym, situated in the same street. Dorms ①, doubles and singles ②.

Overseas Visitors' Club Hostel

Map 4, C6. 230 Upper Long St ✆424 6800, fax 423 4870, *hross@ovc.co.za* Cape Town station.
Well-organized lodge above some some shops with high ceilings, airy spaces and off-white interiors, run more along the lines of a guesthouse than a hostel. Small by Long Street standards, with three dorms (each sleeping six) with balconies. The absence of a bar makes it more tranquil than most lodges in the vicinity. A TV lounge leads onto a wraparound balcony that offers views of the street. ①.

B&BS, GUESTHOUSES AND SELF-CATERING

Harbour View Cottages

Map 5, F6. 1 Loader St, De Waterkant ✆418 6081, fax 418 6082, *reservations@hvc.co.za* Cape Town station.
Self-catering accommodation in the rapidly gentrifying nineteenth-century Waterkant district, adjacent to the Bo-Kaap

and less than 1km from the V&A Waterfront and city centre. Twenty-five one-, two- and three-bedroom restored historic cottages located in Waterkant, Loader, Dixon and Napier streets provide varied facilities. Some of the cottages come with garages, swimming pools and harbour or mountain views. Perfect for families looking for somewhere central. No charge for toddlers not occupying a bed. ③–④.

St Paul's B&B Guest House

Map 4, B6. 182 Bree St ☏423 4420, fax 423 1580. Cape Town station. Charming, well-managed guesthouse in a Georgian building (formerly a maternity hospital) in a calm street on the city centre fringes, within easy striking distance of the sights. Attached to the lovely brick-and-stone St Paul's Church and its rectory, the rooms are large, comfortable and light with huge windows. Shared bathroom facilities. Kitchen available to guests. ③.

Travellers' Inn

Map 4, C6. 208 Long St ☏424 9272, fax 424 9278. Cape Town station.
Pleasant budget accommodation in a turn-of-the-century building above some shops; a wraparound balcony dotted with pot plants overlooks Bloem and Long streets. With no bar and no backpacker scene, this could be a good bet for travellers wanting to avoid the hectic social atmosphere of the city centre hostels. Apart from the light and spacious family rooms (twin beds and a double bunk), accommodation is small and sparely furnished, but clean and quite adequate. Shared bathroom facilities. ②.

HOTELS

Cape Heritage Hotel

Map 4, B3. 90 Bree St ☏424 4646, fax 424 4949, *chrelais@satis.co.za* Cape Town station.

Elegant and tastefully restored hotel located in a row of houses dating back to 1771, in Heritage Square, just below the Bo-Kaap. Fifteen spacious rooms are each furnished in a unique theme, among them African, Japanese and Dutch. Although there's no garden, there is a nice courtyard. ⑧.

Cape Gardens Lodge Hotel

Map 4, C7. 88 Queen Victoria St, Gardens © 423 1260, fax 423 2088, *lodge@dockside.co.za* Cape Town station.
Smart multistorey hotel with 56 air-conditioned rooms with cable TV, baths and showers, bang in the centre, opposite the Gardens. Two minutes from the South African Museum and Art Gallery and an easy and pleasant walk through the Company's Gardens to the city centre. ⑤–⑥.

V&A WATERFRONT

In keeping with the gentrified ambience of the **Waterfront**, accommodation here tends to be upmarket; this is where Bill and Hillary Clinton stayed when they visited the city in 1998. There are a couple of reasonably priced places to stay if the presidential suite isn't an option.

Breakwater Lodge

Map 5, E4. Portswood Road, Waterfront ©406 1911 (ask for Lodge Reservations), fax 406 1070, *brkwater@fortesking-hotels.co.za* Waterfront buses.
The most affordable place to stay on the doorstep of the Waterfront, this is a sparkling white hotel linked to the Graduate School of Business and housed in a nineteenth-century prison building, a five-minute walk from the V&A Waterfront. Although it lacks personality, the lodge's 200 or so standard en-suite rooms are functional and come equipped with TVs and phones, while the 110 budget units share a bathroom with one other room. Rate excludes breakfast. ③–④.

The Cape Grace

Map 5, F4. West Quay, V&A Waterfront ⓒ410 7100, fax 419 7622. Waterfront buses.

One of Cape Town's most expensive and most exclusive hotels, spectacularly sited on a slender spit that overlooks the V&A Waterfront's small vessel marina to one side and the Alfred Basin to the other. The hotel's 102 rooms have either harbour or Table Mountain views and are stylishly furnished in pared-back French period style. ⑨.

City Lodge

Map 5, G4. Corner of Alfred and Dock roads, Waterfront ⓒ419 9450, fax 419 0460, *clva.resv@citylodge.co.za* Waterfront buses.

Rather austere but perfectly adequate hotel poised between the V&A Waterfront and the city centre, and less than 1km from both. Rooms have TVs and there's a small swimming pool. While not as close to the V&A action as *Breakwater Lodge*, this is still one of the few reasonably priced places this close to the Waterfront. ⑤.

Victoria & Alfred Hotel

Map 5, E3. Pierhead, Waterfront ⓒ419 6677, fax 419 8955, *resvanda@ambassador.co.za* Waterfront buses.

Four-star squeaky clean hotel on North Quay, bang in the heart of the Waterfront. Occupying a converted turn-of-the-century dock warehouse, within spitting distance of numerous bars and restaurants, it overlooks the Alfred Basin. Some rooms have stunning views of Table Mountain. Decor is in the Cape Dutch Revival style. ⑨.

CITY BOWL SUBURBS

The **City Bowl suburbs** are popular for accommodation, and the most southerly sections are just five to ten minutes' walk from the Gardens and museums. A few backpacker lodges can be found along Kloof Street, the continuation of trendy Long Street. The further up you go the leafier the suburbs become, and you'll find the pricier and more comfortable B&Bs, guesthouses and hotels along the lower slopes of Table Mountain, overlooking the city centre and Duncan Dock.

There's no public transport to the City Bowl Suburbs, but most accommodation listed here is under 3km from Cape Town station.

BACKPACKER LODGES

The Albergo

Map 4, C7. 5 Beckham St, Gardens ℗422 1849, fax 423 0515, *absolut@mweb.co.za*

Two pleasant adjacent houses along a side street, just off the busy restaurant strip of Kloof Street and a ten-minute walk from the city centre. The livelier house (no. 5) has dorms only and these lead off a large lounge and yard with outdoor seating. The other house tends to be quieter with rooms (mainly doubles) leading off a small communal space. Pool room and cable TV, but no bar. Dorms ①, doubles, triples and family room ②.

Ashanti Lodge

Map 7, D1. 11 Hof St, Gardens ℗423 8721, fax 423 8790, *ashanti@iafrica.com*

King of the Cape Town lodges, this is a massive, superbly refurbished two-storey Victorian mansion five minutes' walk from the Gardens. Details that give it the edge are stripped timber, chic marbling and ethnic decor, soaring ceilings, a beautifully kept front garden, cosy TV lounge and a swimming pool with sun terrace. A terrific upstairs café/bar has a deck with epic views of Table Mountain. Twelve private rooms (twin or double beds) and ten dorms (sleeping six to eight) are furnished with custom-made wrought iron bunks and beds. Facilities include international phone booths (pay when you leave), laundry, free pick-up from station or airport and an efficient travel centre. Camping ①, dorms and doubles ②.

The Backpack

Map 4, B7. 74 New Church St, Tamboerskloof ©423 4530, fax 423 0065, *backpack@gem.co.za*

One of the few lodges in a similar league to *Ashanti*, in three interleading houses on the cusp of the City Bowl suburbs and the city centre and easily walkable to both. Professionally run and service oriented, it's pleasantly furnished with bold colours and ethnic fabrics. Plenty of outdoor space, including a pool terrace that leads off the bar. Accommodation is in six dorms (sleeping six to ten) and eleven private rooms (with two or four beds and some doubles, one of which is en suite). Some rooms are suitable for families, although there's an unfenced pool. ②.

The Backpackers' Lodge

Map 4, C8. 15 & 26 Faure St, Gardens © 423 5485, fax 423 5471, *bella@iafrica.co.za*

Two bungalows across the road from each other in a quiet back street five minutes' walk from the Gardens. Psychedelic blue, mauve and silver decor and ethnic wall hangings give a Sixties commune feel and the compact size of the two places – four dorms (sleeping a total of nineteen) and four doubles – makes this a good bet to meet people or just chill out on the floor cushions in the lounge. Bar and Internet facilities available. Dorms ①, doubles ②.

Cloudbreak Backpackers' Lodge

Map 4, G8. 219 Upper Buitenkant St, Gardens ©461 6892, fax 461 1458, *cloudbrk@gem.co.za*

Friendly and fun place on a busy road close to a large shopping centre. Comprises eight doubles in a house with a garden, and three dorms sleeping six to twelve people in another house across the road. Surfing is a high priority, and daily trips are organized to good breaks and beaches. Free airport pick-up, and there's a travel and booking centre. Dorms ①, doubles ②.

Oak Lodge

Map 4, F9. 21 Breda St, Gardens ℂ465 6182, fax 465 6308, *oak-lodge@intekom.co.za*

More an event than a lodge, this highly recommended hostel in an 1860s Victorian house has dramatic dungeons, dragon murals, and a lively atmosphere. Spacious, well serviced and with an immaculate kitchen. Dorms ①, doubles ②.

Zebra Crossing

Map 4, B8. 82 New Church St ℂ & fax 422 1265, *zebracross@intekom.co.za*

Cape Town's only backpacker lodge that boasts about being quiet. On the northern edge of the City Bowl suburbs, it's an easy walk to the Kloof Street restaurants and pubs as well as those in the city centre. A café/bar (which closes at 9pm) serves full meals and decent coffee and there are two pleasant terraces under vines. Accommodation is in three spacious dorms (sleeping eight), ten doubles and four singles. The best rooms are the three doubles in the annex outside, with a balcony that has views of the mountain. Child friendly. Dorms ①, doubles ②.

SELF-CATERING AND GUESTHOUSES

African Sun

Map 7, H1. 3 Florida Rd, Vredehoek ℂ & fax 461 1601, *afpress@iafrica.com*

Small, secluded, self-catering apartment, attached to a family house a little over 1km from the city centre. Furnished with pared-back ethnic decor, it's run by friendly, well-informed and interesting owners, one a children's author and the other a travel writer. Great value. ②.

Ambleside Guesthouse

Map 7, F4. 11 Forest Rd, Oranjezicht ℗465 2503, fax 465 3814.
The guesthouse has been going for fifty years and comprises eight, inexpensive, comfortable though slightly stuffy en-suite rooms, all with great views across the city to the harbour, and cable car watching from the back patio. A hot breakfast is served in the rooms and you can prepare your own meals in a communal kitchen. ②.

Belmont House

Map 7, F3. 10 Belmont Ave, Oranjezicht ℗461 5417, fax 461 6642, *belmont@dockside.co.za*
Tastefully restored 1920s house with seven fresh rooms, each with its own shower or bath. Either take the B&B option or self-cater in their communal kitchen. Discount of five percent if you produce this book. ③.

Flower Street Villa Guest House

Map 7, G1. 3 Flower St, Oranjezicht ℗465 7517.
Spacious rooms in a former nursing home. There's a small extra charge for breakfast, but guests have use of kitchen. Doubles and triples (with or without bathroom). ②.

Saasveld Lodge

Map 4, B8. 73 Kloof St, Tamboerskloof ℗424 6169, fax 424 5397, *info@saasveldlodge.co.za*
Clean but rather impersonal 1950s-style, four-storey lodge on a buzzing thoroughfare that's lined with good eateries, less than 1km from the centre. Rooms have TV and phone, and the rate excludes breakfast. Reasonable value with no frills. ③.

GUESTHOUSES AND HOTELS

Cape Swiss Hotel

Map 7, D2. Corner of Kloof and Camp streets, Tamboerskloof ⓒ423 8190, fax 426 1795.

Unprepossessing high-rise 1960s block whose main attraction is its location in trendy Kloof Street, which has a respectable range of restaurants; it's about 1km from the city centre and 2km from the Lower Cable Station. Three-star comfort, though no mountain views. ④.

Lady Hamilton Hotel

Map 7, D1. 10 Union St, Gardens ⓒ424 1460, fax 423 7788, *serting@ mweb.co.za*

Reasonably priced smart hotel in a quiet street off lively Kloof Street and under 1km from the Gardens. Rooms are light and pleasant and you'll find a swimming pool, restaurant and bar on the premises. ④.

Leeuwenvoet House

Map 4, B8. 93 New Church St, Tamboerskloof ⓒ424 1133, fax 424 0495, *leeuwen@iafrica.com*

Tranquil restored Victorian guesthouse with eleven en-suite rooms kitted out with pine, wicker and all the hotel trimmings of TV, phone, fan and radio alarm. Situated on a major thoroughfare with secure parking, it's a fifteen-minute walk from the city centre with airport transfers also available. ⑥.

Lezard Bleu

Map 7, G3. 30 Upper Orange St, Oranjezicht ⓒ461 4601, fax 461 4657, *welcome@lezardbleu.co.za*

Five en-suite rooms furnished with maple beds and cupboards in a spacious open-plan 1960s house. Sliding doors from each room open onto a garden. Located in a pleasant part of town, it's 1km from the centre and about half that distance to a nature reserve on the lower slopes of Table Mountain. Good views, pool and generous breakfasts. **⑥**.

Mijlhof Manor Hotel

Map 4, A8. 2a Milner Rd, Tamboerskloof ✆426 1476, fax 422 2046, *mijlof@gem.co.za*

Decent hotel in a restored 1710 building with seventy rooms – it's situated at the foot of Signal Hill about 1km from the centre. Rooms are comfortably furnished in Cape Dutch style and there's a courtyard and small pool. Rate excludes breakfast. **⑤**.

Mount Nelson Hotel

Map 4, D8. 76 Orange St, Gardens ✆423 1000, fax 424 7472 *nelress@iafrica.com*

Cape Town's grande dame: a fine and famous high-colonial Victorian hotel, built in 1899 (and extended in the late 1990s in response to demand). Set in extensive established gardens, with arrival along a palm-lined colonnade, it takes itself terribly seriously and charges accordingly. Rate excludes breakfast. **⑨**.

Underberg Guest House

Map 4, A8. 6 Tamboerskloof Rd, Tamboerskloof ✆426 2262, fax 424 4059, *underberg@netactive.co.za*

Located in the upmarket suburb of Tamboerskloof, this Victorian guesthouse offers possibly the best City Bowl value in its price band. Its high ceilings and compact size (there are only eleven rooms) create an atmosphere that is both intimate and airy. **⑤**.

Villa Belmonte

Map 7, F3. 33 Belmont Ave, Oranjezicht ✆462 1576, fax 462 1579, *villabel@iafrica.com*

South Africa's smallest four-star hotel, on the lower slopes of Table Mountain and 1km from the city centre, feels like an

CITY BOWL SUBURBS: GUESTHOUSES AND HOTELS

elegant Italian country villa. Rooms are themed and prices vary according to size. Book six months ahead for balcony rooms with views of sea and mountain. ⑧–⑨.

GREENPOINT TO SEA POINT

Down the **Atlantic seaboard** lie the seaside suburbs of Green Point, Three Anchor Bay and Sea Point. Historically Cape Town's hotel and high-rise land, this is now packed with accommodation, making it a good alternative to the City Bowl if your budget is tight.

BACKPACKER LODGES

A la Maison Lodge
Map 6, F3. 339b Main Rd, Sea Point ✆439 8838, fax 434 4064, *alamaison@iafrica.com* Sea Point bus.
Small hostel in a two-storey 1950s apartment block which, despite being on the corner of Sea Point's busy main drag, is a relaxed place, with ethnic rugs on pine floors and spacious rooms and dorms furnished with steel beds. There's a comfortable lounge, and pick-ups can be arranged from the airport or station with the prospect of a complementary cold beer on arrival. Dorms ①, double rooms ②.

Carnaby the Backpacker
Map 6, I7. 219 Main Rd, Three Anchor Bay ✆439 7410, fax 439 1222, *carnaby@netactive.co.za* Sea Point bus.
Extraordinary and fun hostel, previously an old-fashioned three-star hotel, located about 100m from the sea (too rocky for swimming). The 1970s Spanish-style stucco decor has been retained for kitsch effect. A big attraction is that almost all of its eight dorms (sleeping three to six) and fourteen double rooms are en suite and have phones which receive calls. There's even a honeymoon suite with its own TV. Shady

outdoor pool terrace, bar, pool, pinball and travel centre. ②.

St John's Waterfront Lodge

Map 5, E5. 4–6 Braemar Rd, Green Point ℗439 1404, fax 439 1424, *fredgeof@mweb.co.za* Sea Point bus.

The closest hostel to the V&A Waterfront, ten minutes away on foot, and well run by friendly and helpful staff. Accommodation is in four dorms (sleeping eight or nine) as well as some doubles, one of which is en suite. In addition to two swimming pools, a great garden and a bar, the restaurant serves reasonably priced light meals till midnight. They also have Internet access, a coin-operated washing machine and a travel centre. The main drawback is that it's in a major red-light district. Dorms ①, doubles ②.

Sunflower Stop

Map 5, C6. 179 Main Rd, Green Point ℗434 6535, fax 434 6501 *devine@sunflowerstop.co.za* Sea Point bus.

Bright yellow lodge that claims to be the cleanest in Cape Town (it's serviced twice a day), in a two-storey 1940s house 1km from the Waterfront. Accommodation is in five dorms (sleeping six to twelve) and five doubles. This child-friendly lodge has a bar, pool room, swimming pool, coin-operated washing machine, safe, travel centre and Internet access. Dorms ①, doubles ②.

GUESTHOUSES

Altona Lodge

Map 5, C6. 19 Croxteth Rd, Green Point ℗ & fax 434 2572. Sea Point bus.

Quiet and friendly guesthouse in a Victorian house close to the city centre, with seventeen B&B rooms, five of which are en suite. Cheaper rooms share a bathroom, though each room has its own hand basin. Service is good, rates very reasonable, there's a small garden and the atmosphere is homely. ③.

GREENPOINT TO SEA POINT: GUESTHOUSES

Dungarvin House

Map 5, C6. 163 Main Rd, Green Point ℂ & fax 434 0677, *kom@ ilink.nis.za* Sea Point bus.

A grand Edwardian villa with moulded pediments on a busy road not far from the Sea Point restaurant action, with gracious, well-appointed rooms. ⑤.

Jambo Guest House

Map 5, C6. 1 Grove Rd, Green Point ℂ439 4219, fax 434 0672, *jambo@.iafrica.com* Sea Point bus.

Small atmospheric establishment with five double rooms in a quiet cul-de-sac off Main Road, just over 1km from the V&A Waterfront. Despite being in the inner-city suburbs, its lush leafy exterior and enclosed garden with pond are delightfully relaxing and the service is excellent. A luxury suite has a large sitting area, jacuzzi and French doors opening onto the garden. ⑤–⑥.

Lion's Head Lodge

Map 6, F3. Corner Conifer and 319 Main Rd, Sea Point ℂ434 4163, fax 439 3813, *lionhead@cif.co.za* Sea Point bus.

Plain but very comfortable en-suite hotel-style rooms that are clean and well maintained, despite the weather-worn exterior of the four-storey building. Some face the busy main road at the heart of Sea Point's restaurant strip, but there are quieter ones overlooking the courtyard. All have phones and TV and the lodge features a swimming pool, its own bar, beer terrace and an à la carte restaurant. Also offers fully equipped apartments that sleep two. Rooms and apartments ③.

Olaf's Guest House

Map 6, F2. 24 Wisbeach Rd, Sea Point ℂ439 8943, fax 439 5057, *olafs@icon.co.za* Sea Point bus.

Clean, comfortable and pleasantly decorated Victorian bungalow with a friendly owner, five minutes from the beachfront promenade and 3km from the city centre. Its eight en-suite

ACCOMMODATION

rooms all have cable TV and telephones, and you can have
breakfast on the patio beside the swimming pool. ⑤.

Oliver Guest House

Map 6, E2. 8 Oliver Rd, Sea Point ℂ439 9237, fax 434 8998. Sea
Point bus.
Comfortable guesthouse in the heart of Sea Point, two minutes' walk from the Main Road restaurant strip and the seafront
promenade. Sister to the Kinneret Guest House, it's less
ostentatiously furnished and better value, with satellite TV
and fridges in all rooms. ④.

Stonehurst Guest House

Map 6, G3. 3 Frere Rd, Sea Point ℂ434 9670, fax 439 8131. Sea
Point bus.
Airy tin-roofed Victorian residence with original fittings,
Cape furniture and a pleasant front garden. No meals are pro-
vided, but there's a kitchen and guest lounge. Some rooms have
balconies and not all have baths. ②–③.

Villa Rosa

Map 6, D4. 277 High Level Rd, Sea Point ℂ434 2768, fax 434 3526,
villaros@mweb.co.za Sea Point bus.
Friendly eight-room guesthouse in a salmon-pink two-storey
Victorian house on the lower slopes of Signal Hill, two blocks
from the beachfront promenade. Decorated with simplicity and
style, all rooms have TVs, phones and safes, but only some on
the upper floor have sea views. ④.

SELF-CATERING

Don Suite Hotel

Map 6, E2. 249 Beach Rd, Sea Point ℂ434 1083, fax 434 4808,
seapoint@don.co.za Sea Point bus.
Five-storey block of 27 self-catering apartments across the road

GREENPOINT TO SEA POINT: SELF-CATERING

155

from the beachfront promenade, 300m from the lively Main Road restaurant strip and 4km from the V&A Waterfront. All the flats, studio and one- and two-bedroom units are spanking new and well equipped. Rates depend on whether or not you get a view. ⑤–⑥.

HOTELS

Ritz Inn

Map 6, H2. Corner of Main and Camberwell roads, Three Anchor Bay ℰ439 6010, fax 434 0809, *ctritz@iafrica.com* Sea Point bus.
Enormous 27-storey 1960s block with 222 rooms and no balconies, best known for the revolving restaurant on the twenty-second floor. Less than 2km from the V&A Waterfront, it's in the heart of the Sea Point wining and dining district. Although starting to look like the oldest swinger in town, it's still good value. Price excludes breakfast. ④.

Winchester Mansions Hotel

Map 6, F1. 221 Beach Rd, Sea Point. ℰ434 2351, fax 434 0215, *winman@mweb.co.za* Sea Point bus.
Self-consciously colonial-style 1920s hotel, in a prime spot across the road from the seashore, with an ambience straight from the pages of Agatha Christie. Palm trees at the front of the three-storey Cape Dutch Revival building hint at the interior: rooms have ceiling fans, and a cool Italianate courtyard restaurant is overlooked by balconies draped in luxuriant creepers. ⑦–⑨.

SOUTHERN SUBURBS

The **southern suburbs** – the formerly whites-only areas closest to the mountain – are convenient for the Simon's Town train line, providing easy access to both the city centre and the False Bay seaboard. Closest to town, Observatory (see p.91), with its streets of tightly packed Victorian cottages, large student population, congenial cafés and live music joints, can rival the city centre. The more southerly suburbs of Rosebank, Claremont, Newlands and Rondebosch are leafier and quieter.

BACKPACKER LODGES

The Green Elephant
Map 3, H5. 57 Milton Rd, Observatory ℂ 448 6359, fax 448 0510, *greenelephant@iafrica.com* Observatory station.
Five basic dorms and six doubles in a large, vibey house just off Main Road, with a jacuzzi, braai, solar-heated plunge pool and Internet facilities. The owner leads outdoor expeditions up Table Mountain and Lion's Head. Camping is permitted in the garden. Dorms ①, doubles ②.

The Lodge
Map 3, H5. 36 Milton Rd, Observatory ℂ & fax 448 6536, *thelodge@ mweb.co.za* Observatory station.
One of Cape Town's cheapest options is a collection of six clean and homely self-catering houses, run from and close to the above address. Each house has dorms and doubles and a garden or patio, plus shared kitchens and bathrooms. Not part of the backpacker scene, the accommodation is available for longer stays only, anything from a week upwards. Dorms ①, doubles ②.

Riverview Lodge
Map 3, H5. 5 Anson/Station roads, Observatory ℂ447 9056, fax 447 5192, *info@riverview.co.za* Observatory station.
Huge professionally run lodge with 43 single, double and dorm rooms in a converted two-storey former apartment block, two minutes' walk from Observatory station. It tends to attract large groups but has several small, comfortable lounges, outdoor

spaces and quiet nooks if you need some solitude. A massive plus is the large breakfast that's included in the price. ②.

The Tin Roof Backpackers' Lodge

Map 3, H5. Corner 22 Barrington and Ossian roads, Observatory ☏447 4400, fax 448 0546, *info@tinroofbackpackers.co.za* Observatory station.

Small, calm and airy hostel with four dorms that sleep four or six people in a bungalow with a small front verandah. Facilities include a large and well-equipped self-catering kitchen, capacious lockable cupboards and ingenious three-storey pine-log bunks that maximize floor space. A shady pergola and grape vines provide some pleasant outdoor space on the terrace. ②.

B&BS AND SELF-CATERING

Baxter Suites

Map 3, H7. 20 Lyle Rd, opposite Baxter Theatre, Rondebosch ☏689 7070, fax 689 7295, *baxter@ambassador.co.za* Rosebank station.

Serviced apartments in a seven-storey 1960s hotel 200m from Rosebank station, giving easy train access to the city centre (6km) and the False Bay coast. Its 48 units each have an open-plan lounge/diner and kitchenette equipped with a fridge and stove, making this a reasonable self-catering option. Breakfast available, but not included in the rate. ④.

Carmichael House

Map 3, H6. 11 Wolmunster Rd, Rosebank ☏689 8350, fax 689 8097, *carmichael@webmaster.co.za* Rosebank station.

Turn-of-the-century two-storey house with six big rooms kitted out with phones, safes and hairdryers, with fax and email access. There's a peaceful garden, swimming pool and secure parking. It's a ten-minute walk to Rhodes Memorial and the Contour Path, while the Rondebosch shops are 1km away. ④.

Gloucester House Bed & Breakfast

Map 2, E3. 54 Weltevreden Ave, Rondebosch ✆ & fax 689 3894.
Rondebosch station.

Private house with two bedrooms, and a lounge/dining room
for self-catering. Guests may use the large garden, swimming
pool and barbecue area, and there's the plus of being close to
Rondebosch station. Price excludes breakfast. ②.

Ivydene

Map 2, E3. off Glebe Road, Rondebosch ✆685 1747,
ivydene@mweb.co.za Rondebosch station.

Delightful old Cape Dutch farmhouse near the university, with
an artistic and friendly atmosphere, divided into self-catering
apartments. Garden and swimming pool. ③.

Koornhoop Manor House

Map 3, H5. Corner of Wrensch and Nuttal roads, Observatory ✆ &
fax 448 0595. Observatory station.

Pleasant rooms in a spacious Victorian house with a tranquil,
enclosed garden and small playground, close to the station,
with secure parking and grounds. Besides B&B accommodation in seven double rooms, two of which are suitable for
families, there's the option of a self-catering suite, which has
three bedrooms and its own entrance. ③.

HOTELS

The Courtyard

Map 3, I7. Liesbeek Avenue, Mowbray ✆448 3929, fax 448 5494,
cyct.res@citylodge.co.za Observatory/Mowbray stations.

Exceptional value considering the high level of luxury. A beautiful early nineteenth-century Cape Dutch homestead under
thatch, with terracotta floors, brass chandeliers and large lawns
in a semi-rural setting. There's a hotel minibus (chargeable).
Breakfast is extra. ⑤.

SOUTHERN SUBURBS: HOTELS

The Vineyard Hotel

Map 2, E4. Corner of Colinton and Protea roads, Newlands ℗683 3044, fax 683 7725, *hotel@vineyard.co.za* Claremont station.
Arguably Cape Town's finest hotel, in a restored country villa built for Lady Anne Barnard in 1799. Decorated in elegant Cape Dutch style, there's an outstanding panorama of Table Mountain from the extensive garden. For the level of four-star luxury, it offers good value. Courtyard rooms ⑥, mountain-facing ⑦.

CONSTANTIA AND TOKAI

Lush **Constantia** is one of Cape Town's most salubrious suburbs, only twenty minutes' drive from either coast as well as the V&A Waterfront. Sharing the same valley is the adjoining suburb of **Tokai**, worth considering if you want to be well out of the centre; it's close to forest walks and ten minutes from the beach. Inexpensive accommodation is rare, but if money's no object and you're looking for somewhere exceptional and romantic, you might just find it in a Cape Dutch manor house.

....

**A car is essential if you're staying in
Constantia as there's no public transport.
Rental companies are listed on p.251.**

....

B&BS AND SELF-CATERING

Allandale Holiday Cottages

Map 2, D6. 72 Zwaanswyk Rd, Tokai ℗715 3320, fax 712 7944, *stay@allandale.co.za*
Sixteen one-, two- and three-bedroom self-catering brick cottages on a smallholding on the slopes of Constantiaberg, two minutes from the motorway and twenty from Cape Town. Each cottage has a garden area with a braai and outdoor

seating, and also a key that opens the gate into adjoining Tokai forest. Features a pool and tennis courts. ③.

Elephant Eye Lodge

Map 2, D6. 9 Sunwood Drive, Tokai ℗ & fax 715 2432, *orsmond@iafrica.com*

Six reasonably priced rooms at a friendly B&B family home, in a converted Cape Dutch farmhouse minutes' walk from Tokai Forest and with its own large grounds. Two rooms offer some basic self-catering facilities, and you can get evening meals delivered. A baby's cot is also available and the swimming pool is safely fenced. ④.

Houtkapperspoort

Map 2, C5. Hout Bay Road ℗794 5216, fax 794 2907, *houtkap@iafrica.com*

Twenty-four rustic one- and two-bedroom stone-and-brick self-catering cottages set up against the Table Mountain Nature Reserve, close to Constantia Nek (around 5km from Hout Bay and 15km from the city centre). You can take paths straight from the estate up the mountain slopes, play tennis or take a dip in the solar-heated pool. Highly recommended. ③–④.

Little Ruo

Map 2, D5. 11 Willow Rd, off Spaanschemat River Road, Constantia ℗794 2052, fax 794 1981, *ruo@netactive.co.za*

Two pretty B&B rooms at the home of friendly architect owners, plus three self-catering units set in a huge landscaped garden with willows, a stream and a saltwater pool, with plenty of opportunity for serenely lazing about. ⑤–⑥.

The Stables

Map 2, D5. Chantercler Lane, Constantia ℗ & fax 794 3653.

Five en-suite doubles, each with their own entrance and patio, in converted stables. They're known for their fabulous six-course breakfasts, and you can relax around the pool in a large garden. ⑤.

Constantia Uitsig Country Hotel

Map 2, D5. Spaanschemat River Road, Constantia ℗794 6500, fax 794 7605, *res@ilink.co.za*

Sixteen custom-built and luxurious Cape Dutch-style cottages, in a garden setting on Constantia Uitsig wine estate, next door to Steenberg. Two fabulous restaurants, *Constantia Uitsig* and *La Colombe* (see p.186 & p.187 respectively), are on site. ⑨.

Steenberg

Map 2, D6. Corner Steenberg and Tokai roads ℗713 2222, fax 713 2221, *hotel@iafrica.com*

A luxurious place on South Africa's oldest wine estate at the foot of the Steenberg Mountain. Accommodation is in the original manor house and three other farm buildings (now national monuments), which are perfect examples of Cape Dutch architecture, dating back to 1682. Arranged around a large formal garden, the buildings have whitewashed walls, thatched roofs, ornate gables and are furnished with seventeenth- and eighteenth-century Cape antiques. ⑨.

ATLANTIC SEABOARD

Moving south from Sea Point along Victoria Drive, the luxury mountainside suburb of **Camps Bay** has soaring views over the Atlantic, with the advantage of being close to the city centre, and with its own restaurants and shops. Nearby **Llandudno** has similar vistas, no shops or restaurants, but a supremely beautiful beach with clusters of granite boulders at either end. **Hout Bay** is the main urban concentration along the lower half of the peninsula, with a harbour, pleasant waterfront development and the only public transport beyond Camps Bay. South of Hout Bay is the semi-rural settlement of **Noordhoek**, close to the Cape of Good Hope Nature Reserve.

BACKPACKER LODGES AND CAMPING

Imhoff Caravan Park
Map 2, B8. 1 Wireless Rd, Kommetjie ℂ783 1634, fax 783 2871, *anderson@icon,co.za*
A hundred metres from spectacular Long Beach, this is the nicest campsite in the area. Two fully equipped self-catering chalets (sleeping four) are available, plus three on-site caravans (bring bedding). Camping ①, chalets ②.

Stan's Halt
Map 3, B5. The Glen ℂ & fax 438 9037, *stanh@new.co.za* Camps Bay bus.
This tranquil backpacker hostel has six-bed dorms in a former nineteenth-century hunting lodge in the heart of woodlands, a fifteen-minute walk from Clifton beach. Ideal if you want to hike or explore the coast. The easiest way to get there is by minibus, rikki or Golden Arrow bus to Camps Bay and walk ten minutes uphill on a forest path. Otherwise, it's a thirty-minute walk downhill from Kloofnek. ①.

B&BS AND SELF-CATERING

Bay Cottage
Map 2, B8. Benning Drive, Kommetjie ℂ & fax 783 3601.
En-suite room adjoining a family house, with a second room available if you are in a group; it's situated on Long Beach and

has basic self-catering facilities and a garden. The owners will help you catch fish to braai, and they lend out wet suits and boogie boards. ③.

Beach House

Map 2, C5. Royal Avenue, Hout Bay ℂ & fax 790 4228.
Modern guesthouse with seven perfectly adequate en-suite rooms, a five-minute walk from Mariner's Wharf and the beach. Features a patio with tables and chairs. ③.

11 Sunset Avenue

Map 2, B4. Llandudno, ℂ & fax 790 2103, *alcock@mweb.co.za*.
Self-contained, open-plan studio suitable for a couple and one child, and a two-bed apartment close to the beach. They feature indigenous garden, a pool, and magnificent sea and mountain views. Both are rented only as self-catering units. There's off-street parking – pretty essential in sheer-sided Llandudno. ②–③.

Leeukop

Map 3, B6. 25 Sedgemoor Rd, Camps Bay ℂ438 1361, fax 438 1675. Camps Bay bus.
Best B&B accommodation in Camps Bay, near the beach and cafés, in two stylishly arty and comfortable apartments adjoining the proprietor's home. The flats, the bigger one being pricier, are fully equipped, and you can either self-cater or stay on a B&B basis. ④–⑤.

Monkey Valley Beach

Map 2, C7. Mountain Road, Noordhoek ℂ789 1391, fax 789 1143, *monkey@iafrica.com*
Attractive group of mainly wooden and thatched two-storey chalets spread over several acres of Chapman's Peak, overlooking the seven-kilometre Noordhoek beach, 40km south of the city centre. Surrounded by indigenous vegetation

and with no other houses in sight, and there's an emphasis on natural products throughout. Either eat in the restaurant, self-cater or stay on a B&B basis. Cottages sleep six to eight people and work out reasonably for a group. The cheaper rooms face the courtyard, while the priciest are sea facing. ⑥.

HOTELS

Bay Hotel

Map 3, B6. Victoria Road ℂ438 4444, fax 438 4455, *jacky@thebay.co.za*
Luxurious, glitzy five-star hotel on the fashionable beachfront strip. Its late-1980s construction blends neo-Cape Dutch with Mediterranean styles and cane furniture, to conjure up a laid-back colonial fantasy. ⑨.

Chapman's Peak Hotel

Map 2, C6. Main Road, Hout Bay ℂ790 1036, fax 790 1089.
Impressive seaside setting overlooking Hout Bay beach, though not all of the rather ordinary rooms are seafacing. The pubby restaurant does great calamari, though the other seafood is not particularly recommended. ⑤–⑥.

FALSE BAY SEABOARD

The Cape Town–Simon's Town Metrorail line runs through the southern suburbs to hit the coast at **Muizenberg**, the oldest of Cape Town's seaside suburbs. To its south are a series of settlements, including salubrious **St James**, **Kalk Bay** with its working harbour and great cafés, and **Fish Hoek**, which is known for the best swimming beach along the False Bay seaboard. At the end of the line is the handsome and historic village of Simon's Town (see separate heading below).

FALSE BAY SEABOARD: BACKPACKER LODGES, CAMPING, B&BS, GUESTHOUSES AND HOTELS

BACKPACKER LODGES AND CAMPING

Abe Bailey Youth Hostel

Map 2, E7. Corner of Maynard and Westbury roads, Muizenberg ℗ & fax 788 2301, *abeb@new.co.za* Muizenberg station.

A respectable hostel five minutes' walk from the beach, hosting South African groups as well as backpackers. Seven dorms sleep six to fourteen people, and there are two double rooms. False Bay (Valsbaai) station, a few minutes' walk away, is closer than Muizenberg itself. Dorms ①, doubles ②.

Harbourside Backpackers

Map 2, D8. 136 Main Rd, Kalk Bay ℗788 2943, fax 788 6452. Kalk Bay station.

Popular hangout, with beds on platforms offering views of the harbour. A party atmosphere prevails, but there are quieter doubles on the lower of its upstairs floors. The hostel, two minutes' walk from the station, is on the same road as several cafés and very browsable antique shops, and it's a ten-minute walk to the lovely Dalebrook tidal pool. Dorms ①, doubles ②.

The Wave Backpackers

Map 2, D8. 288 Main Rd, Clovelly ℗ & fax 782 3659. Clovelly station. Dorms and doubles and a very reasonable B&B rate in a house on the busy main road between Kalk Bay and Fish Hoek. There's good swimming just across the railway line on Clovelly beach, and it's ten minutes along the sand to Fish Hoek Station. A kitchen is available for self-catering and the owners offer free airport pick-ups. ①.

B&BS, GUESTHOUSES AND HOTELS

Chartfield Guest House

Map 2, D8. Corner of 30 Gatesville and Norman roads, Kalk Bay

©788 3793, fax 788 8674, *info@chartfield.co.za* Kalk Bay station.
Unpretentious accommodation, 100m from Kalk Bay station,
in a well-kept rambling house halfway up the hill overlooking
the harbour – there are terrific panoramas of the Hottentots
Holland Mountains across False Bay. The best rooms are the
one in the loft with its own balcony and a semicircular one on
the corner with 180-degree views. ③.

Castle Hill

Map 2, D8. 37 Gatesville Rd, Kalk Bay ©788 2554, fax 788 3843.
Kalk Bay station.
Stylishly restored two-storey Edwardian guesthouse up a hill
with grand views of the sun rising across False Bay and
whale-watching in season. Five large bedrooms with high
ceilings and timber floors are simply furnished. The best unit is
the Rose Room, which is the most spacious and has French
doors opening onto the upstairs verandah; avoid the
disappointingly small and viewless back room. ④.

Sunny Cove Manor

Map 2, D8. 72 Simon's Town Rd, Fish Hoek © 782 2274, fax 782
6043, *imagine@iafrica.com* Sunny Cove station.
Outstanding sea views (except for the back room) in this
cheerful B&B, three minutes' walk to Sunny Cove station,
with safe parking on the property. There are four suites, three
of them with two bedrooms each, and if you cross the road and
over the railway line, you're on Jager's walkway, which leads to
Fish Hoek beach. ④.

SELF-CATERING

The Avenue Hotel

Map 2, D8. 7 First Ave, Fish Hoek ©782 6026, fax 782 5693,
reservations@avenuehotel.co.za Fish Hoek station.
Unglamorous two-storey hotel within walking distance of the

beach and shops, but with no sea view. Well priced and perfectly adequate rooms make it popular with tour groups. Outside there's a pool with loungers and umbrellas, if it's too windy for the beach. ④.

The Innisfail

Map 2, D8. 6 Dalebrook Rd, Kalk Bay ⓒ788 8928, fax 788 8929, *innis@iafrica.com* Kalk Bay station.

Modest hotel with simple but comfortable rooms, off Kalk Bay Main Road, and a short hop under the railway line to the beach and lovely Dalebrook sea-water pool. Has a 1950s feel and home comforts. ③.

Muizenberg Cottage

Map 2, D7. 7 Mount Rd, Muizenberg ⓒ & fax 788 5098, *jclarke@gem.co.za* Muizenberg station.

One-bedroom self-catering garden cottage at the foot of Muizenberg Peak, five minutes' walk to the station, giving easy access to all the False Bay seaboard destinations. A ten-minute stroll gets you to the start of mountain trails into Silvermine Nature Reserve, or down to the beach. Owned by a friendly couple, it's done out in ethnic style, and has a phone and fully equipped kitchen. Discounts for stays of a week or longer. ②.

Nautilus Lodge

Map 2, D8. 39 Simon's Town Rd, Fish Hoek ⓒ & fax 782 4168, *nautilus@global.co.za* Sunny Cove station.

Three self-catering units next to Tudor House, on Jager's Walk leading to Fish Hoek Beach. Each unit has magnificent sea views and a patio with garden furniture. ③.

Tides

Map 2, D8. 37 Simon's Town Rd, Fish Hoek. ⓒ782 6933 or 082/781 4492. Sunny Cove station.

Luxury two-storey townhouse on the shore with two double bedrooms, which open out onto a balcony, with excellent views of False Bay. Fully equipped kitchen. ④.

Tudor House by the Sea

Map 2, D8. 43 Simon's Town Rd, Fish Hoek ⓒ782 6238, fax 782 5027, *ericab@tudorhouse.co.za* Sunny Cove station.

Luxury self-catering apartments with slightly stuffy decor, but wide uninterrupted views of False Bay across the train tracks; each unit has its own balcony or garden. Sunny Cove Station is two minutes away on foot, providing transport to both the city centre (35km) and Simon's Town (5km). It's a five-minute walk along a coastal path to the wide, safe and sandy Fish Hoek swimming beach. Book as far ahead as possible. ③–⑤.

SIMON'S TOWN

Simon's Town (see p.127) is regarded by most Capetonians as a separate village, which it originally was, although it's now quite definitely part of the metropolis. During the day, all trains are met by rikki taxis, which will take you anywhere in the Simon's Town vicinity.

B&BS AND SELF-CATERING

Ark Studio

Map 2, E10. 4 Grant Ave, Boulders ⓒ786 2526, fax 786 3512. Simon's Town station.

Two rather luxurious and fully equipped self-catering units sleeping two to four people, with unimpeded sweeping views across False Bay, a couple of minutes' walk from Boulders Beach. Guests have the use of the garden, a small heated plunge pool and off-street parking. Breakfast is available. ④.

Boulders Beach Guest House

Map 2, E10. 4 Boulders Place, Boulders Beach ℂ786 1758, fax 786 1825, *boulders@iafrica.com* Simon's Town station.

Thirteen B&B rooms and two self-catering flats above the Boulders Beach car park, two minutes from Boulders Coastal Park. The self-catering units sleeping two to six people have patios for outdoor breakfasts, and braai facilities. Meals available at the adjacent restaurant (Mon–Sun 7.30am–9.30pm). ⑤–⑥.

Blue Lantern Holiday Cabins

Map 2, E10. Main Road, Froggy Pond ℂ & fax 786 2113, *blue-lantern@intekom.co.za* Simon's Town station.

Modest, fully equipped timber cabins of varying sizes, 4km from the centre of Simon's Town, just beyond the Boulders Beach turn-off. The least expensive has a double bed and kitchen in one room with an en-suite bathroom, and there's also a swimming pool and TV room. Bring your own bed-linen. ②–③.

British Hotel Apartments

Map 2, D9. 90 St George's St ℂ & fax 790 4930. Simon's Town station.

Three-bedroom self-catering apartments in a grand 1898 Victorian hotel that's part of a highly picturesque main street. This is an experience rather than just somewhere to stay. Huge units with high ceilings and enormous balconies overlooking the street and the docks, and there are more modest doubles (with bath). ③–④.

Kijabe Lodge

Map 2, E10. 32 Disa Rd, Murdock Valley ℂ & fax 786 2433. Simon's Town station.

Two en-suite bedrooms in the modern mountainside home of friendly Belgian owners, five minutes by car from Simon's Town centre, and a ten-minute walk to Boulders Beach. The reasonably priced rooms have good sea views, and there's a big pool with chairs and tables around it plus braai facilities. One of the rooms can accommodate parents and a child. ③.

Oatlands Holiday Village

Map 2, E10. Froggy Pond ⓒ786 1410, fax 786 1162, *oatlands@netactive.co.za* Simon's Town station.

Near the golf course, 3km from Simon's Town and 1km from Boulders Beach, *Oatlands* has over twenty self-catering chalets of various sizes, sleeping two to six people. The cheapest of the lot are uncarpeted, without TV, and have bunks, while the best have all you need for a family holiday. The grounds are large, with a pool, playground and trampoline – and you'll find a pub and restaurant on the premises. ②–③.

Sans Tache

Map 2, D9. 10 Neptune Close ⓒ & fax 786 3934. Simon's Town station.

Two B&B rooms in a friendly, modern house on the mountainside just north of Simon's Town. Views from the patio, where breakfast is served, are stunning. Both rooms have their own separate entrances, and one boasts simple self-catering facilities. ③.

Seaforth Beach Bungalows

Map 2, D9. Queen's/Seaforth roads ⓒ & fax 786 1463. Simon's Town station.

Cheapest of the self-catering cottages, less than 2km from the centre of Simon's Town and a minute's walk to Seaforth Beach, with safe swimming. Seven tiny shed-like timber units sleeping two to four people share washing facilities, while four slightly pricier brick chalets sleep two to six people and have their own bathrooms. Bedding can be hired. Each unit has its own braai spot, and outdoor seating under trees. ①–②.

SIMON'S TOWN: B&BS AND SELF-CATERING

Whale Rock

Map 2, D10. 438 Main Rd, corner Ixia Crescent, Murdock Valley ℭ & fax 786 2187. Simon's Town station.

Self-catering family apartment with modern decor, dishwasher, microwave, sea views and a terrace, sleeping four to six people, and a self-catering studio with a king-size bed. Both options are part of a private house, but have separate entrances. Fisherman's Beach is 300m away, and the house is 3–4km from Simon's Town, within walking distance of Boulders Beach. ③.

HOTELS

Lord Nelson Inn

Map 2, D9. 58 St George's St ℭ786 1386, fax 557 4228. Simon's Town station.

A comfortable and busy little inn, along the main road in the centre of town, whose name recalls the fact that Nelson once spent time convalescing here. The best of the hotel's compact rooms, all furnished in country style with pine, have balconies and harbour views. Reasonable value. ③–④.

Quayside Lodge

Map 2, D9. St George's Street, off Jubilee Square ℭ786 3838, fax 786 2241, *info@quayside.co.za* Simon's Town station.

Luxury hotel with 28 rooms, occupying a good part of the Simon's Town marina right in the centre of town, and with an annex across the road above the post office. Views from the balconies of the sea-facing rooms take in the mountain-edged False Bay, the yacht basin and Naval Dock Yard; the hotel is awash with nautical artefacts. ⑨.

Eating

Cape Town has a large number of relaxed and convivial restaurants, which generally serve imaginative and healthy food of a high quality. The range of styles is broad – with a full range of international cuisines available.

Cape cuisine, the only truly local food, is a spicy hybrid of the cooking styles brought to South Africa and adapted by slaves, principally from Asia and Madagascar. Mild and semi-sweet curries with a strong Indonesian influence predominate, and include: *bredie* (stew), of which *waterblommetjiebredie*, made using water hyacinths, is a speciality; *bobotie*, a spicy minced dish served under a savoury custard; and *sosaties*, a local version of kebab using mincemeat. For dessert, dates stuffed with almonds make a light and delicious end to a meal, while *malva* pudding is a rich combination of milk, sugar, cream and apricot jam. There are only a few restaurants dedicated to this style of cooking, but dishes influenced by Cape cuisine are relatively common elsewhere. A recent development is the emergence of a modern Cape style that combines international and local cuisines. Many of the restaurants listed here, especially the more upmarket ones, fit into this category.

As far as **seafood** goes, Cape Town offers cold-water

fish such as kingklip and snoek, not found along the coast to the east; every fish'n'chip shop in town offers fried snoek in season.

Given Cape cuisine's strong links with the local (teetotal) Muslim community, you'll rarely be able to enjoy Cape wines at restaurants serving Cape food, particularly in the Bo-Kaap. However, just about everywhere else in Cape Town, **wine** drinking is a matter of fierce local loyalty and most meals are accompanied by it. In no other city in the country does it feel more right to be sampling Cape wines than under the gaze of Table Mountain.

For the best delis and places to buy food
and wine for picnics and self-catering,
see p.203, and for top picnic spots see p.240.

BREAKFAST, SNACKS AND OUTDOOR EATING

Recently Cape Town's city centre has begun to enjoy a renaissance, and plenty of continental-style **cafés** are springing up. Service tends to be efficient and friendly, and most cafés stay open till around 11pm.

CITY CENTRE

Gallery Café

Map 4, D6. South African National Gallery, Government Avenue.
Cape Town station.
Tues–Sun 10am–5pm.

Breakfast, lunch and tea with a small but good menu that includes pasta, salads and sandwiches in a pleasant space inside the gallery – the best place for refreshment if you're exploring the museums in the Gardens.

Long Street Café
Map 4, C5. 259 Long St. Cape Town station.
Mon–Sat 9.30am–midnight, Sun 6–11pm.
Cool bar/deli/restaurant in the city centre's most happening
street, with tasteful open-plan decor and fresh continental-style
food. Also good if you just want a drink.

Mr Pickwick's
Map 4, C5. 158 Long St. Cape Town station.
Mon & Tues 8am–2pm, Wed–Sat 8am–4pm
Hearty and cheap "tin-plate" meals, including a range
of hot and cold "foot-long" sandwiches, which are quite a
challenge.

Sunflower Health Café
Map 4, C4. 161 Longmarket St. Cape Town station.
Mon–Fri 9.45am–5.30pm, Sat 9am–2pm.
Vegetarian restaurant attached to a health food shop. Menu
includes two hot meals each day, of the lentil bake or vegetable
lasagne variety, as well as salads and tasty cold food.

Yellow Pepper
Map 4, C5. 138 Long St. Cape Town station.
Mon–Sat 8.30am–5pm, plus dinner Fri & Sat.
Good lunch spot near town centre, featuring big plate-glass
windows to gawk at bustling Long Street, and pasta bakes that
will set you up for an afternoon's sightseeing or shopping.

V&A WATERFRONT

Bayfront Blu
Map 5, E4. Two Oceans Aquarium. Waterfront buses.
Daily 9am–11.30pm.
All-day breakfasts and fine coffee in an unbeatable location
attached to the aquarium, with seating on a quayside deck that

gives views of boats cutting across the water and clouds drifting over Table Mountain.

Mugg & Bean

Map 5, E3. Victoria Wharf. Waterfront buses.

Daily 9am–midnight.

Choose from a range of excellent coffees (if you need to tank up on caffeine try their bottomless cup of java). Light meals include toasted sandwiches and salads, but the location inside a shopping mall doesn't make the most of the Waterfront setting.

Zerban's

Map 5, E3. Victoria Wharf. Waterfront buses.

Daily 8am–11pm.

The Waterfront incarnation of a Cape Town institution, previously known for its European-style cakes, bread and coffee but now successfully branching out into breakfasts as well as brunch and lunch.

CITY BOWL SUBURBS

Café Bardeli

Map 4, C7. Long Street Studios, off Kloof Street, Gardens. 1.5km from Cape Town station.

Daily lunch & dinner till late.

Excruciatingly stylish, *Café Bardeli* is the epitome of café society: the food is chic and delicious. A film-set favourite, with Cape Town's highest quotient of supermodels per square metre.

Happy Wok

Map 7, D1. 62a Kloof St, Gardens. 1.5km from Cape Town station.

Daily 5.30pm–late, Mon–Fri noon–2.30pm.

Very informal and inexpensive café-style eatery serving a range of dishes from China, Japan and Vietnam, plus self-service jasmine tea.

BREAKFAST, SNACKS AND OUTDOOR EATING: CITY BOWL SUBURBS

Hartlief Gourmet

Map 4, G8. Gardens Centre, Mill Street, Gardens. 2km from Cape Town station.

Mon–Fri until 6pm, Sat until 1pm.

Essentially a takeaway, this meat-centred deli has an exceptional selection of foods. German specialities include sauerkraut fried with strips of bacon.

Melissa's

Map 7, D2. 94 Kloof St, Gardens ℄424 5540. 3km from Cape Town station.

Daily 8.30am–8pm.

In the food emporium you can buy freshly made Mediterranean fare, while the small café serves light meals and fine desserts.

> There's no convenient public transport in the City Bowl suburbs, but most of the eateries listed here are walkable from the city centre and, if you're exploring the museums and Gardens, few will be more than ten to fifteen minutes' away.

SEA POINT AND GREEN POINT

Aladdin Coffee Shop

Map 6, D3. Nedbank Centre, 15 Kloof Rd, Sea Point. Sea Point bus.

Mon–Sat 8am–5pm.

Patio coffee shop with views of Table Mountain, serving up breakfasts and light lunches.

Chariots Italian Coffee Bar

Map 5, D6. 107 Main Rd, Green Point. Sea Point bus.

Daily until 11.30pm.

Stylish decor and great inexpensive food make this a fashionable haunt for Cape Town's yuppies. Come for *foccaccia* and decent coffee.

Giovanni's Deliworld
Map 5, D5. 103 Main Rd, Green Point. Sea Point bus.
Daily 8.30am–9pm.
No outdoor seating, but this trendy Italian deli/coffee shop is handy for a coffee, snack or takeaway.

New York Bagels
Map 6, C2. 51 Regent Rd, Sea Point. Sea Point bus.
Daily till late.
Fantastic supermarket of a deli with a sit-down section. Choose from a dizzying array of bagels and homemade fillings, from chopped liver to herring, plus stir-fry, pasta and pastries. Highly recommended.

Rieses Delicatessen
Map 6, D3. 367 Main Rd, Sea Point. Sea Point bus.
Daily until mid-evening.
Fine sandwiches served up at a local institution, with outdoor seating. Try their salt beef on rye.

SOUTHERN SUBURBS

Café Carte Blanche
Map 3, H5. 42a Trill Rd, Observatory. Observatory station.
Daily 7pm till late.
Former curio shop decorated with Eastern artefacts, where you can sip wine under a hanging Persian carpet or quaff beer on a Mongolian bedspread. Small, unique and exotic.

Gardener's Cottage
Map 2, E3. 31 Newlands Ave, Montebello Estate, Newlands.
Tues–Fri 8am–4.30pm, Sat & Sun 8.30am–4.30pm.

Set in a complex of old farm buildings under ancient pine trees, and serving hearty breakfasts and lunches as well as tea and coffee. Worthwhile if you want to browse through the neighbouring arts and crafts workshops.

Jonkershuis

Map 2, D5. Groot Constantia Wine Estate, off Ladies Mile Extension, Constantia.
Breakfast, tea & lunch daily, dinner Tues–Sat.
Rustic informal place, where you can enjoy traditional Cape dishes or tea, surrounded by vineyards and mountains. A children's playground adjacent to outdoor seating makes this congenial and easygoing for a family outing.

Kirstenbosch Restaurant

Map 2, D4. Kirstenbosch National Botanical Gardens, Rhodes Drive, Newlands. Shuttle bus from Cape Town Tourism.
Mon–Sat 9am–5pm & Sun 8.30am–5pm.
Capetonians complain bitterly about the price of teas, coffees and sandwiches (not high by European standards) at the coffee shop in the Gardens, but the outdoor setting in tended parkland at the foot of Table Mountain is unbeatable.

Obz Café

Map 3, H5. 115 Lower Main Rd, Observatory. Observatory station.
Daily all day till late.
Trendy deli/café/bar, where you can get tasty deli meals, bacon-and-egg breakfasts and Danish pastries, or nurse a drink all evening.

Rhodes Memorial Restaurant

Map 3, H6. Groote Schuur Estate, Rondebosch.
Daily 9am–5pm.
Set on the side of Devil's Peak, this is one of Cape Town's best tea gardens, offering views across the city to the sea. A great

BREAKFAST, SNACKS AND OUTDOOR EATING: SOUTHERN SUBURBS

place for imaginative continental breakfasts – also good for salads and tasty snack lunches and teas.

ATLANTIC SEABOARD

Fish on the Rocks

Map 2, B6. Beyond Mariner's Wharf, Hout Bay, drive through the dock and factory. Hout Bay bus.
Daily 9am–7pm.
Delicious fresh fish'n'chips, served under red umbrellas or eaten on the rocks overlooking the bay. A fabulous place, during the season, to watch whales.

Mariners Wharf Bistro

Map 2, B5. The Harbour, Hout Bay. Hout Bay bus.
Daily 10am–6pm.
Relaxed, well-run place with terrace seating overlooking the harbour. Good for seafood to eat in or take away.

Red Herring

Map 2, B7. Beach Road/Pine Road, Noordhoek.
Tues–Sun lunch & dinner.
Snacks and drinks on the upstairs deck, which offers marvellous sea and mountain views, attached to a country restaurant that does good home-style roasts, fish dishes and vegetarian options.

Suikerbossie

Map 2, B5. Victoria Drive, Hout Bay.
Tues–Sun breakfast & lunch.
Cape Town outdoor institution with great views of Hout Bay, making it popular with tourists: a fine spot for lunch.

FALSE BAY SEABOARD

Bertha's Grill & Coffee House

Map 2, D9. Quayside, Simon's Town. Simon's Town station, then rikki taxi.

Daily 8am–10pm.

Great place for breakfast or a coffee in the delightful setting of the Simon's Town marina complex, which is small and low-key compared with the V&A Waterfront but has equally impressive sea and mountain views.

Café Matisse

Map 2, D8. 76 Main Rd, Kalk Bay. Kalk Bay station.

Daily 9.30am–11pm.

Popular, relaxed café serving all-day breakfasts, pizzas, light meals and wine by the glass. The work of local artists is exhibited on the walls.

The Olympia Café & Deli

Map 2, D8. Main Road, Kalk Bay. Kalk Bay station.

Tues–Sat 7am–7pm, Sun 7am–3pm.

Breakfast at the buzzing *Olympia* is part of the Kalk Bay routine for locals. Good for coffee or freshly squeezed orange juice with a choice of sticky pastries. Huge, delicious sandwiches make a filling lunch.

RESTAURANTS

The greatest concentration of **restaurants** is in the city centre and the surrounding areas, with Sea Point and, more recently, the Waterfront having well-established reputations for good food. An even younger newcomer is Kloof Street in the City Bowl suburbs, with new places springing up all the time. For **Cape cuisine**, the best places are *Biesmiellah* in the Bo-Kaap, or *Kaapse Tafel* in the city centre.

As far as **prices** go, expect to pay under R30 for a main course at an inexpensive restaurant, up to R60 at a moderately priced one, and over R60 at an expensive place.

CITY CENTRE AND V&A WATERFRONT

Anatoli
Map 5, G5. 24 Napier St ℗419 2501. Cape Town station.
Tues–Sun until 11pm. Moderate.
Turkish restaurant in a turn-of-the-century warehouse that buzzes with atmosphere. Excellent *meze* include exceptionally delicious *dolmades*, and there are superb deserts such as pressed dates topped with a puff of cream.

Bayfront Blu
Map 5, E4. Two Oceans Aquarium, Waterfront ℗419 9068. Waterfront buses.
Daily lunch & dinner. Moderate–expensive.
Traditional African food as well as Californian dishes, a good vegetarian selection and some exciting seafood options such as Swahili prawn curry. Best of all is its situation on the edge of the marina, with outdoor seating that offers a stunning view of Table Mountain.

Biesmiellah
Map 5, G7. Upper WaleStreet/Pentz Street ℗423 0850. Cape Town station.
Daily noon–3pm & 6–11pm. Moderate.
One of the oldest and best-known restaurants for traditional Cape cuisine. Try their spicy stews and round things off with a wickedly rich *malva* pudding made with apricot jam and cream. No alcohol.

Col'Cacchio
Map 4, B1. Seeff House, 42 Hans Strijdom Ave. Cape Town station.
Lunch Mon–Fri, dinner daily. Inexpensive.
Offbeat pizza restaurant, which also serves pasta and often spills

onto the pavement outside. Has over forty different and original pizza toppings, such as smoked salmon, sour cream and caviar. No bookings.

Floris Smit Huijs

Map 4, C4. 55 Church St ℂ423 3414. Cape Town station.
Daily until 10.30pm. Moderate.

The beautiful decor in this eighteenth-century town house is as big an attraction as the eclectic international cuisine, which features some local specialities such as Malay chicken salad, and kudu venison served with a delicious apple sauce.

Jewel Tavern

Map 3, G3. Off Vanguard Road, Duncan Docks ℂ448 1977.
Daily mid-morning till 10pm. Moderate.

Unpretentious Taiwanese sailors' eating house, which has been "discovered" by Cape Town's *bon viveurs*. Located in the middle of the docks, it serves superb food, including great hot and sour soup and spring rolls made while you watch.

Kaapse Tafel

Map 4, C7. Montreux Building, 90 Queen Victoria St ℂ423 1651.
Cape Town station.
Lunch Mon–Fri, dinner Mon–Sat. Moderate.

Twenty years in the business of traditional Cape cuisine hasn't diminished this popular restaurant's excellent reputation. Good for *bobotie* and Cape seafood.

Mama Africa

Map 4, C5. 178 Long St ℂ424 8634. Cape Town station.
Dinner Mon–Sat. Moderate.

Food from around the continent, including local Cape specialities and succulent Karoo lamb, served in a relaxed atmosphere. The highlight is a twelve-metre bar in the form of a sinuous green mamba.

RESTAURANTS: CITY CENTRE AND V&A WATERFRONT

Mexican Kitchen Café

Map 4, C6. 13 Bloem St ✆423 1541. Cape Town station.
Daily until midnight. Inexpensive.
Excellent casual restaurant serving up good-value burritos, enchiladas, nachos and *calamari fajitas*, with some fine vegetarian options. They also do deli-style takeaways.

Musselcracker Restaurant

Map 5, E3. Shop 222, First Floor, Victoria Wharf, Waterfront ✆419 4300. Waterfront buses.
Daily 12.30–2.30pm & 6.30–10.30pm. Moderate.
Work your way through the excellent seafood buffet starting with bread and anchovy butter, paté and/or soup; move on to cold gravdlax, herring and fish *bobotie* or a choice of casseroles, and finish it all off with a delicious pudding.

Vasco da Gama Tavern

Map 4, A2. 3 Alfred St. ✆425 2157. Cape Town station.
Daily 10am–9pm. Inexpensive.
Known locally as the "Portuguese embassy", this unpretentious restaurant with a blaring TV is a genuine working man's pub. Grilled tongue with bread, accompanied by wine mixed with Coke – a Portuguese "speciality" called *catemba* – are standard. It's also a great seafood restaurant at half the usual price, and better than many of the upmarket joints.

CITY BOWL SUBURBS

Al Dente

Map 7, D2. 88 Kloof St, Gardens ✆423 7617. 3km from Cape Town station.
Daily except Tues 11am–10.30pm. Moderate.
A sprawling and beautifully decorated restaurant that serves fresh and fragrant Mediterranean food with an Italian emphasis. Try their roast game fish or lamb Toscana done in a pizza oven.

Amigos Mediterranean Restaurant

Map 7, D3. 158 Kloof St, Gardens ℗423 6805. 2.5km from Cape Town station.

Lunch and dinner daily until midnight. Moderate.

A tasty mixture of Greek *meze* combined with Italian and Spanish food. Lively joint with some tables outside and a loyal clientele.

The Blue Plate Restaurant and Bar

Map 4, C7. 35 Kloof St, Gardens ℗424 1515. 1.5km from Cape Town station.

Dinner daily till late, lunch Fri only. Moderate.

Spacious restaurant in an elegant Victorian home offering global cuisine. Friendly and well-informed waiters and some outdoor seating along the sidewalk.

Buccaneer Steakhouse

Map 4, C7. 64 Orange St, Gardens ℗424 4966. 1.5km from Cape Town station.

Dinner daily, lunch Mon–Fri. Inexpensive.

Swiss-owned eatery that does good steaks and great sauces. The atmosphere borders on dowdy, but it makes for a relaxed and low-cost evening.

Café Paradiso

Map 7, D3. 110 Kloof St, Gardens ℗423 8653.

Daily lunch & dinner. Moderate.

Good Greek and Mediterranean dishes, including a weigh-your-plate *meze* bar and outside terrace with views up to the mountain and down over the city and docks.

Ocean Basket Southern Africa

Map 4, C9. 75 Kloof St, Gardens ℗422 0322. 2.5km from Cape Town station.

Lunch Mon–Sat & dinner every evening. Moderate.

Long queues and delicious aromas speak eloquently of the

outstanding dishes – from fish'n'chips to prawns and calamari – at this slick quick-in, quick-out seafood chain.

Yindees

Map 7, D1. 22 Camp St, Tamboerskloof ⌀422 1012. 3km from Cape Town station.

Lunch Mon–Sat, dinner Mon–Sat. Moderate.

The best Thai restaurant in Cape Town, whose deserved growth in size is a powerful advert of its popularity. Great food and brilliant spicy prawn soup served by dour waiters.

SOUTHERN SUBURBS

Africa Café

Map 3, H5. 213 Lower Main Rd, Observatory ⌀447 9553. Observatory station.

Dinner Mon–Sat. Inexpensive–moderate.

Probably the best restaurant in Cape Town for African cuisine, with a fantastic selection from around the continent. Given that you're served a communal feast of sixteen dishes and can have as many refills as you like, its R80 per head price tag is pretty reasonable. Booking essential.

Buitenverwachting

Map 2, D5. Buitenverwachting Estate, Klein Constantia Road ⌀794 3522.

Tues–Fri lunch & dinner, Sat lunch. Expensive.

One of South Africa's top restaurants, wonderfully located on the Buitenverwachting wine estate with views of the vineyards and mountains from the terrace. The food is of a high standard and consistently imaginative, fusing international and Cape flavours.

Constantia Uitsig Restaurant

Map 2, D5. Spaanschemat River Road, Constantia ⌀794 4480.

Lunch Tues–Sun, dinner daily. Expensive.

Located on a wine estate, this very successful place has views of mountains and vineyards across the Constantia Valley. Rooted in good Provençale and Tuscan cuisine, it is one of South Africa's best restaurants.

Emily's Bistro

Map 3, G5. 77 Roodebloem Rd, Woodstock ℗448 2366.

Tues–Fri lunch, Mon–Sat dinner. Moderate–expensive.

Flamboyant and chic South African creations such as sweet potato fondue combined with honeybush tea and garnished with pumpkin seeds have earned this restaurant a reputation as one of the city's top ten. Located in an intimate house (formerly a brothel), done out in deep blue with zebra stripes, *Emily's* describes itself, rather mystifyingly, as "Cape Town's first Afro Euro Trash Restaurant".

Enrica Rocca

Map 2, E4. 19 Wolfe St, Wynberg ℗762 3855. Wynberg station.

Mon–Sat lunch & dinner. Moderate–expensive.

A real authentic Italian, with a vast antipasto spread followed by a limited range of interesting pasta dishes. Fixed-price set menu options are a good deal if you want to have the works: antipasta, pasta, main dish and dessert.

La Colombe

Map 2, D5. Constantia Uitsig Wine Estate, Spaanschemat River Road, Constantia ℗794 2390.

Lunch & dinner; closed Sun dinner & all day Tues. Expensive.

Airy restaurant, rated one of South Africa's best, overlooking a swimming pool and beautiful gardens. An imaginative Provençale menu dreamed up by the French chef varies from day to day, depending on what's in season.

Pancho's Mexican Kitchen
Map 3, H5. 127 Lower Main Rd, Observatory ©447 4854. Observatory station.
Daily–late. Inexpensive.
Highly popular and inexpensive cantina-style restaurant serving Mexican dishes.

Parks
Map 2, E4. 114 Constantia Rd, Wynberg ©797 8202. Wittebome station.
Dinner Mon–Sat. Moderate–expensive.
The most elegant and expensive eating in the southern suburbs outside the wine estates, in a restored Victorian town house with an original menu that always includes a Cape dish, seafood and something delicious for vegetarians. Noted for its personal, almost pedantic service and attention to detail.

SEA POINT AND GREEN POINT

Aris Souvlaki
Map 6, B2. 83a Regent Rd, Sea Point ©439 6683. Sea Point bus.
Daily until 11pm. Inexpensive.
Reliable terrace restaurant for Greek *shwarma* and *souvlaki*. You can also get takeaways.

Mario's Restaurant
Map 5, D5. 89 Main Rd, Green Point ©439 6644. Sea Point bus.
Lunch Tues–Fri, dinner Tues–Sun. Moderate.
Excellent Italian casseroles and pastas. Game appears on the menu when available: try their guinea fowl.

Nando's Chickenland
Map 6, F2. 128 Main Rd, Sea Point ©439 7999. Sea Point bus.
Daily until 10pm. Inexpensive.

South Africa's answer to KFC. Surprisingly good grilled Portuguese-style *peri-peri* poultry with a choice of seasoning.

Pizzeria Napoletana

Map 6, D3. 178 Main Rd, Sea Point. Sea Point bus.
Closed Mon. Moderate.
A family business since 1956, the best pizza joint in Cape Town offers good value and tasty cuisine. Try the veal parmigiano or their crayfish – the largest you'll find on the Peninsula.

San Marco

Map 6, G2. 92 Main Rd, Sea Point ©439 2758. Sea Point bus.
Lunch Sun, dinner Wed–Mon. Moderate–expensive.
Stunning Italian seafood as well as pasta. The grilled *calamari* tossed in chilli and garlic is wonderful, and their antipasto trolley is especially good for vegetarians. Finish up with wonderful ice cream.

Theo's Steaks

Map 5, B5. Beach Road, Mouille Point ©439 3494. Sea Point bus.
Lunch Mon–Fri, dinner Mon–Sat. Moderate.
Upmarket atmospheric place right on the beachfront, offering superb Greek-style steaks and seafood.

ATLANTIC SEABOARD

Blues Restaurant

Map 3, B6. 9 The Promenade, Victoria Road, Camps Bay ©438 2040. Hout Bay bus.
Daily noon until after midnight. Expensive.
Spectacular views make this pricey Californian-style restaurant one of the most popular in town. The food is uneven, but on a good day the dishes, such as spicy red pepper soup or lamb with leeks and garlic, can be delicious.

Red Herring

Map 2, C7. Beach Road/Pine Street, Noordhoek ℗789 1783.
Lunch & dinner Tues–Sun. Moderate.

Beautiful sea and mountain views at this relaxed out-of-town restaurant. Choices include springbok and kudu, plus a good choice of vegetarian options or fresh fish.

The Round House

Map 3, B6. The Glen, Camps Bay ℗438 2320.
Lunch Mon–Fri, dinner Mon–Sat. Moderate–expensive.

Nouvelle – and old-style – French cuisine at this old-fashioned restaurant, housed in Lord Charles Somerset's eighteenth-century hunting lodge. Somerset was governor of the Cape (1814–1826), and the lodge is set in a secluded spot, with Regency features including an elevated curving verandah and a circular lookout facing the sea.

FALSE BAY SEABOARD

Brass Bell

Map 2, D8. Main Road, Kalk Bay ℗788 5456. Kalk Bay station.
Daily until late. Moderate.

Arguably the best location on the peninsula to eat, this unpretentious Cape Town institution is located in the station building and has False Bay's waves breaking against the wall of its outdoor terrace. Unbeatable views of both Table and the Hottentots Holland mountains, but the seafood meals don't always match the magnificent setting. There's also a pub with live music some nights.

Fish Hoek Galley Seafood Restaurant

Map 2, D8. Beach Road, Fish Hoek ℗782 3354. Fish Hoek station.
Lunch & dinner daily. Moderate.

Informal restaurant right on the beach. They do steaks, but it's their excellent-value seafood platter that attracts busloads of tourists.

Gaylords Indian Cuisine

Map 2, E7. 65 Main Rd, Muizenberg ✆788 5470. Muizenberg station. Dinner & lunch Wed–Sun, dinner only Wed. Inexpensive–moderate. The tacky interior belies an imaginative menu that adapts great North Indian cooking and local ingredients to create something unique – and reasonably priced.

Harbour House Restaurant

Map 2, D8. Kalk Bay Harbour ✆788 4133. Kalk Bay station. Lunch & dinner daily. Moderate–expensive. Seafood and Mediterranean fare, at a venue situated spectacularly on the breakwater of Kalk Bay Harbour. Freshly caught fish bought from the Kalk Bay fishing boats is a speciality.

Shopping

The V&A Waterfront is the city's most popular shopping venue; there's a good range of shops, but you should expect to pay above the odds for everything. The city centre also offers variety and, for some people's taste, a grittier and more interesting venue for browsing, especially if you're looking for collectables, antiques and secondhand books. The city's suburbanites tend to do their shopping closer to home at the upmarket Cavendish Square Mall in Claremont. There are other smaller shopping areas dotted about the suburbs.

Core **shopping hours** have traditionally been Monday to Friday 8.30am–5pm, and Saturday till 1pm. But this has begun to change and lots of supermarkets, bookshops and other specialist outlets now stay open on Sundays and beyond 5pm.

MALLS AND SHOPPING CENTRES

South African shopping tends to follow an American rather than European model, with huge **malls** where you can browse in a bookshop as well as bank, buy clothes and groceries and go to the movies. They always have several coffee shops and restaurants.

Cavendish Square

Map 2, E3. Vineyard Road, Claremont. Claremont station.

Mon–Thurs 9am–6pm, Fri 9am–9pm, Sat 9am–6pm, Sun 10am–4pm.

Huge upmarket multistorey complex that is the major shopping focus for the southern suburbs. With 200 shops, fifteen restaurants, sixteen cinemas and parking for 1800 cars, this is the best place in Cape Town to shop, but its scale can be a bit overwhelming.

Golden Acre

Map 4, D3. Adderley Street. Cape Town station.

Mall 6am–midnight; most shops 8.30am–5pm.

Dark and not entirely pleasant complex linked by walkway to the station. Handy if you're about to catch a train, but otherwise best avoided.

Blue Route Mall

Map 2, D6. Tokai Road, Tokai.

Mon–Fri 9am–5.30pm, Sat & Sun 9am–5pm.

Pretty functional single-storey centre that's handy if you're staying in Constantia or along the False Bay. Has branches of Pick'n'Pay and Woolworths.

V&A Waterfront

Map 5, E2–E4. Waterfront buses.

Mon–Sat 9am–9pm, Sun 10am–9pm.

It would be possible to visit Cape Town and never leave the Waterfront complex, which has a vast range of upmarket shops packed into the Victoria Wharf Shopping Centre, including outlets of all the major South African chains, selling books, clothes, food and crafts.

ARTS AND CRAFTS

Cape Town is not known for its indigenous **arts and crafts**

ARTS AND CRAFTS

in the way that Durban is, and much of the stuff you'll buy here is from elsewhere in Africa: goods from Zimbabwe and Zambia are particularly well represented. There are several places in the city centre and the V&A Waterfront, but you'll often pick up the same arts and crafts for a lot less money at the sidewalk **markets** scattered around town. Don't expect exotic West African-style market places however; Cape Town's venues are more like European or North American flea markets.

....

For some of the best arts, crafts, collectors'
china and Africana antiques and books,
make for Main Road at Kalk Bay (see p.126),
which has a strip of trendy outlets and
cafés clustered around the station.

....

SHOPS

Africa Nova

Map 2, C5. Main Road, Hout Bay ©790 4454. Hout Bay bus.
April–Sept Mon–Fri 9am–5pm, Sat & Sun 10am–2pm; Oct–March Mon–Fri 9am–5pm, Sat & Sun10am–4pm.

A better than average selection of ethnic crafts and curios as well as contemporary African textiles and artwork, with an emphasis on the individual and handmade.

African Image

Map 4, C4. Church Street/Burg Street ©423 8385. Cape Town station.
Mon–Fri 9am–9pm, Sat 9am–1.30pm.
Map 5, E3. Shop 6228, Victoria Wharf, V&A Waterfront ©419 0382. Waterfront buses.
Mon–Sat 9am–9pm, Sun 10am–9pm.

One of the best places for authentic traditional and contemporary African arts and crafts, from fabrics and antique sculpture to beadwork, but goods are a little over-priced.

Ethno Bongo

Map 2, C5. Main Road, Hout Bay ℭ790 0802. Hout Bay bus.

Mon–Fri 10am–5pm, Sat 10am–3pm, Sun 10am–5pm.

Charming shop in a fisherman's cottage selling wonderful and well-priced crafts, jewellery and accessories made from recycled metal and wood. Also quirky kaftans and ethnic clothing. Highly recommended for genuinely unique gifts and souvenirs.

Kalk Bay Gallery

Map 2, D8. 62 Main Rd, Kalk Bay ℭ788 1674. Kalk Bay station.

Daily 9am–5pm

Graphics, engravings as well as African art and artefacts – good value, with the chance of picking up something very collectible.

Le Bon Ton . . . & Art

Map 4, B6. 209 Bree St ℭ423 3631. Cape Town station.

Tues–Sat 10am–7pm, Sun 11am–4pm.

Art supermarket incorporating over forty small galleries which show interesting material, including sculpture and African works. Light snacks available.

Out of Africa

Map 5, E3. Shop 125, Victoria Wharf, V&A Waterfront ℭ418 5505. Waterfront buses.

Daily 9am–9pm.

Expensive baskets, beads and African arts and antiques, in the pleasant spending fields of the Waterfront.

Rose Korber Art Consultancy

Map 3, B6. 48 Sedgemoor Rd, Camps Bay ℭ438 9152. Hout Bay bus.

Mon–Fri 9am–5pm.

This should be the first stop for the serious collector, with an

ARTS AND CRAFTS: SHOPS

exceptional selection of contemporary art and craft, including ceramics and beadwork from around the continent.

Yellow Door

Map 4, G8. Upper Floor, Gardens Centre, Gardens ℗465 4702. 1.5km from Cape Town station.

Mon–Fri 9am–6pm, Sat 9am–4pm.

One of the largest and best selections of local crafts and design, including ceramics, fabrics, jewellery, basketry, metalwork and interior decor.

MARKETS

Cape Town Station

Map 4, D2. Forecourt, Adderley Street. Cape Town station.

Mon–Fri 8am–5pm, Sat 8am–2pm.

Thronging ranks of market traders selling radios, leather goods and African crafts. Not principally aimed at tourists, so it's pretty authentic.

Constantia Craft Market

Map 2, D5. Alphen Common, corner of Spaanschemat River and Ladies Mile roads, Constantia.

First and last Sat and first Sun of the month.

Sizeable outdoor flea market where you can pick up good local crafts and items from around the continent, ride a camel or a pony and have a cup of tea.

Greenmarket Square

Map 4, C4. Burg Street. Cape Town station.

Mon–Fri 8am–5pm, Sat 8am–2pm.

Open-air market that's the best place in town for colourful handmade Cape Town beachwear, from T-shirts to shorts and sandals, as well as being a showcase for antiques and knick-knacks.

The Pan African Market
Map 4, C4. 76 Long St. Cape Town station.
Mon–Fri 9am–5pm, Sat 9am–3pm.
Multicultural hothouse of township and contemporary art, artefacts, curios and crafts. There's music, a café specializing in African cuisine, a bookshop, a Cameroonian hairbraider and West African tailor.

The Red Shed Craft Workshop
Map 5, E3. Victoria Wharf, V&A Waterfront. Waterfront buses.
Mon–Sat 9am–9pm, Sun 10am–9pm.
Market where craftworkers make and sell ceramics, textiles, candles and jewellery and you can see glassblowers at work.

Victoria Road Market
Map 2, C3. 1km south of Bakoven along the coast road.
Daily.
Carvings, beads, fabrics and baskets sold from a spectacularly sited market – on a clifftop viewpoint overlooking the Atlantic.

BOOKS AND MUSIC

South Africa produces a lot of **books** given the size of its reading population: you'll find scores of good locally produced novels and endless volumes on history, politics and natural history. For new books there are some pleasant places in the suburbs or at the Waterfront to browse for half an hour, while Upper Long Street has over half a dozen second-hand book and specialist comic shops in close proximity, interspersed with congenial cafés.

Most **music** is sold on CD, and the ubiquitous chains such as CNA and Musica tend to stock pretty unadventurous selections of mainly British and American sounds. For South African bands and music from the rest of the continent, the outlets listed below are by far the best.

....

**Recommended books on South Africa
are listed on p.330.**

....

Clarke's Antiquarian

Map 4, C6. 211 Long St ℂ423 5739. Cape Town station.
Mon–Fri 8.45am–5pm, Sat 8.45am–1pm.

The best place in Cape Town for South African books, with a huge selection of locally published titles covering literature, history, politics, natural history and the arts, plus very well-informed staff. They also deal in collectors' editions of South African books.

Exclusive Books

Map 5, E3. Victoria Wharf, V&A Waterfront ℂ419 0905. Waterfront buses.
Mon–Thurs 9am–10.30pm, Fri & Sat 9am–11pm, Sun 10am–9pm.
Map 2, E3. Lower Mall, Cavendish Square, Claremont ℂ464 3030. Claremont station.
Mon–Fri 9am–9pm, Sat 9am–11pm, Sun 10am–9pm.
Map 2, D5. Constantia Village Shopping Centre, Spaanschemat River Road, Constantia ℂ794 7800.
Mon–Sat 9am–9pm, Sun 10am–5pm.

Friendly bookshop, ideal for browsing. Well-stocked shelves include magazines and a wide choice of coffee-table books on Cape Town and South African topics.

Kirstenbosch Shop

Map 2, D4. Kirstenbosch National Botanical Garden ℂ762 2510. Shuttle bus from Cape Town Tourism.
Daily 9am–6pm.

Excellent and well-chosen selection of natural-history books, field guides and travel guides covering Southern Africa, as well as a range of titles for kids.

The Travellers Bookshop
Map 5, E3. King's Warehouse, Victoria Wharf, V&A Waterfront ©425 6880. Waterfront buses.
Daily 9am–9pm.
Cape Town's only specialist travel bookshop stocks a good range of titles, mainly about South Africa and especially the Cape, covering history, politics, natural history and the arts as well as travel guides.

MUSIC

Sessions Music
Map 5, E3. Lower Level, Victoria Wharf, V&A Waterfront ©419 7892. Waterfront buses.
Mon–Thurs & Sun 9am–9pm, Fri & Sat 9am–10pm.
One of the best places in Cape Town to buy music, with an extensive selection of South African and African sounds and helpful staff.

The Max Megastore
Map 2, E3. Shop F14, Upper Level, Cavendish Square, Claremont ©683 1810. Claremont station.
Mon–Thurs 9am–9pm, Fri–Sun 9am–11pm.
Africa's first music megastore, with late-night opening seven days a week and a vast selection of all kinds of music, including good local jazz.

FOOD AND PROVISIONS

Self-catering is the cheapest way to eat in Cape Town, and it can also be good fun. Apart from **braais**, which happen anywhere with any excuse, there are countless places on beaches, in the forests or up Table Mountain where you can enjoy a terrific **picnic**, or you may just want to buy stuff to cook at your accommodation. Lots of delis can be found

FOOD AND PROVISIONS

down Kloof Street and in Green Point and Sea Point. By far the most atmospheric places to buy seafood are the Hout Bay and Kalk Bay harbours (see p.119 & p.126 respectively).

SUPERMARKETS

The easiest places to shop for food are at the big **supermarket** chains. The larger branches of the better supermarkets also have fishmonger counters where you can buy fresh fish.

Woolworths
Map 4, D3. Adderley Street. Cape Town station.
Mon–Fri 8.30am–5.30pm, Sat 8am–2pm.
Map 5, E3. V & A Waterfront. Waterfront buses.
Daily 9am–9pm.
Map 2, E3. Cavendish Square Mall, Claremont. Claremont station.
Mon–Thurs 9am–6pm, Fri 8.30am–8pm, Sat 8am–6pm, Sun 9am–5pm.
Map 2, D6. Blue Route Mall, Tokai.
Mon–Thurs 9am–5.30pm, Fri 8.30am–7pm, Sat 8.30am–5pm, Sun 9am–2pm.
The South African version of Britain's Marks & Spencer stores is excellent for quality fast-cook meals, fresh produce and cold foods, such as olives, humus and various Mediterranean dips, but can be pricey.

Pick'n'Pay
Map 5, E3. V&A Waterfront. Waterfront buses.
Daily 9am–8pm.
Map 3, B6. Main Road, Camps Bay. Hout Bay bus.
Daily 9am–7pm.
Map 3, H5. Main Road, Observatory. Observatory station.
Mon–Thurs 7am–8.30pm, Fri 7am–10pm, Sat 7am–10pm, Sun 8am–2pm.

Map 2, E3. Corner Main Road and Campground Road, Claremont. Newlands station.

Mon–Thurs 8am–6pm, Fri 8am–7pm, Sat 8am–4pm, Sun 9am–2pm.

Map 2, D6. Blue Route Mall, Tokai.

Mon–Thurs 8.30am–6pm, Fri 8.30am–7pm, Sat 8am–2pm, Sun 9am–2pm.

In a similar vein to Woolworths but considerably larger and cheaper with a good deli counter and a choice of prepared meals, among which you'll find their excellent-value ready-grilled whole chickens. Also one of the best places for dry goods and a range of groceries.

DELICATESSENS AND FARM STALLS

Thanks to the city's cosmopolitan population there are some excellent (if pricey) delicatessens, several of which are strung along Main Road, Green Point and Sea Point. You'll also find delicious food and some unusual fruit and vegetables at the more sophisticated farm stalls.

The Barnyard Farm Stall

Map 2, D6. Steenberg Road, adjacent to the well-signposted Steenberg Wine Estate, Tokai.

Mon–Fri, Sat & Sun 9am–6pm.

One of Cape Town's nicest farm stalls, with a selection of high-class cheeses, breads, home-baked cakes, wines, patés, coffee beans and many other delights. Also has the major attraction of a very good outdoor café with a children's playground attached.

Giovanni's

Map 5, D5. 103 Main Rd, Green Point. Sea Point bus.

Mon–Sun 8.30am–9pm.

Excellent breads and delicious Italian foods to take away and – if temptation overcomes you – there's always the option of sitting down for a coffee and a snack.

Melissa's

Map 7, D2. 94 Kloof St, Gardens. 2.5km from Cape Town station.
Mon–Fri 7.30am–8pm, Sat & Sun 8.30am–8pm.

Expensive imported and local specialities, which you can either eat in or take away.

New York Bagel Deli

Map 6, C2. 51 Regent Rd, Sea Point. Sea Point bus.
Daily 8am–8pm.

Sea Point has the best bagels in town and a great selection of Eastern European Jewish fillings – salt beef, gherkins, chopped liver and pickled herring – and an array of delicious pastries.

Old Cape Farm Stall

Map 2, D5. Turnoff to Groot Constantia, on Constantia Nek Road.
Daily 8.15am–6pm.

A good place to pick up a picnic, where you can choose from their delicious selection of dips and ready-made foods such as olive bread, couscous and other salads, as well as fresh fruit and vegetables.

FRESH FISH

Kalk Bay Harbour

Map 2, D8. Harbourside, Kalk Bay. Kalk Bay station.
Buy fresh fish directly from the fishermen and have it gutted and scaled on the spot. Availability is subject to weather.

Fish Market

Map 2, C5. Mariner's Wharf, Hout Bay Harbour. Hout Bay bus.
Mon–Fri 9am–5.30pm, Sat & Sun 9am–6pm.

Fresh seafood from the South Africa's original waterfront emporium, but slicker and less atmospheric than Kalk Bay harbour.

WINE

Supermarkets tend to have decent **wine** at competitive prices, but for more interesting labels and well-informed staff, there are some first-rate specialist wine merchants in town.

....

The best – and cheapest – places to buy wines are at the estates that produce them. Coverage of the Constantia wineries begins on p.99, and the estates outside Cape Town on p.274.

....

Vaughan Johnson's
Map 5, E3. Dock Road, the V&A Waterfront. Waterfront buses.
Mon–Fri 9am–6pm, Sat & Sun 10am–5pm.
One of Cape Town's best-known wine shops, which has a huge range of labels from all over the country, but can be a bit pricy.

Enoteca
Map 4, B3. Corner 125c Buitengracht and Bloem streets. Cape Town station.
Mon–Fri 9am–8pm, Sat 9am–5pm.
Map 2, E3. Castle Building, corner of Kildare Lane and Mains Road, Newlands. 1.5km from Newlands station.
Mon–Fri 10am–9pm, Sat 9am–7pm.
Good broad selection of South African and foreign wines from a knowledgeable and helpful outfit.

Woolworths
Map 4, D3. Adderley Street. Cape Town station.
Mon–Fri 8.30am–5.30pm, Sat 8am–2pm.
Map 5, E3. V & A Waterfront. Waterfront buses.
Daily 9am–9pm.

Map 2, E3. Cavendish Square Mall, Claremont. Claremont station.
Mon–Thurs 9am–6pm, Fri 8.30am–8pm, Sat 8am–6pm, Sun 9am–5pm.
Map 2, D6. Blue Route Mall, Tokai.
Mon–Thurs 9am–5.30pm, Fri 8.30am–7pm, Sat 8.30am–5pm, Sun 9am–2pm.

The own-label wines of South Africa's upmarket supermarket chain have come a long way since the days when you'd sneakily decant them so no one would know their source. Cognoscenti now happily flaunt these competitively priced wines, which consistently represent good quality and value.

HOLISM

Cape Town is South Africa's alternative-culture and **holism** capital. To find out what's on, the best **publications** are *Link-Up,* a free listings magazine, and the glossier *Odyssey* (R12), which is also the place to track down sources of Southern African crystals, gemstones and essential oils – disappointingly though, there are few oils from Cape plants except for geraniums. Both publications are available from health-food shops and alternative health venues.

Fields Health Store
Map 7, D1. 84 Kloof Street, Gardens ©423 9587. 2.5km from Cape Town station.
Mon–Fri 8am–7pm, Sat 9.30am–4pm.
Sells health and beauty products, with a juice bar serving a daily vegetarian lunch buffet and cakes. Upstairs you can get massage, shiatsu, acupuncture and the like, but appointments are essential.

Natural Remedies
Map 2, E3. Pearce Street, Claremont ©674 1692. Claremont station.
Mon–Fri 9am–5.15pm, Sat 8.30am–1pm.
The best place in the southern suburbs for homeopathic and

herbal remedies, aromatherapy oils, beauty products and a range of health foods.

Waldorf School Shop

Map 2, D5. Spaanschemat River Road, 400m west of Ladies Mile, Constantia ℗794 4997.

Mon–Fri 9am–3.30pm, Sat 9am–1.30pm.

Excellent fresh organic (biodynamic) vegetables, rye bread, cheeses, homeopathic and other health products, as well as a small range of handmade toys at the school's shop, next to the car park. The outdoor café, which serves teas and healthy snacks, may tempt you to dally a while.

The Wellstead

Map 2, E4. 1 Wellington Avenue, Wynberg ℗797 8982. Wittebome station.

Mon–Fri 9am–5pm.

The major source of New Age information and literature in Cape Town; has a library and bookshop with new and second-hand books. Their shop sells the usual goodies: crystals, wind chimes, cards, prints and music. It also has meeting room, regular video showings and meditation evenings on Mondays (7–7.30pm).

White's Chemist

Map 4, E4. 77 Plein Park, Plein Street ℗465 3332. Cape Town station.

Mon–Fri 7.30am–5pm, Sat 7.30am–12.30pm.

A long-established manufacturer and supplier of homeopathic remedies, powders, tinctures and books. They also sell homeopathic first-aid kits and herbal products.

HOLISM

Theatre and cinema

S o far, democracy hasn't been good for South Africa's theatre scene. Resources are scarce (state funds have been redirected to more pressing areas), and political protest theatre, a fertile genre in the oppressive 1970s and 1980s, is now obsolete. A steady trickle of new plays are being written and performed in Cape Town, some of them innovative and hard-hitting. As yet there is no real successor to Athol Fugard, the world-renowned playwright, several of whose works were first staged here, but writers and directors to look out for include Brett Bailey, Marthinus Basson, Reza de Wet and Fred Abrahamse.

On the **musical** front, David Kramer and Taliep Petersen have produced several hit shows that celebrate the history and culture of Cape Town. Their latest, *Kat and the Kings*, recently had an award-winning run on London's West End. Comedies, musicals and musical tribute shows are well attended and make up the staple fare of the major theatres, tickets ranging between R30 and R100.

Despite a recent boom in **film** production in Cape Town, local feature films are scarce. Mainstream Hollywood releases are shown at several commercial cinemas, all of which advertise daily in the *Cape Times* and *Cape Argus*, while a couple of independent cinemas include art-house films in their programmes.

Virtually all events in Cape Town, including theatre, cinema, concerts and sport, can be booked by phone through Computicket ℂ918 8910 or 918 8950, or online at *www.computicket.com*

THEATRES

Baxter Theatre Centre
Map 3, H7. Main Road, Rondebosch ℂ689 5991.
A mammoth face-brick theatre complex whose design was inspired by Soviet Moscow's central railway station. Mounts an eclectic programme of shows, ranging from comedy festivals to jazz concerts to kids' theatre.

Gauloises Warehouse
Map 5, F6. 6 Dixon Rd, Green Point ℂ421 0777.
A new 280-seat venue that provides a minimalist space for modern drama. One of the few genuinely adventurous, youth-oriented theatres in town.

Little Theatre
Map 3, H7. University of Cape Town, Orange Street ℂ480 7129.
Showcase for innovative work from the University of Cape Town drama school. Productions can be self-indulgent and/or breathtaking. The drama school has a long tradition of producing fine actors, and counts Richard E. Grant among its graduates.

Maynardville Open Air Theatre
Map 2, E4. Church Street/Wolfe Street, Wynberg ℂ421 5470.
Every year in January and February, a Shakespeare comedy is staged under the summer stars in Maynardville Park. The setting

THEATRES

is pure romance and the plays are presented with great imagination by the cream of Cape Town's actors and designers.

Nico Theatre Centre

Map 5, I4. DF Malan Street ℂ421 5470.

Once the Camelot of state-funded white performing arts, the Nico has reinvented itself as a more popular, less elitist theatre. High-quality ballet and opera continues to be produced in the new era, while adventurous new dramas appear periodically. Don't be intimidated by the monumental 1970s architecture.

Theatre On The Bay

Map 3, B6. Link Street, Camps Bay ℂ438 3300.

Upmarket theatre catering to a mature establishment audience. Productions include contemporary mainstream plays, farces, musical tributes and revues. Rather predictable fare, but generally good-quality performances.

CINEMAS

The **mainstream cinemas** most convenient for visitors are: the Nu-Metro and Ster-Kinekor at the V&A Waterfront (ℂ419 9700); the Ster-Kinekor Cavendish Commercial (ℂ683 6328–9) at Cavendish Square Shopping Centre, Claremont; and, at the same shopping centre, the Ster-Kinekor Cinema Nouveau (ℂ683 4063–4), which specializes in art-house and foreign-language films. The Ster-Kinekor complex at the Blue Route Mall in Tokai (ℂ713 1280) is convenient if you're staying along the False Bay seaboard.

   Independent cinemas are listed below. Tickets cost around R25 and many cinemas have discounted tickets one day a week, which you'll find advertised in the press.

The Labia

Map 4, C8. 69 Orange St, Gardens ℂ424 5927.

Formerly the flea-ridden temple of alternative cinema in Cape Town, the Labia has been spruced up in recent times and now screens an intelligent mix of art films, cult classics and new releases. Three screens, and tasty snacks for sale. Screenings are advertised in the daily papers and programmes are distributed at various outlets.

Independent Armchair Theatre

Map 3, H5. 135 Lower Main Rd, Observatory ℂ447 1514.

An adventurous club/cinema which screens cult and art movies with a video projector. Sprawl in one of an extended family of comfy couches, have a drink and enjoy the show. Screenings are on Monday to Friday evenings – contact the venue for details, or pick up a programme when you're in the area.

....

For megascreen movies, Cape Town's Imax cinema on the V&A Waterfront is covered on p.80.

....

CINEMAS |

Clubs, bars and live music

Cape Town's nightlife has traditionally been a little sleepy compared with Johannesburg's, but this is changing. Things have become much more open and cosmopolitan in recent years, spiced up by thousands of African and European visitors and immigrants. A bright economy and a general loosening up of the city's staid personality has made Cape Town a diverse and exciting place to go out in.

The city is passionate about music – while mainstream house is very popular, there are strong followings for drum'n'bass, trance, hip hop, dub and Latin grooves, as well as **kwaito**, the dance style of young black Jo'burg. Much more laid-back than European club sounds, *kwaito* can be described as slowed-down, bass-heavy house fused with township pop. Sexy and jubilant, it makes for a positive and uproarious party. Though *kwaito* is still predominately a black scene, coloured and white youth are gradually getting into it.

Many dance **clubs** have a short lifespan – and many of the best regular parties hop from venue to venue. Some of the more enduring clubs are listed below, but watch the press for up-to-the-minute information. The daily newspapers, the

Pop music and Cape Jazz

Cape Town's greatest musical treasure is **Cape Jazz**, a subgenre of South African township jazz whose greatest exponent is the internationally acclaimed **Abdullah Ibrahim** (known as Dollar Brand before his conversion to Islam). Born and raised in District Six, Ibrahim is a supremely gifted pianist and composer, who for decades has produced a hypnotic fusion of African, American and Cape Muslim idioms. In his greatest recordings, *Mannenberg* and *African Marketplace*, the fluttering rhythms of *goema* – traditional Cape carnival music – are combined with the cascading call-and-answer structure of African gospel. This is emotional jazz, full of simple, euphoric melody and enchanting brass lines.

Other Cape Town jazz legends are the late Basil Coetzee, a phenomenal tenor saxophonist who played on *Mannenberg*; Robbie Jansen, another saxman with a raunchy, fiery style who worked with Afro-pop greats Juluka; and alto saxman Winston "Ngozi" Mankunku, an old-school hepcat whose gigs are an exercise in good vibes. Both Jansen and Mankunku can occasionally be heard live in the city – watch the press. Other veteran stars to look out for are guitarist Errol Dyers, pianist Hotep Galeta and bassist Spencer Mbadu.

Two young stars stand out as talented heirs to the Cape Jazz tradition: astronomically cool guitarist Jimmy Dludlu and subtle, mellow pianist Paul Hanmer. Catch them live if you can. Also watch out for the powerful singer Judith Sephuma, and Jo'burg-based maestros Moses Molelekwa, McCoy Mrubata and Sipho Gumede. Check the press for upcoming performances and venues.

Cape Town is also well stocked with charismatic **rock**, **reggae** and **pop** bands. Notable exports include township bubblegum star Brenda Fassie, radical hip-hop crew Prophets Of Da City and R'n'B crooner Jonathan Butler. The best live acts are the Springbok Nude Girls, cheesy funk merchants The Honeymoon Suites, funk-reggae crew Firing Squad and the innovative live trance ouftit Colorfields.

Cape Argus and the *Cape Times*, run weekly club columns on Thursdays and Fridays respectively, and the monthly listings magazine *Cape Review* is also useful. Otherwise, collect flyers and keep your ears open – often the best parties are scantily promoted. Cover charges vary from R10 to over R100 for big events with international DJs. It's worth being aware that all drugs are illegal in South Africa, and aggressive police raids on clubs are by no means unknown.

Cape Town is well populated with **bars**, ranging from the hip to the eccentric to the seedy. Most liquor licences stipulate that the last round is served at 2am, but this is far from strictly followed. Expect a cover charge if live music is featured. Traditional pubs are not a big feature: where they do exist they're generally either cod-Irish franchises or depressing empty dives.

Gay and lesbian clubs are listed from p.228.

CITY CENTRE AND CITY BOWL SUBURBS

Clubland tends to be very concentrated, extending from Kloof Street in the **City Bowl** suburbs down a long spine that runs into the city centre along Long and Loop streets and ends around Waterkant Street in the **Lower City Centre**. This makes for an abundance of entertainment, but the venues are sometimes separated by dark and empty blocks. Nearby, Somerset Road in Green Point, with its string of gay bars, comes alive on weekend nights.

There's no public transport in Cape Town after mid-evening and walking around the city centre alone and at night is a poor idea. If you're out clubbing or partying arrange reliable transport beforehand, or call one of the metered taxis listed on p.255.

Café Camissa

Map 7, D2. 80 Kloof St, Gardens ℂ424 2289.

Daily 11am–late.

Small, rootsy and studiedly relaxed, *Café Camissa* is the jewel of Kloof Street. You can lounge outside with a beer, a meal or a boardgame, and let a hot city afternoon ease past. By night *Camissa* tends to buzz, with weekly doses of low-key live music (Wednesdays and Sundays). Poetry readings are also held regularly.

Chilli'n'Lime

Map 4, B7. Annex A, Longkloof Studios, Darter's Road, Gardens ℂ426 4469.

A stylish split-level club which hosts pulsing house and hip-hop parties on weekend nights. Frequented by a left-field student crowd.

Club Georgia

Map 4, B7. 30 Georgia St, off Buitensingel ℂ422 0261.

Tues–Sat 9.30pm–late.

Lively over-25s club that celebrates music from across Africa, including *kwassa-kwassa, kwaito, ndombolo, rai, kizamba* and *makossa*.

Drum Café

Map 4, F6. 32 Glynn St, Gardens.

Mon, Wed, Fri & Sat 8pm–late.

Have a drink and hire a drum for a communal drumming session. If you prefer to leave things to the professionals, percussion and rock acts perform on weekend nights. Light meals available. Fully licensed.

The Jam

Map 3, E4. 43 De Villiers St, District Six ℂ465 2106.

Quality live music and underground hip-hop parties at a

minimalist venue with space to move in. No rigid schedule, but there's an event on most nights – watch the press for details.

Jo'burg

Map 4, C6. 218 Long St, City Centre ℂ422 0241.

Daily 5pm–2am.

Great decor, and a good place to schmooze to a funky sound-track. Frequented by a hip art-school and media crowd. Live music on Sunday nights.

The Lounge

Map 4, C6. 194 Long St, City Centre.

Mon–Sat 8pm–2am.

Unabashedly trendy long-serving refuge for Cape Town's smart and glamorous. Once upstairs, make for the superb balcony and grab a table overlooking vibrant Long Street. House and jungle dominate the turntables.

Mama Africa

Map 4, C6. 178 Long St, City Centre ℂ424 8634.

Mon–Sat 8.30pm–late.

A relaxed and spacious restaurant-bar in the heart of Long Street clubland, *Mama Africa* boasts a twelve-metre bar in the form of a green mamba. Traditional percussion groups and African jazz outfits perform regularly. Popular with European and North American visitors.

On Broadway

Map 5, F5. 21 Somerset Rd, Green Point ℂ418 8338.

Daily 9pm–late.

Cabaret restaurant-bar, on the fringes of the city centre, with Mediterranean-style food and live performances every night. One of the few venues committed to the city's small but sassy cabaret scene. Drag shows on Sunday and Tuesday; cover charge R40.

The Purple Turtle

Map 4, C4. Corner Shortmarket and Long streets, City Centre.

Daily 11am–late.

A cavernous, vaguely seedy bar frequented by Goths, metal-heads and other nocturnal creatures. Catch live music on Saturday nights, but don't expect easy listening.

Yeah Bo

Map 4, C3. 83 Castle Street, City Centre.

Fri & Sat 9pm–late.

A big, vibrant *kwaito* club that jumps on weekends with one of the few young black crowds on the inner-city club scene. *Kwaito* sounds predominate, but international house is also a crowd pleaser.

V&A WATERFRONT

The **V&A Waterfront** offers a lot if you want to eat well and your budget is generous. You'll also find a reasonable amount of mainstream after-dark nightlife in safe surroundings: the area has an emphatically clean-cut atmosphere.

Den Anker Restaurant and Bar

Map 5, E3. Victoria and Alfred Pierhead.

Daily 11am–midnight.

A smart busy pub populated by tourists and well-heeled locals. Den Anker specializes in imported Belgian beers, both on tap and in a bottle. One of the more spirited places to visit at the Waterfront.

Green Dolphin

Map 5, E3. Victoria and Alfred Pierhead ℂ421 7471.

Daily noon–midnight (music from 8.30pm).

Upmarket jazz venue, serving excellent seafood and hosting quality jazz bands nightly. R15 cover charge for a

V&A WATERFRONT

table with a limited view, otherwise R20.

SOUTHERN SUBURBS

If you're on foot, **Observatory** is a good destination: in and around Lower Main Road is compact and safe. The buildings are old and characterful, the vibe is warm, mellow and multiethnic, and there's a gaggle of bohemian restaurants and bars. Of the neighbouring suburbs, **Woodstock** is in the same vein, while upmarket **Newlands** has more sedate offerings, as does **Constantia**, Cape Town's leafiest and richest suburb.

Café Ganesh

Map 3, H5. 66 Lower Main Rd/Trill Road, Observatory.
Daily 6pm–late. Closed during July.
Café Ganesh is the cosmopolitan heart of Observatory, and the place to meet artists, writers, performers and students. Spontaneous *kwaito* parties sometimes break out.

Café Sirens

Map 2, E4. 80 Main Rd, Claremont.
A lively club, catering to a mixed suburban crowd, with live jazz on Tuesday nights and comedy acts on Wednesdays. Students take over on Thursdays. Dress code is "smart–casual" (closed shoes, long trousers and shirts with collars).

Don Pedros

Map 3, G5. 113 Roodebloem Rd, Woodstock.
Daily 9am–late.
Since the 1980s, when it was chosen haunt of struggling activists, *Don Pedros* has been a place for good cheap food and scruffy Capetonian ambience. Linger all evening over a beer or a coffee without feeling hassled.

89 on Roodebloem
Map 3, G5. 89 Roodebloem Rd, Woodstock.
Tues–Sat 6pm–2am.
A friendly and intimate bar filled with elegant decor. Once
an artisan's cottage, *89* offers a welcoming hearthfire in winter
and – for the rest of the year – a great space to chill out in.

Foresters' Arms
Map 2, E3. 52 Newlands Ave, Newlands.
Mon–Sat 10am–11pm, Sun 9am–4pm.
Preppie students and professionals gather to quaff draught beer
at "Forries", in the heart of leafy Newlands. A big wood-
panelled pub in the Anglo-Celtic tradition, it boasts a beautiful
hedged-in courtyard. Grab a bench for a drowsy afternoon pint
in the great outdoors.

Independent Armchair Theatre
Map 3, H5. 135 Lower Main Rd, Observatory ℗447 1514.
A spacious club with several lounge suites, the *Independent Arm-
chair Theatre* is a stylish, innovative venue with a small art
gallery attached. Cult and art-house films are screened on week
nights, and a steady stream of notable bands plays here.

Pedlars on the Bend
Map 2, D5. Spaanschemat River Road, Constantia.
Daily 11am–11pm.
Upmarket bar at one of the posher restaurants in this ritzy
suburb, with a delightful outdoor area shaded by oaks. A good
place to drop in to after a mountain stroll.

Ruby Inna Dust
Map 3, H5. 122 Lower Main Rd, Observatory.
Daily 7pm–late.
Dim, seedy and decrepit underground institution, which
for decades has nurtured Cape Town's rasta, punk and hippy

SOUTHERN SUBURBS

subcultures. Catch some young and energetic live music downstairs, shoot pool upstairs, or simply space out on the upstairs balcony. You won't find a less pretentious bar.

FALSE BAY SEABOARD

A string of seaside villages, the **False Bay** coast has a just a couple of bars worth making a beeline for.

Brass Bell
Map 2, D8. Kalk Bay station.
Daily 11am–late.
A pub and restaurant tucked neatly between the sea and the railway line that's a superb place to be on a summer afternoon. Eat chips and seafood, nurse a pint of draught Guinness, admire the mountains across the bay and take a splash in the tidal pool.

Red Herring
Map 2, C7. Corner of Pine and Beach roads. Noordhoek.
Tues–Sun 11am–midnight.
An upmarket pub above a smart restaurant with an outdoor deck overlooking the panoramic Noordhoek valley: ideal for a refreshing break while you're driving down the peninsula. Busy on warm weekend afternoons when a clean-cut twenty-something crowd gathers.

ATLANTIC SEABOARD

Sea Point is still a good place for a night out; otherwise head for the places listed here, in Camps Bay and Clifton.

Dizzy Jazz Café
Map 3, B6. 41 Camps Bay Drive, Camps Bay ©438 2686.
Daily noon–2am (music from 8.30pm).
Crowded and lively nightspot with a big verandah, draught

beer and sea views. Live jazz on Fridays and Saturdays, otherwise the sounds alternate between African and mainstream.

La Med Bar and Restaurant

Map 3, B5. Glen Country Club, Victoria Road, Clifton.
Tues–Sun 11am–2am.

Overlooking the rocks at Clifton, this spot draws a sporty, mainstream crowd; it's a favourite place for hang-gliders from Lion's Head to drop in to after landing in the adjacent field.

CAPE FLATS

The **townships** are blessed with countless backyard bars and shebeens, but there are few established and formal clubs. The best nightlife option is to join a township jazz tour (see p.39).

Club Images

Map 2, F3. Claude Street, Athlone Industria ✆637 9038.
Thurs–Sat 8.30pm–late.

A big brash venue including a karaoke bar, a sports bar and a roomy dancefloor. Live jazz on Thursday nights, while DJs follow the spirit of the crowd on Fridays and Saturdays. R'n'B and mainstream house are the staple sounds.

Club Vibe

Map 2, F4. Rigel Road/Castor Road, Lansdowne ✆762 8962.
Fri & Sat 9pm–late.

A vast nightclub catering mainly to a well-dressed coloured crowd. Features two dance floors (mainstream and uplifting house), a hundred television screens and a groundbreaking sound technology feature known as "The Earthquake". Security is strong, the door policy is smart–casual and strictly no under-18s can enter.

West End & Club Galaxy

Map 2, F3. College Road, Rylands ℗637 9132.
Thurs, Fri & Sat 8pm–late.

Two nightclubs in one building – you can circulate between them in the course of an evening. *West End* is Cape Town's top jazz venue, with regular performances by sizzling African jazz and fusion outfits. The last Sunday of every month sees several acts sharing the bill (call the club for details). Dress up, and book a good table if you want to be seated and see the stage. *Club Galaxy* is a straight-up dance club playing R'n'B and mainstream house to a young and smart crowd.

Sports and outdoor activities

C apetonians take their sport seriously: the city provides every opportunity for pitting yourself against the elements, whether you're on a sailboard, hang-glider or a surfboard, or coming down the mountain on a rope or bike. Alternatively, just let everyone else get on with it while you sink a few beers and watch the cricket.

Tickets for all the sports events listed here
can be booked through Computicket outlets
(℡918 8910 or 918 8950; *www.computicket.com*).

CRICKET

Cricket is keenly followed by a wide range of Capetonians. The city's **cricketing** heart beats at Newlands Cricket Ground, 61 Campground Rd, Newlands (℡674 4146). One of the most beautiful grounds in the world, Newlands nestles beneath venerable oaks and the elegant profile of Devil's Peak. Provincial, test and one-day international matches are played here. **Tickets** range from R25–30 for provincial matches to R90–160 for internationals.

RUGBY

The Western Cape is one of the world's **rugby** heartlands, and the game enjoys religious support. Provincial, international and Super 12 contests are fought on the hallowed turf of Newlands Rugby Stadium, Boundary Road, Newlands (©689 4921). Find out whether either Western Province or the Stormers (the Western Cape regional team) are on a winning run – and then get a ticket. The stadium will be packed and the atmosphere exhilarating. Expect to pay R15–20 for stand **tickets** for lower profile events and up to R75 for crowd-pullers like the Super 12.

SOCCER

Though never as well attended as cricket or rugby, Cape Town **soccer** is burgeoning with talent. The dusty streets of the Cape Flats have recently produced superb young footballers such as Benni McCarthy (Ajax Amsterdam, Celta Vigo) and Quinton Fortune (Atletico Madrid, Manchester United). The most ambitious and professional club in the city is Ajax Cape Town (©408 3800), jointly owned by its Amsterdam namesake. The most exciting games to attend are those between a local outfit and either of the Soweto glamour teams, Orlando Pirates and Kaizer Chiefs: they draw a buzzing crowd wherever they play. Matches are at Green Point Stadium, off Beach Road; Athlone Stadium, off Klipfontein Road, Athlone; and Newlands Rugby Stadium (see above). Tickets for league matches are cheap at around R15–20.

RUGBY AND SOCCER

PARTICIPATION SPORTS

Abseiling
You can **abseil** off Table Mountain or Chapman's Peak with Abseil Africa (©424 1580) for around R200 for a half-day trip.

Bird-watching
The peninsula's varied habitats attract nearly 400 different species of **birds**. Fertile ground for the activity is on Lion's Head, in Kirstenbosch Gardens and the Cape of Good Hope Nature Reserve, as well as at Kommetjie and Hout Bay; you can find out about guided outings with knowledgeable guides through the Cape Bird Club (©686 8795). For a more institutionalized experience, there's World of Birds, Valley Road, Hout Bay (©790 2730; see p.119 for more).

Golf
The Milnerton **golf** course, Bridge Road, Milnerton (©752 1047), is tucked in between a lagoon and the Table Bay and boasts classic views of Table Mountain. Other popular local courses are at Rondebosch Golf Club, Klipfontein Road, Rondebosch (©689 4176), and Royal Cape Golf Club, 174 Ottery Rd, Wynberg (©761 6551) Prices are around R145/R210 for 9/18 holes; clubs can be rented for R80; and caddy fees are R50. Booking is essential.

Gyms
"Health and Racquet" clubs are upmarket but well-appointed **gyms** dotted around the peninsula. Contact their head office (©710 8500) to find out where the nearest one is to you.

Horse-riding
Horse Trail Safaris, Indicator Lodge, Skaapskraal Road, Ottery (©73 4396 or 082/575 5669) offer **riding** along

Strandfontein and Muizenberg beaches; Sleepy Hollow Horse Riding, Sleepy Hollow Lane, Noordhoek (©789 2341) cover the spectacular Noordhoek Beach. Both cost around R150 for 2hr 30min.

Inline skating (roller-blading)

Especially popular along the long smooth promenade that runs from Mouille Point to Sea Point, **inline skating** is a growing activity. You can rent blades from Rent 'n' Ride, 1 Park Rd, Mouille Point (©434 1122; around R30 for 2hr).

Kite-flying

The Kite Shop (©421 6231), Shop 110, Ground Floor, Main Shopping Complex, V&A Waterfront, sells **kites** of all shapes, colours and sizes.

Mountain-biking

Downhill Adventures (©082/459 2422), whose meeting point is outside *Hopkins Cycle Inn* on the corner of Bree and Wale streets in the city centre, take organized **mountain biking** trips down Table Mountain, around Cape Point and through the Winelands (from R180 for a full day). Also try Rent 'n' Ride, 1 Park Rd, Mouille Point (©434 1122), for bike rental, from R60 a day.

Paragliding

Fun 2 Fly (©557 9735) offer one-day, one-and-a-half day and full-licence **paragliding** courses, from R350 to R2500.

Road cycling

Cycling (see above for rental outlets) is popular all over the peninsula, and is a great way to take in the scenery. For information about the Cape Argus Pick'n'Pay Cycle Tour (see p.245), the largest individually timed **bike race** in the world, contact The Pedal Power Association (©689

PARTICIPATION SPORTS: INLINE SKATING (ROLLERBLADING) TO ROAD CYCLING

8420), who also organize fun rides from September to May.

Rock climbing

You can learn how to rock climb up Table Mountain's famous facade with the Cape Town School of Mountaineering (℅619 604), who charge R750 for a four-day **rock-climbing** course. For recommended climbing leaders, see p.252.

Scuba diving

Cape waters are cold but can be clear and are good for seeing wrecks and reefs. Because it's invariably warmer than the Atlantic seaboard, False Bay is preferred in winter. **Dives** cost from R30 for a short dive from the shore to around R70 from a boat; prices include dive gear. An internationally recognized PADI open-water diving qualification can be completed for around R1400. For information and arranging scuba-diving courses and equipment rental, contact: Atlantic Underwater Club, Bay Road, Mouille Point (℅439 9322); Ocean Divers International, Protea Ritz, Main Road, Sea Point (℅439 1803); Orca Industries, Herschel Road/Bowwood Road, Claremont (℅461 9673); and Time Out Adventures, Avalon Building, 8 Mill St, Gardens (℅461 2709).

Surfing

Top **surfing** spots include Big Bay at Bloubergstrand, where competitions are held every summer, Llandudno, Muizenberg, Kalk Bay and Long Beach at Kommetjie and Noordhoek. For further information, contact the Western Province Surfing Association (℅674 2972).

Swimming and snorkelling

There are surf livesaver patrols on duty at Milnerton, Camps Bay, Llandudno, Muizenberg and Fish Hoek beaches.

Snorkelling trips to swim with seals at Seal Island are arranged by Hout Bay Two Ocean Divers (℡438 9317), from R180 including all gear. For **pools**, try Long Street Swimming Pool, Long Street (℡400 3302), Cape Town's only heated indoor pool; or Newlands Swimming Pool, corner of Main and San Souci roads, Newlands (℡464 4197), an Olympic-sized chlorinated pool. Sea Point Swimming Pool, Beach Road, Sea Point (℡434 3341), is an enormous and wonderful sea-water pool.

Walking

The best places for gentle **strolls** are Newlands Forest, up from Rhodes Memorial, and the beaches. For longer **walks**, head for anywhere on Table Mountain (see p.109), Tokai Forest, Silvermine Nature Reserve or Cape Point Nature Reserve. For recommended walking guides, see p.252.

Windsurfing

In summer, most Capetonians moan about the howling southeaster – handy, though, if you're into **windsurfing**. Langebaan, 75 minutes' drive north of town, is one of the best spots; for further help contact Cape Windsurf Centre, Langebaan (℡022/772 1114). Otherwise, the place to go in Cape Town is Bloubergstrand. The Blouberg Windsurf Centre (℡554 1663, *blouwind@mweb.co.za*) rents equipment, cars with racks and has long-term accommodation at Bloubergstrand, as well as being able to offer general advice to its clients, for example on which airlines offer free carriage of windsurfing equipment.

Gay Cape Town

South Africa boasts one of the world's few gay- and lesbian-friendly constitutions, and Africa's most developed and diverse gay and lesbian scene. Cape Town has always had a strident and vibrant gay culture, and is on its way to becoming an African Sydney, attracting gay travellers from across the country and the globe.

INFORMATION

The Cape Town **Gay Help and Information Line** (©422 2500; daily 1-8pm) is an excellent resource, covering organizations as well as entertainment. In addition, two national **publications** are worth getting hold of for listings and general information. The bimonthly glossy lifestyle mag *Outright* is aimed at gay and lesbian readers (with an emphasis on men). Available at international airports, major booksellers and newsagents, it serves as a good starting point for making contacts and finding out where to go. The monthly newspaper *Exit* carries listings and has a strong political focus. SA's gay nervecentre in **cyberspace** is *q on line*: visit *www.q.co.za* for chatrooms, virtual cruising, dating services and news on gay issues, gay travel and nightlife.

The Triangle Project, 41 Salt River Rd, Salt River (©448 3812), is a dedicated and efficient organization that provides HIV tests and professional counselling to gay men and lesbians. They also offer legal advice, run educational projects and manage a growing library.

....

An excellent guide to gay Cape Town is the free *Pink Map*, published by A&C Maps, which gives a lively and comprehensive coverage to gay entertainment, shopping and accommodation in the city. It is available at Cape Town Tourism's visitor centre, good bookstores, tourist centres and gay clubs and restaurants.

....

SPORT AND EVENTS

If you're up for some **sport** in the company of gay and gay-friendly Capetonians and visitors, contact COGS (Cape Organization Of Gay Sport, ℗788 9310, fax 683 1269, *cogs@africamail.com*). COGS co-ordinates hikes around the peninsula and various sporting and social outings, and travellers are warmly welcomed.

An annual highlight is the popular and comprehensive **Gay Film Festival** (℗424 1532; *www.oia.co.za*), showcasing gay and lesbian films, features and documentaries from across the globe. It happens simultaneously in Cape Town, Pretoria and Johannesburg; dates and venues vary from year to year. The city also hosts an annual **Mother City Queer Project** party, a hugely popular event usually held in early December (see p.247).

CLUBS AND PUBS

55

Map 5, F5. 22 Somerset Rd, Green Point ℗425 2739. Sea Point bus. Daily noon–late.

A young and sassy theatre/club/bistro attracting a cosmopolitan crowd. The decor can be described as "warehouse chic", and regular live entertainment includes drag shows (Wednesdays) and revues (Thursdays) – cover charge R35. It takes on its club persona on Fridays and Saturdays.

89 on Roodebloem

Map 3, G5. 89 Roodebloem Rd Woodstock ℭ447 0982.

Tues–Sat 6pm–2am.

Elegant, beautifully outfitted gay-friendly pub in a Victorian house. Nestled in increasingly trendy upper Woodstock, it strikes a refreshing chord, halfway between an intimate local and a sleekly cosmopolitan meeting-place.

BAD – The Bronx, Angels, Detour

Map 5, F6. Corner Somerset and Napier streets, Green Point ℭ419 9216.

Daily till late.

A complex of clubs that share a courtyard and a reputation as the heartbeat of Cape Town's gay nightlife. *Angels* and *Detour* are two cavernous dance venues (R'n'B and hard house respectively) with a common cover charge of R40; *Bronx* is a hugely popular and energetic bar where you can get down to commercial house, cheesy and Latino grooves. The crowd here is mixed, unpretentious and committed to having a good time.

Blah Bar

Map 5, F5. 21a Somerset Rd, Green Point ℭ421 7643.

Daily 5pm–late.

A stylish upmarket bar in the heart of Green Point's "gay village". The *Blah Bar* was the victim of an unclaimed and unsolved bomb attack in 1999, but reopened within weeks and remains a friendly, chic and petal-strewn haven. A relaxed stopover-point before or after a night of dancing.

Evita se Perron Theatre/Café

Darling Station, Darling ©022/492 2831. 55min north of Cape Town by train or car.

Evita Bezuidenhout (aka Pieter Dirk Uys) is South Africa's Dame Edna Everidge, a socialite, diplomat and sharp commentator on current affairs. Catch her and Uys' other alter egos at *Evita se Perron* ("Evita's Platform") a theatre-café on Darling railway station in the interior. Enjoy traditional South African food at *Tannie's Station Café* (vegetarian meals available), drink at *Bambi's Berlin Bar*, or shop at the Bapetikosweti Duty-Free Shop. Shows are on weekends, or seven days a week during the festive season. Darling has several guesthouses, making it practical for an overnight stay if you're arriving and leaving by rail. Contact Metro Rail (©403 9080) for information on trains to Darling.

Café Manhattan

Map 5, G6. 74 Waterkant St, Green Point ©421 6666. 1km from Cape Town station.

Mon–Sat noon–late, Sun 6pm–late.

A cultured, relaxed restaurant-bar which serves good affordable food and hosts live Latin music every Sunday night (no cover charge). Ladies' night is on the last Thursday of every month. Decor changes regularly as new exhibitions are mounted. Also features an outside terrace beneath oak trees. Straight-friendly.

On Broadway

Map 5, G6. 21 Somerset Rd, Green Point ©4188338. 1km from Cape Town station.

Daily.

Cabaret restaurant-bar with Mediterranean-style food and live performances every night of the week. One of the few venues committed to the city's small but sassy cabaret scene. Drag shows on Sunday and Tuesday, starting at 9pm (R40).

CLUBS AND PUBS

Rainbow
Map 2, H2. 1st floor, *Park Court Lodge Hotel*, Voortrekker Road, Belville ©948 0911. Bellville station.

Daily 10am–late.

The only openly gay bar in the very drab and conservative northern suburbs, the *Rainbow* is defiantly vibey and raunchy, with a multiracial mixed-age crowd. Karaoke nights, strip shows and disco evenings happen every week.

STEAMBATHS

The Hothouse Steam and Leisure
Map 5, F6. 18 Jarvis St, Green Point ©418 3889, *info@hothouse.co.za* 1km from Cape Town station.

Mon–Fri noon–2am, Sat & Sun 24hr.

Luxurious pleasure complex featuring jacuzzis, sauna, a sun-deck with a superb view, a full bar with a limited food menu, video room, fireplace and satellite TV. Entrance R30–35 week-days, R40-45 weekends.

Steamers
Map 4, G7. Corner Wembley and Solan roads, Gardens ©461 6210, *info@steamers.co.za* 1km from Cape Town station.

Feb–Nov daily noon–3am; Dec & Jan Mon–Fri noon–8am, Sat & Sun 24hr.

The ultimate cruise venue featuring a swimming pool, steam room, sauna, jacuzzi, glory holes, leather room, cabins, voyeurs' room, sunbed and more.

Kids' Cape Town

ape Town is an excellent place to travel with children. The city enjoys fine weather, and activities in its many nature reserves, gardens and historic estates let under-10s work off some energy in a safe environment. Much of what there is to do for kids is either free or inexpensive, though renting a car is pretty well essential given the poor public transport.

Where the prices in this chapter refer to children, they mean under-16s, unless specified.

The V&A Waterfront is a good place to go with kids: several of its attractions are listed below. But it also has the added appeal of ships and seals in the harbour, boat rides and umpteen child-friendly fast-food outlets.

MUSEUMS AND SIGHTS

Cable Car

Map 3, C6. Lower Cable Station, Tafelberg Road. Kloofnek bus, then walk; shuttle bus from Cape Town Tourism.

Cable car return fares: mid-April to mid-Sept R45, under-16s R20;

CHAPTER 15 • KIDS' CAPE TOWN

mid-Sept to Nov R60, scholars R45; Dec to mid-April R65, scholars R35; under-4s free.

A ride in the cable car can't fail to thrill, and once on the tabletop there are views, pathways to explore, and outdoor and indoor refreshments, albeit expensive. The furry little dassies (see p.110) always provide some amusement, but they shouldn't be fed as they may bite.

Groot Constantia

Map 2, D5. Groot Constantia Wine Estate, off Ladies Mile Extension, Constantia.

Museum daily 10am–5pm, R5; cellar tours daily: April–Sept 11am & 3pm, Oct–March hourly 10am–4pm; R10 (booking essential ☏794 5128); wine tasting daily: April–Sept 10am–4.30pm, Oct–March 9am–5.30pm; R12; grounds free.

Beautiful seventeenth-century Cape Dutch manor house with large grounds that are ideal for a wander. The most child-friendly of the Constantia wine estates, its congenial outdoor *Jonkershuis* restaurant has an adjoining playground.

SA Museum and Planetarium

Map 4, C–D7. 25 Queen Victoria St ☏424 3330. Cape Town central station.

Daily 10am–5pm; adults: museum R5, planetarium R7, combined R10; kids: museum free, planetarium R5. Cape Town station.

The museum is great for rainy days, especially for five- to twelve-year-olds, who'll enjoy the four-storey whale well and African animal dioramas, as well as the dinosaur displays. The Museum's Discovery Room (weekdays 10am–3pm, Sat & Sun 11am–4.30pm) features live ants, massive spiders, and a crocodile display. For exceedingly cheap Internet access (R5 for 30min), there are ten computers with natural-history Web sites bookmarked and interactive CD-ROMs. The Planetarium has special children's shows over weekends and in school holidays, while the adjoining Gardens are full of friendly squirrels.

MUSEUMS AND SIGHTS

Telkom Exploratorium

Map 5, E3. Union Castle Building, V&A Waterfront. Waterfront buses.

Tues–Sun 9am–6pm; R10, under-18s R5.

Interactive science museum where kids over 4 are invited to let their itchy fingers loose on knobs, buttons and dials. Activities include stomach-turning rotation inside a gyroscope, simulated speeding at 315kph in a Ferrari, virtual-reality rides as well as fairground favourites such as distorting mirrors.

Two Oceans Aquarium

Map 5, E4. V&A Waterfront. Waterfront buses.

Daily 9.30am–6pm; R34, kids R18.

One of Cape Town's most rewarding museums (see also p.83) has loads for kids to do, apart from the excitement of just looking at the weird and wonderful sea creatures. The touch pool provides the chance to handle a few species – sometimes this includes a small shark or sea urchins – while the Apha Activity Centre usually has puppet shows or face painting as well as computer terminals where older kids can learn about marine ecology.

AMUSEMENT AND THEME PARKS

Ratanga Junction

Map 2, F1. N1 to Bellville, take exit 10 (Sable Street exit) ✆0861/200 300. Regular shuttle departures from Cape Town Tourism, V&A Waterfront & *Holiday Inn Newlands*.

Rides: Wed–Sun (Mon–Sun during school holidays) 10am–6pm; riders R90, junior & non-riders R55; under-3s free.

Spectacular multimillion-rand theme park that recreates a mythological late nineteenth-century mining town, with loads of activities and eateries. The real attractions are the 24 rides, which include family rides, thrill rides, steam trains and boats.

The biggie is the Cobra, a towering spine-like roller coaster which takes you 34m to the first drop, speeds you along at 100kph and delivers four-times gravity traction around the bends. A rider ticket entitles you to sample all the rides as many times as you wish. Certain rides are restricted to people over 1.3m tall.

Scratch Patch and Mineral World
Map 2, D9. Dido Valley Road, off Main Road, Simon's Town ℗786 2020.
Map 5, E3. V&A Waterfront ℗419 9429. Waterfront buses.
Mon–Fri 8.30am–4.45pm, Sat & Sun 9am–5.30pm; R6–25, depending on size of container.
Over-3s will enjoy taking a bag and filling it with the reject polished gemstones which literally cover the floor. From the Simon's Town Scratch Patch, you can cross the catwalk to see one of the world's biggest gemstone tumbling plants in operation (Mon–Fri).

Spier
Map 1, E3. 50km from Cape Town, along the R310 ℗809 1100, *info@spier.co.za*
Daily 9am–5pm, free.
A brilliant family outing that dovetails nicely with a tour of the Winelands. Spier is a historic manor house in vast grounds with a large lake – a good setting for picnics. There's a kids' playground and space to run about, as well as guided pony rides (April–Oct Sat & Sun 11am–4pm; Nov–March daily 11am–4pm; R7 for ten minutes). Another highlight is the cheetah park, part of a breeding programme, where you can enter the enclosure to pet a purring big cat (viewing free; cheetah encounter R30, kids R15). You're not allowed to consume your own food on the estate, but their farmstall and coffee shop has a deli that bakes delicious fresh bread and pastries and sells cheeses, cold meats and dips, from which

AMUSEMENT AND THEME PARKS

you can compile your own picnic basket. There's also a choice
of four eateries: the *Jonkershuis Restaurant*, *Spier Café*, the
Taphuis Grill and the *Riverside Pub*.

World of Birds

Map 2, C5. Valley Road, Hout Bay ℡790 2730.
Daily 9am–5pm, R25, kids R15, under-3s free.
Allow at least two hours to see the more than 3000 birds and
small animals housed in surprisingly pleasant and peaceful
walk-through aviaries. You can watch penguins being fed at
11.30am and 3.30pm, pelicans at 12.30pm and owls at 4.10pm.
There's a café and restaurant serving light lunches, or you can
picnic at the Flamingo Terrace.

BEACHES

Cape Town is literally surrounded by **beaches** – a classic
and easy summer weekend family outing. This selection is
particularly suitable for toddlers and smaller kids and generally also offers something for parents. Most beaches are
pretty undeveloped, so it's best to take what you need in the
way of food and drinks with you. Sea water and swimming
pool temperatures are published each day in the *Cape Times*
in the weather section.

> **Get to the beach as early as possible so you can
> leave by 10–11am before the sun gets too strong,
> and to avoid the wind which often gusts up in
> the late morning.**

FALSE BAY SEABOARD

The warmer **False Bay seaboard** has the advantage of
being accessible by Metro Rail train from central Cape

Town. By car, take the M3 in the direction of Muizenberg; it'll take about 40 minutes from central Cape Town to Fish Hoek.

Boulders Beach

Map 2, E10. Entry R10. 39km south of central Cape Town. Simon's Town station, then rikki taxi.

One of the only places to go when the southeaster is blowing, Boulders has safe, flat water, making it ideal for kids – and its resident penguin breeding colony. The granite boulders create a beautiful, protected setting, and there's some shade in the morning. It's an extremely popular beach, and fills up fast during the December school holidays, so go as early in the day as you can.

Fish Hoek

Map 2, D8. 30km south of central Cape Town. Fish Hoek station.

One of the best peninsula beaches has gentle waves that are warm in summer, and a long stretch of sand. There's a playground, and a reasonable café on the beach, and with a pushchair you can stroll along Jager's Walk, a paved pathway along the rocky coast which has beautiful views of the Hottentots Holland mountains. When it's windy, you'll find the small grassy area next to the showers the most protected area for sunbathing.

St James

Map 2, D8. 38km south of central Cape Town. St James station.

A safe tidal pool with a small sandy beach next to the photogenic bathing boxes. With a pushchair, you can walk to Muizenberg along a concreted coastal pathway, with views of the distant mountains across the water. St James can get overcrowded at weekends and parking can be inadequate. There are no tea shops on site, but there are tea and scones at the Labia Museum on Main Road, between St James and Muizenberg, and an Italian restaurant across the road from St James Station.

BEACHES: FALSE BAY SEABOARD

ATLANTIC SEABOARD

The **Atlantic seaboard** is too cold for serious swimming, but does have some lovely stretches of sand, boulders and rock pools – and astonishing scenery. Beaches are excellent for picnics, and on calm summer evenings idyllic for sundowners and sunsets. In the summer they are less windy than the False Bay beaches, but tend to absolutely bake in the afternoons. South of Hout Bay, there's no public transport.

Camps Bay

Map 3, B6. 8km southwest of central Cape Town. Hout Bay bus.

Sandy beach with some grass and shade-giving palm trees, lying below the impressive Twelve Apostles rampart. There's a tidal pool and small rock pools to explore, and its easily reachable from the centre by car or bus.

Noordhoek and Kommetjie

Map 2, B7–8. 41km southwest of central Cape Town.

The eight-kilometre stretch of white sand from Noordhoek to Kommetjie provides fine walking, kite-flying and horse-riding, with stupendous views of Chapman's Peak. Some good restaurants and farmstalls in the rural and wooded Noordhoek area make for a pleasant outing, and if you're going to Kommetjie, there's camel riding (see below). Kommetjie itself has some nice groves of milkwood trees, and rocks and pathways to explore. You'll need your own transport to get out here.

Sea Point Promenade

Map 6. 4km west of central Cape Town. Sea Point bus.

Stretching 3km from the Lighthouse in Mouille Point to Sea Point Pavilion, the paved promenade, bordered by lawns, hotels and apartment blocks hugs the rocky coastline. It's the closest stretch of coast to the centre, with several parking spots along the promenade, and is ideal for pram pushing or roller-blading. There's also the draw of playgrounds and ice-cream sellers. While there are two little beaches strewn with slimy kelp, they are not safe for swimming, although you could take a bucket and spade to them. For swimming, head for the pool at the Sea Point Pavilion.

SWIMMING POOLS

Long Street Baths
Map 4, C6–7. Corner Long Street and Buitensingel ℂ400 3302. Cape Town station.
Mon–Fri 7am–8pm, Sat 7am–7pm, Sun 8am–6pm. R6, kids R3.
Conveniently central, Cape Town's only heated indoor pool is great when the weather is poor.

Newlands Pool
Map 2, E3. Corner Main Road and Sans Souci roads, Newlands. Newlands station.
Daily: April–Sept 9am–5pm; Oct–March 7am–6.30pm; R6, kids R3.
Olympic-sized unheated pool surrounded by lawns and mountain views. Its summer high temperature of 24°C drops to an unappealing 15°C in winter.

Sea Point Pool
Map 6, C2. Sea Point Pavilion, Beach Road. 5km west of central Cape Town. Sea Point bus.
Daily: April–Sept 9am–5pm; Oct–March 7am–6.45pm; adults R6, kids R3.
Marvellous Olympic-sized chlorinated seawater pool on the sea edge, with two paddling pools for children, and seagulls flapping about.

SWIMMING POOLS

OUTDOOR AND PICNIC SPOTS

The Barnyard Farmstall

Map 2, D6. Steenberg Road (M42), next to Steenberg Estate, between Tokai Road and the Ou Kaapse Weg.

Excellent place for an outdoor snack or cup of coffee at a small farmyard with ducks and chickens wandering around, and an unusually good kids' playground. The farmstall itself has delectable breads, dips, baked goods and deli fare and is a good stop if you're doing the Constantia winelands.

Imhoff Farm

Map 2, B8. Kommetjie Road, opposite Ocean view turn-off ©789 1711.

Camel rides are laid on daily between noon and 4pm at Imhoff Farm, where you can also see ostriches and other flightless birds, stroke farm animals or gawp at snakes in boxes. Camel rides cost R12 for six minutes, R40 for thirty minutes or R75 for an hour. Walks lead into the surrounding trees and sandy areas, but not on the beach itself. Toddlers can ride with a parent in the same saddle, and 4-year-olds and upwards can do it alone.

Kirstenbosch National Botanical Garden

Map 2, D4. Rhodes Drive ©762 1166. Shuttle bus from Cape Town Tourism.

Daily April–Aug 8am–6pm, Sept–March 8am–7pm; R10, kids R5.

Without doubt top of the list for a family outing, the extensive lawns here offer miles of space for running about, there are trees to climb, rocks to jump off and streams to paddle in. There's no litter, no dogs, it's extremely safe and you can push a pram all over the walkways. Great for picnics or to have tea outdoors at the café. For older kids there are short waymarked walks, the Stinkwood and Yellowwood trails (1.2km and 2.5km), or you can scale the mountain up Skeleton Gorge (see p.115).

Newlands Forest

Map 2, D3. 9km south of the centre, off the M3 to Muizenberg.

Dawn to dusk; free.

Gentle walks in and around pine forests and streams on the wooded southern slopes of Table Mountain, with a flattish pathway suitable for pushchairs. It's good for picnics if you want to get out of the city and don't have time to go further afield. Safest at weekends and in the afternoons when the joggers and dog walkers are out. Use the access point off the M3 signposted "Forestry Office", where there's ample parking.

Noordhoek Farm Village

Map 2, C7. Noordhoek Main Road, just before the road climbs up to Chapman's Peak ℃789 1317.

Mon–Sun 8.30am–5.30pm.

Very much geared to the tour buses en route to Cape Point via Chapman's Peak, but nevertheless a delightfully tranquil place under oak trees, where you can buy fresh produce, clothes, souvenirs and Zimbabwean sculpture. Best of all is the shady playground next to the café with outdoor seating, which can be a life-saver if you're doing Chapman's Peak with restless children in the car.

Silvermine Nature Reserve

Map 2, D7. Ou Kaapse Weg (M64).

Dawn to dusk; R8.

Beautiful nature reserve on the mountains above Muizenberg and Kalk Bay, about 25km from the centre, accessed from a signposted entry gate at the top of Ou Kaapseweg (M64). It's a good place to see fynbos vegetation at close quarters, stroll around the pine-fringed lake and picnic with small children. It is exposed though, and not recommended in heavy winds or mist. With older children there are some mountain-top walks with relatively gentle gradients, which give spectacular views over both sides of the peninsula. Friends of Silvermine (℃782

OUTDOOR AND PICNIC SPOTS

5079 or 785 1477) offer free walks with members at various times of the week.

Tokai Forest Arboretum

Map 2, C–D6. Tokai Road; take the Tokai exit from the M3 towards Muizenberg, then head to the mountains at the end of Tokai Road, or access it from the signpost on the M42.

Dawn to dusk; R2.

Peaceful forest with trees from all over the world, established in 1885 on the slopes of Constantiaberg. A wonderful place to escape to when the southeast wind blows, it offers walks and mountain biking, as well as a thatched tea shop with outdoor seating. A great place for young children to explore, with logs to jump off and a gentle walk to a stream.

SHOPS

If you're looking for something local to take home, your best bet is to check out some of the bright cotton printed **clothes** that have a uniquely Cape Town ethnic look. While there are many labels about, the ones listed tend to be superior (and more expensive). Locally made toys and other goods are generally inferior in quality to what you'd find in Europe or North America.

Baby City

Map 5, F6. 53 Somerset Rd, Green Point ✆419 6040.

Warehouse-style shop that offers rather indifferent service, but stocks a wide range of baby gear such as toys, pushchairs and cots. Amongst the cheapest places in Cape Town for disposable nappies and babywipes.

Mad Dogs

Map 5, E3. Barrow Mall, Lower Level, Victoria Wharf, V&A Waterfront ✆421 7426. Waterfront buses.

Map 2, E3. Cavendish Shopping Centre, Claremont ✆671 8477.
Claremont station.

Zany kids clothes which are durable and well made.

Naartjie and Naartjie factory shop
Map 5, E3. Lower Level, Victoria Wharf, V&A Waterfront ✆418 0733.
Waterfront buses.
Map 2, E3. Cavendish Shopping Centre, Claremont ✆683 7184.
Claremont station.
Map 2, B5. Naartjie factory shop, above the Spar Supermarket, Victoria Avenue, Hout Bay ✆790 3093. Hout Bay bus.

Funky kids' clothing of a similar quality to Mad Dogs. Cheaper
seconds are available from their factory shop in Hout Bay, near
the harbour.

Reggies
Map 4, D3. Golden Acre Shopping Centre, Adderley Street ✆419
2955. Cape Town central station.
Map 2, E3. Cavendish Shopping Centre, Claremont ✆683 2312.
Claremont station.
Map 2, D6. Blue Route Shopping Centre, Tokai ✆712 0120.

Reliable, countrywide chain of shops that sells baby goods and
toys for all ages, with a couple of branches in the southern suburbs.

Peggity's Toys
Map 5, E3. Lower Level, Victoria Wharf, V&A Waterfront ✆419 6873.
Waterfront buses.

Conveniently central but slightly pricey shop, stuffed to the
brim with good-quality toys for all ages, including beach
goods, books and tapes.

SHOPS

Festivals and events

Many of Cape Town's events take place outdoors in summer, and make full use of the city's wonderful setting. They include the Coon Carnival (the name it's widely known by despite the pejorative connotations), a unique event rooted in the city's coloured community, while the Kirstenbosch Summer Sunset Concerts, which run from December to March, are a must. Winter tends to be quiet, but it does herald the arrival of calving whales, and in their wake the Hermanus Whale Festival in September, which packs out this small southern Cape settlement.

JANUARY

The Coon Carnival

January 2, and following 3 Saturdays. South Africa's longest and most raucous annual party, the **Coon Carnival** (aka the Cape Minstrel Carnival), brings over ten thousand spectators to Green Point stadium (Map 5, C5). It starts on

January 2 for the *Tweedenuwejaar* or "Second New Year" celebrations – an extension of New Year's Day unique to the Western Cape. Central to the festivities are the brightly decked-out coloured minstrel troupes that vie in singing and dancing contests.

One good reason to come is to hear the locally evolved style of singing known as *ghommaliedjies* (drum songs), accompanied by banjos, which began as slave songs performed at new year and evolved in the twentieth century into a part of working-class coloured culture. The style of minstrelsy that characterizes the carnival dates back to the 1880s, when minstrel entertainers from visiting US ocean liners joined in the city's new year revelry. Up to the 1970s, an important part of the carnival was a parade from District Six through the streets of Cape Town; sadly this died out when District Six was razed, and with it some of the spontaneity and vigour of the event. Many coloureds were moved out to the Cape Flats, and now have to be bussed to stadiums.

Tickets (R20–30) to watch the event at Green Point Stadium on January 2 and the following three Saturdays can be reserved through Computicket (see p.255); you won't get such a good view if you buy tickets at the gate on the day (R15).

FEBRUARY

Cape to Rio Yacht Race

Held in February in even years. Cape Town's largest seafaring event is the biennial **Cape to Rio Yacht Race**, a 3640-nautical-mile run held in even years. Yachts set sail from Cape Town's docks; good free vantage points are the breakwater at the V&A Waterfront and Signal Hill.

MARCH

Cape Argus Pick'n'Pay Cycle Tour
Early March. The 105-kilometre **Cape Argus Pick'n'Pay Cycle Tour** is the largest individually timed bike race in the world with 35,000 participants. You can pick up entry forms from Pick'n'Pay supermarkets or enter online at *www.cycletour.org.za*

North Sea Jazz Festival Cape Town
End of March/beginning of April. Initiated as a two-day event in 2000, the Cape Town counterpart of the world-famous **North Sea Jazz Festival** combines international jazz with African sounds. Notable performers at the launch event included Courtney Pine, Herbie Hancock, Jimmy Dludlu, Moses Molelekwa and Hugh Masakela. Day/weekend passes (R235/360) can be bought through Computicket (see p.255); the programme and latest information can be checked out via *www.mweb.co.za/NorthSeaJazzFestivalCapeTown*

APRIL

Two Oceans Marathon
Second half of April. The **Two Oceans Marathon**, another of the Cape's big sports events, is in fact a marathon and a half (56km), and takes place every April. Information and entry forms can be obtained from Old Mutual Two Oceans Marathon, PO Box 2276, Clareinch 7740 ℃671 8724, *raceadmin@TwoOceansMarathon.org.za, www.TwoOceansMarathon.org.za* (Mon–Fri 8.30am–4.30pm).

JULY

Whale Migrations

There's obviously no fixed schedule for the annual migration of calving **southern right whales**, but they usually start appearing any time from July, and remain along the Cape Town and Western Cape coast as late as December. For details about whale-watching off the Cape Peninsula see p.272, and off the Whale Coast p.259.

SEPTEMBER/OCTOBER

Hermanus Whale Festival

End of September/beginning of October. To coincide with peak whale-watching season, the western Cape town of Hermanus (see p.260) stages the week-long annual **Whale Festival** of arts and the environment. Held in September/October, its activities include plays, a craft market, a children's festival and live music (further information ℂ028/313 0928).

DECEMBER

Mother City Queer Project

Early December. Mother City Queer Project is a hugely popular party, usually held in early December, for which a vast venue is chartered (thus far, Observatory's River Club and the Nico Theatre). Thousands of gay revellers form teams and converge in outrageous fancy dress following a pre-advertised theme – past ones have been "The Secret Garden," "The Twinkly Sea," "The Shopping Trolley" and "Heavenly Bodies". Many partygoers spend frenetic months conceiving and preparing their costumes for an MCQP party. Outlandish get-ups, fabulous decor, multiple dance-floors and a mood of sustained delirium make this event a real draw (further information ©426 5709, *www.mcqp.co.za*).

Kirstenbosch Summer Sunset Concerts

Late December to early March. Amongst the musical highlights of the Cape Town calendar are the popular **Kirstenbosch Summer Sunset Concerts**, held on Sunday evenings from December to March on the magnificent lawns of the botanical gardens at the foot of Table Mountain. Performances begin at 5.30pm and cover a range of genres, from local jazz to classical music. Come early to find a parking place, bring a picnic and some Cape fizz – and enjoy. Tickets, available at the gate, cost R20 for adults and R10 for kids. Watch the press to find out what's on.

Directory

ACCOMMODATION AGENCIES Cape Town Tourism
runs a Hotel and Accommodation Booking Desk from its visitor centre in the central business district, on the corner of Burg
and Castle streets (Mon–Fri 8am–5pm, Sat 8.30am–1pm, Sun
9am–1pm; ©426 4260, fax 426 4266, *info@cape-town.org*).
Bed'n'Breakfast, PO Box 2739, Clareinch 7740, Claremont
(©683 3505, fax 683 5159, *holtz@intekom.co.za*) has places
from R160–200 per person per night, while for self-catering
accommodation during December and January, A–Z Holiday
Accommodation, 15 Winton Crescent, Woodbridge Island
7441 (©551 2785, *louise@a-zholidayhomes.co.za*) can provide
apartments and houses for R400–4000. Home Accommodation (©715 7130, fax 712 3340, *homeaccm@iafrica.com*) produces
a South African accommodation guide, which lists about fifty
properties in Cape Town with rooms for R100–175 per person
per night – choose your place and book directly with the host.
The booklet is available free from Satour offices worldwide, can
be posted (small charge for airmail, surface mail free), or you
can visit their Web site (*www.travelselection.co.za*).

AIRLINES Air France (©418 8180); Air Namibia (©421
6685); Air New Zealand (©419 9382); Air Portugal (©421
7224); Air Zimbabwe (Compass Tours ©419 4370); Alitalia
(©418 3386); British Airways (©683 4203, or toll-free

©0800/01 1747); KLM Royal Dutch Airlines (©421 1870 or ©934 3495); Lufthansa (©425 1490 or ©934 8534); Nationwide (©936 2050); Olympic Airways (©423 0260); Qantas (©683 4203); Sabena (©421 7957); SA Airlink (toll-free ©0800/11 4799); South African Airways (domestic and international ©936 1111); Swissair (©421 4938).

AIRPORT INFORMATION ©934 0407.

AIRPORT TAX is included in the price of domestic and international fares.

AMERICAN EXPRESS Thibault House, Thibault Square, city centre (©421 5586). Offers full Amex facilities, including help with lost cards.

BANKS Main branches are easy to find in the shopping areas of the city centre, the middle-class suburbs and at the Waterfront (Mon–Fri 8.30am–3.30pm, Sat 8–11am). Wherever you find banks, you'll also find automatic teller machines (ATMs) that take cards on the Cirrus and Maestro networks.

BUREAUX DE CHANGE For foreign exchange transactions outside normal banking hours, try one of the following: American Express, Shop 11a, Alfred Mall, Waterfront (Mon–Fri 9am–7pm, Sat & Sun 9am–5pm; ©419 3917); Rennies Foreign Exchange, Victoria Wharf, V&A Waterfront (Mon–Sat 9am–7pm, Sun 10am–7pm; ©418 3744); Rennies Travel, Riebeeck Street, City Centre (Mon–Thurs 8.30am–5pm, Fri 9–11.30am, Sat 9am–noon; ©425 2370); Absa Bank, Cape Town International Airport (daily 6am–10pm; ©934 0223).

BIKE RENTAL Mountain bikes are available from Rent 'n' Ride, Park Road, Mouille Point (©434 1122; R60 a day).

CAR PARKS These are dotted all over the place in this car-friendly city. At pay-and-display car parks at street level all around the centre, hustlers will offer to look after your car and clean it for a tip, especially on the Grand Parade and Loop and Church streets. If you want to park in peace, head for one of the multistorey parking garages; there's one attached to the Golden Acre complex, and another at the north end of Lower Burg Street. Most hotels and a large number of B&Bs and guest houses offer secure parking.

CAR RENTAL One of the cheapest is Discount Drive Car Hire (𝒞511 6802, 083/250 1222), who rent out older vehicles for as little as R700 a week (including 700km free), while Berea Car and Bakkie Hire (𝒞386 4054) offer an unlimited mileage rate of R226 a day for three to six days. For one-way rental (to drive down the Garden Route and fly back from Port Elizabeth, for example), you'll have to rely on one of the bigger companies, such as Avis (𝒞423 0823), Hertz (𝒞386 1560) and Imperial (𝒞421 5190). Although pricier, they have nation-wide offices. You'll need a credit card to arrange car rental.

CREDIT CARDS For lost credit cards call freephone to be put through to their global service centres: Mastercard 𝒞0800/990 418; Visa 𝒞0800/990 475. You'll be asked to give the card number in order to block it.

DENTAL CARE Dentists are listed in the Yellow Pages telephone directory and are well up to British and North American standards, and generally no more expensive.

DISABLED TRAVELLERS A growing number of tourist attractions in Cape Town are being designed to accommodate disabled travellers. For example, the Kirstenbosch National Botanical Gardens have Braille and wheelchair trails and the V&A Waterfront has been designed as a wheelchair-friendly venue. More details about specific sites can be found on the excellent "Enabled Traveller" Web site (*enabled.24.com*) hosted by Cheshire Homes (*info@enabled.24.com*), who can help with all aspects of travel for disabled visitors.

EDUCATIONAL TOURS For arranging specialist educational exchanges, cultural visits or fact-finding missions, there are few better operators in Cape Town than Ida Cooper Associates (*©683 4648, fax 683 9169, idaca@iafrica.com*), who facilitate contacts with a wide range of South Africans, including leading academics, artists, writers and government ministers.

ELECTRICITY Electricity runs on 220/230V, 50Hz AC, and sockets take unique round-pinned plugs. Most hotel rooms have sockets that will take 110V electric razors, but for other appliances US visitors will need a transformer.

EMBASSIES AND CONSULATES Australia, 14th Floor, BP Centre, Thibault Square (*©419 5425*); Canada, 60 St George's Mall (*©423 5240*); UK, Southern Life Centre, 8 Riebeeck St (*©425 3670*); USA, 4th Floor, Broadway Centre, Heerengracht (*©421 4280*). The main embassies for most countries are in Pretoria, South Africa's executive capital.

EMERGENCIES Ambulance *©10177*; Fire *©535 1100* or 461 4141; Police (Flying Squad) *©10111*; Police (Tourist Assistance Unit) *©418 2853*; Rape Crisis *©447 9762*.

GUIDES For guided rock-climbing (from R600 for two maximum) or mountain walks (from R250 each for two people, reducing to R125 each for groups of five or more), contact Richard Behne (*©448 2697*). Jill Lockley and Margaret Curran (*©715 6136*) are recommended registered guides who can take you along any of the major Table Mountain ascents

and provide informed commentary on natural history for R150
for a half day or R250 for a full day, including refreshments and
transfers; they also do less strenuous outings in the Silvermine
reserve on the lower slopes of the mountain. For guided tours,
see p.38.

HOSPITALS AND DOCTORS Doctors are listed in the
telephone directory under "Medical". The largest state hospital
is Groote Schuur, Hospital Drive, Observatory (✆404 9111),
just off the M3. Somerset Hospital, Beach Road, Mouille Point
(✆402 6911), nearer the centre, has outpatient and emergency
departments and is convenient for the City Bowl and Atlantic
seaboard, although it is generally overcrowded, understaffed
and seemingly under-equipped. If you have medical insurance
you might prefer to be treated at the private, well-staffed and
well-equipped City Park Hospital on Loop Street (✆480
6111).

INOCULATIONS No specific inoculations are compulsory,
and you need take no special precautions unless you're ventur-
ing into remote areas of other provinces or neighbouring
countries.

INTERNET Cape Town is well wired and you should have
no problem finding somewhere to send or receive your email
or do a bit of surfing. Among the numerous places offering the
service you'll find a conveniently central cybercafé at Cape
Town Tourism, at the corner of Burg and Castle streets, while
the cheapest surfing in town is at the South African Museum in
the Gardens (even taking into account the R5 entrance fee for
adults), which costs R5 per half-hour. You can also get Web
access from Cyber Xpress coin-operated Internet kiosks (R5
for 10min), which are located among other places at: the
Dizzie Dassie Restaurant, the Upper Cable Station on top of
Table Mountain; the *Hard Rock Café*, Victoria Wharf, V&A

Waterfront; Rennies, 8 Riebeek St, City Centre; Rennies
Adelphi Centre, Sea Point; and Rennies, Cavendish Square
Shopping Centre, Claremont.

LAUNDRIES Most backpacker hostels have coin-operated
washing machines, while guesthouses, hotels and B&Bs will
usually a offer a laundry service at an extra charge. There are
also laundries in the city centre and most suburban areas that
will do a service wash for you.

LEFT LUGGAGE Virtually every backpacker hostel provides
luggage storage facilities and most other accommodation will
be happy to take care of your luggage for a day or two. The
left-luggage facility at Cape Town station (Mon 8am–7pm,
Tues–Thurs 8am–4pm, Fri 6am–6pm, Sat & Sun 8am–3pm;
℡449 2611) is inexpensive and convenient if you're arriving by
intercity bus or train, or catching an airport shuttle into the
city centre.

MALARIA Malaria is absent from the Western Cape, but is a
real risk in the eastern or northern parts of South Africa as well
as neighbouring countries, and malaria prophylactics may be
necessary.

MOBILE PHONE RENTAL is available from Cellucity,
Shop 6193, Victoria and Alfred Waterfront (℡418 1306) for
around R13 per day for the handset, with calls charged at a
little under R2.50 per minute. For security reasons you'll need
a credit card.

PHARMACIES with extended opening hours include:
Hypermed Pharmacy, corner York and Main roads, Green
Point (daily 8.30am–9pm; ℡434 1414); Sunset Pharmacy, Sea
Point Medical Centre, Kloof Road, Sea Point (daily
8.30am–9pm; ℡434 3333); Tamboerskloof Pharmacy, 16 Kloof

Nek Rd, Tamboerskloof (daily 9.30am–6pm; ℂ424 4450).

POLICE Head office: Caledon Square, Buitenkant Street (ℂ467 8000); Tourist Assistance Unit, Tulbagh Square, City Centre (ℂ418 2853).

POST OFFICE The main branch, on Parliament Street, City Centre (Mon–Tues, Thurs–Fri 8am–4.30pm, Wed 8.30am–4.30pm, Sat 8am–noon; ℂ464 1700), has a poste restante and enquiry desk.

TAXIS There are a number of reliable companies, including Marine Taxi Hire (ℂ434 0434) and Rikkis (ℂ423 4888 or 423 4892).

TELEVISION Cape Town receives broadcasts from SABC 1, 2 & 3 as well as the free-to-air independent channel, e.tv. SABC 3 and e.tv broadcast exclusively in English, while the others mix English-language broadcasts with output in the ten other official languages. Many hotels and guesthouses also get the M-Net satellite service, which has channels offering wall-to-wall sport, movies, news and specialist topics in English.

TELEPHONES There are phone booths all over Cape Town taking phone cards and coins. For cash calls, phones can be found at the Main Post Office, Parliament Street (Mon–Sat 8am–9.45pm, Sun & public holidays 9.30am–8.30pm).

TICKET AGENCY Computicket (ℂ918 8910 or 918 8950, *www.computicket.com*) books most theatre, cinema and sporting events, as well as airline and bus tickets.

TIME In common with the rest of South Africa, Cape Town is two hours ahead of Greenwich Mean Time throughout the year; seven hours ahead of North American Eastern Standard

PHARMACIES–TIME

Time; and eight hours behind Australian Eastern Standard Time. If you're flying from anywhere in Europe, you shouldn't experience any jet lag as you'll be travelling virtually due south.

TRAVEL AGENTS The backpacker-friendly One World Travellers Space, 309 Long Street (©423 0777), is handy for organizing tours or onward travel into the rest of South Africa; and the largest travel franchise in the country is Sure Travel, which has about two dozen centres across Cape Town (©0800/221 656 for the nearest office). Try also STA, 31 Riebeeck Street (©418 6570).

WEIGHTS AND MEASURES South Africa is fully metric, and kilometres, grammes, kilogrammes, litres and degrees Celsius are the norm. Shoe sizes follow the British system.

DAY-TRIPS

The Whale Coast

Until recently, South Africans have been pretty blasé about the fact that hundreds of southern right whales spend the second half of every year close to the southern Cape's shores. However, the Whale Coast, the couple of hundred kilometres east of Cape Town, offers the best shore-based whale-watching in the world. The place most closely associated with their annual migration is Hermanus, the largest town along the shores of Walker Bay, whose warm, shallow waters attract the whales. While the town is a viable day-trip from Cape Town, the coastal scenic route there is so spectacular that it's worth savouring. With whales, fine beaches, some of the best wineries in the Cape and a wonderful cliff-top setting, Hermanus makes a good weekend away, but with a couple more days in hand, you can get a taste of the sparsely populated Overberg ("over the mountain") region that was a wild hinterland to the early white settlers.

East down the coast, the first of the Overburg towns is **De Kelders**, which outshines smarter Hermanus as a whale-watching spot, while, further down the bay, you hit the fishing town of **Gansbaai** (Afrikaans for Goose Bay), which these days is far better known for its sharks than its waterfowl. Curving back to Hermanus, **Danger Point**, at the southern extent of Walker Bay, marks the spot where

HMS *Birkenhead* went down in 1852.

An easy excursion from Hermanus takes you through dry sheeplands and undulating wheatfields to Bredasdorp, a junction town on the R316 that gives you the choice of branching out to Africa's southern tip at **Cape Agulhas**, the well-preserved Moravian mission town of **Elim**, or the fishing village of **Arniston**. And, if you enjoy solitude, then **De Hoop Nature Reserve**, to the east of Arniston, is the best Whale Coast destination, an exciting wilderness of bleached dunes and craggy coast that sometimes sees whales by the score.

....

The phone code for the Whale Coast is ⓒ028.

....

HERMANUS

On the edge of rocky cliffs and backed by mountains, **Hermanus**, 112km east of Cape Town, sits at the northern-most end of Walker Bay. The town trumpets itself as the whale capital of South Africa and, to prove it, has an official whale crier who struts around armed with a mobile phone and a dried kelp horn through which he yells the latest sightings. There is still the barest trace of a once-quiet fishing village around the historic harbour and in some under-stated seaside cottages, but for the most part Hermanus has gorged itself on its whale-generated income that has produced modern shopping malls, supermarkets and craft shops.

Walker Bay does provide some of the finest **shore-based whale-watching** in the world; from about July until November/December, southern right whales start appearing in the warmer sheltered bays of the Western Cape. Whales aside, Hermanus has good swimming and beaches, some excellent wineries, and makes a good base for exploring the coast to either side.

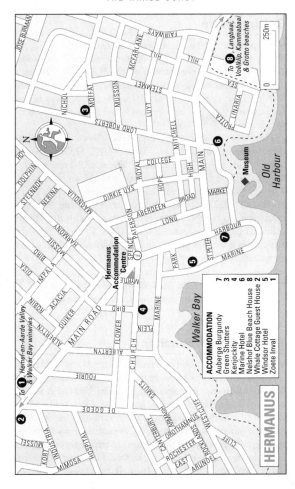

HERMANUS

To **1** Hemel-en-Aarde Valley & Walker Bay wineries

To **8** Langbaai, Voëlklip, Kammabaai & Grotto beaches

Hermanus Accommodation Centre

Museum

Old Harbour

Walker Bay

N

0   250m

ACCOMMODATION

Auberge Burgundy	7
Green Shutters	3
Kenjockity	4
Marine Hotel	6
Nelshof Blue Beach House	8
Whale Cottage Guest House	2
Windsor Hotel	5
Zoete Inval	1

HERMANUS

Getting there

Most people get to Hermanus on a tour (see p.38) or **drive**, which takes about ninety minutes from Cape Town along the N2, striking south onto the R43 at Bot River – the more direct of the two main routes. The **coastal road** that hugs the coast from Strand, leaving the N2 just before Sir Lowrie's Pass, is the more scenic and takes an extra thirty minutes.

The only other transport from Cape Town are **minibus shuttles** operated by Harvey's Travel (℃312 3737; R100 per person) daily to and from Adderley Street, and Traveller's Joy (℃312 3702; R120 per person); you must phone and book. The daily Baz **backpacker bus** from Cape Town (℃021/439 2323) drops people off at Bot River, 28km to the north on the N2, from where you can arrange to be collected by a licensed taxi (℃316 1093; about R25) – the bus carries a mobile phone, and can call a taxi while you're en route.

For the lowdown on whales and their behaviour, and for the best spots to sight them, see the box opposite.

The town and beaches

Main Road, the continuation of the R43, meanders through Hermanus, briefly becoming Seventh Street. **Market Square**, just above the old harbour and to the south of Main Street, is the closest thing to a centre, and here you'll find the highest concentration of restaurants, craft shops and flea markets – the principal forms of entertainment in town when the whales are taking time out.

Just below Market Square is the **Old Harbour Museum** (Mon–Sat 9am–1pm & 2–4pm; R3), whose only real

Whale spotting

The Southern Cape, including Cape Town, provides some of the easiest and best places in the world for **whale-watching**. You don't need to rent a boat or take a pricey tour to get out to sea; if you come at the right time of year, whales are often visible from the shore, although a good pair of binoculars will always come in useful.

All nine of the great whale species of the southern hemisphere pass by South Africa's shores, but the most commonly seen off the Cape coast are **southern right whales** (their name derives from being the "right" one to kill because of their high oil and bone yields and because, conveniently, they float when dead). Southern right whales are black and easily recognized from their pale, brownish **callosities** (rock gardens). These are patches of raised, roughened skin on their snouts and heads, which form a distinct pattern on each individual and can help scientists keep track of them. What gives away the presence of a whale is the blow or spout, a tall smoky plume which disperses after a few seconds and is actually the whale breathing out before it surfaces. If luck is on your side, you may see whales **breaching** – the movement when they thrust high out of the water and fall back with a great splash.

Female whales come inshore for calving in sheltered bays, and stay to nurse their young for up to three months. The period from **August to October** is the best time to see them, although they start appearing in June and some stay around until December. When the calves are big enough, the whales head off south again, to colder stormy waters where they feed on enormous quantities of plankton, making up for the nursing months when the females don't eat at all. Though you're most likely to see females and young, you may see **males** early in the season, boisterously flopping about the females: they neither help rear the calves nor form lasting bonds with females.

Continues overleaf

WHALE SPOTTING

Whale spotting (continued)

In **Hermanus**, the best vantage points to spot whales are from the concreted cliff paths, which ring the rocky shore from New Harbour to Grotto Beach. There are interpretation boards at three of the popular lookouts (Gearing's Point, Die Gang and Bientang's Cave).

Hermanus is the most congested venue during the whale season and there are equally good – if not better – spots elsewhere along the Walker Bay coast. **De Kelders** (see p.268), 39km east of Hermanus, is a good possibility, while **De Hoop Nature Reserve** (see p.272), east of Arniston, is reckoned to be the ultimate place along the entire southern African coast for whale-watching, with far greater numbers of southern rights breaching here than anywhere else.

During the season, the **Whale Information Hotline** (©083/212 1074) can tell you where the latest sightings have been.

attraction is its live transmission of **whale calls** from a hydrophone anchored in the bay (replaced by recordings out of season). An almost continuous five-kilometre **cliff path** through coastal fynbos hugs the rocky coastline from the old harbour to Grotto Beach in the eastern suburbs. For one short stretch the path heads away from the coast and follows Main Street before returning to the shore. East of the Old Harbour, just below the *Marine Hotel*, a beautiful **tidal pool** offers the only sea swimming around the town centre's craggy coast.

For **beaches**, head out east across the Mossel River to the suburbs, where you'll find a decent choice, starting with secluded **Langbaai**, closest to town, a cove beneath cliffs at the bottom of Sixth Avenue. **Voëlklip**, at the bottom of Eighth Avenue, has grassed terraces and is great for picnics.

Adjacent is **Kammabaai**, with the best surfing break around Hermanus and, 1km further east, **Grotto Beach** marks the start of a twelve-kilometre curve of dazzlingly white sand that stretches all the way to De Kelders.

Accommodation

Auberge Burgundy, 16 Harbour Rd ©313 1201, fax 313 1204.
Imitation-Provençal country house in the town centre, projecting a stylish European feel. ⑥.

Green Shutters, 3 Moffat St, Hermanus © & fax 312 3117.
Fully equipped self-catering cottage sleeping four, in a garden set well back from the seafront. ③.

Kenjockity, 15 Church St © & fax 312 1772.
Centrally located and friendly B&B, where you can't see the sea from most rooms but can hear the whales at night in season. ③–④.

Marine Hotel, Marine Drive ©313 1000, fax 313 0160.
Grand seafront hotel with a rather formal ambience – certainly Hermanus's best. If you're shelling out you may as well book early and pay a bit extra for a sea-facing room. There's a jacuzzi and an indoor swimming pool and, a short way down the cliffs, a tidal pool. ⑨.

Nelshof Blue Beach House, 37 Tenth St ©314 0201.
Situated right on Voëlklip Beach in a renovated Victorian house, this is the only B&B in Hermanus where you have the choice of lying in bed or lounging in the jacuzzi to watch whales. ⑥.

Whale Cottage Guest House, 20 Main Rd ©313 0929, fax 313 0912, *relmark@iafrica.com*
Simple, pleasantly furnished guesthouse offering five rooms decorated with marine themes. The only drawback is it's 1.5km from the sea. ④.

HERMANUS

Windsor Hotel, Marine Drive ℂ312 3727, fax 312 2181,
  windsor@hermanus.co.za

The town's second hotel has the best location in town – right on
  the edge of the cliffs – but otherwise isn't a patch on the
  Marine. ④–⑤.

Zoete Inval, 23 Main Rd ℂ & fax 312 1242, *zoetein@hermanus.co.za*

Excellent-value B&B which also doubles as Hermanus's only
  establishment catering to backpackers. Dorms ①, B&B ③.

Eating and drinking

Bientang's Cave, off Marine Drive ℂ312 3454.

Next to the old harbour, this is one of the priciest restaurants in
  town, and is known for its seafood but more particularly its
  fabulous location in a cave on the rocks just above the sea.
  Lunch daily, as well as dinner Friday and Saturday nights during
  season.

The Burgundy, Marine Drive ℂ312 2800.

Above the old harbour, and arguably Hermanus's top restaurant,
  serving fairly expensive French food in one of the town's oldest
  buildings. There's indoor as well as shady outdoor seating.
  Closed Mon.

Fisherman's Cottage, Lemms Corner ℂ312 3642.

Excellent pub off Market Square, with verandah seating in an old
  cottage. Serves reasonably priced fish'n'chips. Closed Sun.

Galjoen Restaurant, Shop 3, Village Square, off Old Market Square
  ℂ312 2282.

Upmarket seafood eatery with a French accent, where the emphasis
  is on excellent presentation. Closed Tues.

Marimba Cafe, 124c Main Rd ℂ312 2148.

Cosy and lively evening joint with a constantly changing mid-price
  menu from across Africa. Booking essential. Closed Tues.

Mogg's Country Cookhouse, Hemel-en-Aarde Valley, 12km north
of Hermanus along the R320 to Caledon ℗312 4321.
An unlikely location for one of Hermanus's most successful restaurants; it's on a working farm in the back country. An intimate
place that's always full and unfailingly excellent – all topped off
with superb views across the valley. Booking essential. Open
Wed–Sun lunch and Fri & Sat evening.

HEMEL-EN-AARDE WINERIES

Some of South Africa's top wines come from the **Hemel-
en-Aarde Valley**, about fifteen minutes' drive west of
Hermanus. Vineyards in the area date back to the early
nineteenth century, when the Klein Hemel-en-Aarde
Vineyard was part of a Moravian mission station, but winemaking has been established here for only just over a
decade. Several small wineries are dotted along a few gravel
kilometres of the R320 to Caledon, which branches off the
main road to Cape Town 2km west of Hermanus, and are
worth a visit for their intimate tasting rooms and first-class
wines, and to see the stark scrubby mountains just inland.

WhaleHaven

200m along the R320 after the Caledon turn-off ℗312 1585,
whwines@itec.co.za
Tastings & sales Mon–Fri 9.30am–5pm, Sat 10.30am–1pm; free.
The first winery you'll reach is WhaleHaven, which released
its first vintage in 1995 – its reputation has been growing
ever since. A small animal farm will help to keep kids busy.

Hamilton Russell

5km along the R320 after the Caledon turn-off ℗312 3595,
hrv@hermanus.co.za
Tasting & sales Mon–Fri 9am–5pm, Sat 9am–1pm; free.

Further on from WhaleHaven you'll come to the longest established of the Walker Bay wineries, which is noted for its exceptionally good Chardonnay. They also bottle a range of wines under the very collectable Southern Right label, which are available at the town liquor stores, where they're popular as souvenirs.

Bouchard Finlayson

6km along the R320 after the Caledon turn-off ℂ312 3515.
Tasting & sales Mon–Fri 9.30am–5pm, Sat 9.30am–12.30pm; free.
Adjacent to Hamilton Russell, towards Caledon, lies Bouchard Finlayson, another establishment with a formidable reputation for its Pinot Noir and Chardonnays.

DE KELDERS

East of Hermanus, the R43 takes a detour inland around the Klein River Lagoon, past the riverside hamlet of Stanford, before reaching **De Kelders**, a haphazard and treeless hamlet that stares from bleak cliffs across Walker Bay to Hermanus. These cliffs offer the best vantage point along the bay for **whale-watching** – find a spot and relax with your binoculars. Despite surpassing fashionable Hermanus as a whale-watching venue and having a marvellous long sandy beach, De Kelders has somehow escaped the hype, and this small cluster of holiday homes remains a backwater devoid of facilities, with only a couple of places renting out rooms.

GANSBAAI

Gansbaai is a workaday place, economically dependent on its fishing industry and the seafood canning factory at the harbour. This all serves to give it a more gutsy feel than the surrounding holidaylands, but there's little reason to spend time here unless you want to engage in **great white shark safaris**, Gansbaai's other major industry. Boats set out from Gansbaai to Dyer Island, east of Danger Point, where great white sharks come to feed on the resident colony of seals.

Shark **diving packages**, including breakfast, lunch, diving gear and a shark T-shirt start at around R1000 (contact the Gansbaai Tourism Bureau ✆ & fax 028/384 1439). Bait is thrown into the water to lure the sharks near the boat, but sightings are certainly not guaranteed, especially over December and January when the abundance of seal pups keeps the sharks well fed and less inclined to show up for tourists. Even if a shark does come along it may not hang around long enough for all the people on the boat to get into the cage for a viewing (only two can fit in at a time).

DANGER POINT

True to its name, **Danger Point** lured the ill-fated HMS *Birkenhead* – bound for Algoa Bay with 600 reinforcements for British regiments fighting the Xhosa in the Eighth Frontier War – onto its hidden rocks on February 26, 1852. As was the custom, the captain of the troopship gave the order: "Every man for himself." Displaying true British pluck though, the soldiers are said to have lined up in their ranks on deck where they stood stock-still, knowing that if one man broke rank it could lead to a rush that might overwhelm the two lifeboats that would carry the seven women and thirteen children to safety. The precedent of "women and children first", which became known as the **Birkenhead Drill**, was thus established, but 445 lives were lost in the disaster, the twenty civilians all surviving.

CAPE AGULHAS

Along the east flank of the Danger Point promontory, a

rocky and shallow coastline with heavy swells and strong currents makes this one of South Africa's most treacherous stretches of coast – one that has seen over 250 wrecks and taken around 2500 lives. Its rocky terrain also accounts for the lack of a coastal road from Gansbaai and Danger Point to **Cape Agulhas** – the southernmost tip of Africa. Apart from this one fact, there's nothing much to recommend the place, which is approached through an ugly sprawl of houses. A stone marker and a sign indicate that this is the southernmost point on the continent – otherwise the rocky shoreline is pretty flat and nondescript.

To get to Agulhas from Hermanus you have to go inland and take the R316 to Bredasdorp, where the road splits; you take the west branch for 43km to Agulhas or the east one for 24km to Arniston (see opposite).

ELIM

A far more rewarding reason than Agulhas to venture along the network of dirt roads that crisscrosses the Whale Coast interior is to visit **Elim**, a mission station 40km to Agulhas's northwest. Founded in 1824 by Moravian missionaries, the whole village is a National Monument of streets lined with thatched, whitewashed houses and fig trees. There's nothing twee about this extraordinarily undeveloped and untouristy place; it doesn't have a bottle store or even a tea shop, and facilities amount to a couple of tiny stores where coloured kids play video games. The beautiful main street, lined with cottages, cuts an axis to the gabled mission church at the far end, behind which there are a number of historic buildings including an old water mill. Nearby, a memorial to emancipation gives thanks to God for the abolition of slavery in 1834 – the only such monument in the country.

ARNISTON

After the cool deep blues of the Atlantic to the west, the tepid azure of the Indian Ocean at **Arniston** is truly startling, and it's made all the more dazzling by its white dunes interspersed with rocky ledges. This is one of the best places to stay in the Overberg and is refreshingly underdeveloped compared with Hermanus and places closer to Cape Town. The village is known to locals by its Afrikaans name, **Waenhuiskrans** (Wagon-house Cliff), after a huge cave 1.5km south of town which trekboers reckoned was spacious enough to accommodate a wagon and span of oxen. The English name derives from a British ship, the *Arniston*, which hit the rocks here in 1815.

Shallow seas that are treacherous for vessels give Arniston the safest swimming waters along the Whale Coast. Apart from sea bathing, **Kassiesbaai**, a collection of starkly beautiful limewashed cottages, occupied by coloured fishermen now collectively declared a National Monument, is the principal attraction of this unspoilt hamlet. You can't stay in the cottages; all the holiday accommodation is in the adjacent new section of town, which has managed miraculously to blend in with the spirit of the old village.

Accommodation

Arniston Hotel, ©445 9000, fax 445 9633, *hotel@arniston.co.za*
Luxurious and well-run hotel in a central position along the seafront. The only place in the village offering sea views from some rooms. ⑦.

Arniston Seaside Cottages, well signposted from the R316 into town, along the street behind the *Arniston* hotel ©445 9772, fax 445 9125.
Limewashed fully equipped self-catering cottages in a mock-Arniston style. ④.

Southwinds, Huxham Street, just behind the hotel ℭ & fax 455
9303, *southwinds@kingsley.co.za*

Three double B&B suites looking onto a courtyard garden. ④.

Waenhuis Caravan Park, along the main road into Arniston ℭ455
9620.

Either pitch your own tent or stay in small, four-bed en-suite
bungalows. Bring your own bedding and towels. Camping ①,
cottages ②.

Eating

Arniston Hotel, see p.271.

Two restaurants with sea views: the informal and reasonably priced
Slipway serves steaks, burgers and the like, while the hotel's main
restaurant is far more formal and quite pricey.

Waenhuis, Du Preez Street (a continuation of the national road).

The only other place in the village, decorated to resemble a
fishermen's tavern, which serves up fish'n'chips and other
seafood.

DE HOOP NATURE RESERVE

Daily 7am–6pm; R10.

De Hoop Nature Reserve is one of the wilderness highlights of the Western Cape and, although the reserve makes
an easy day outing from Hermanus, you'll find it's more
rewarding to come for a night or more, especially as this is
reckoned to be the best place in South Africa to see
southern right whales.

The breathtaking coastline is edged by bleached sand
dunes that stand 90m high in places, and rocky formations
that at one point open to the sea in a massive craggy arch.
The **flora and fauna** are impressive too, encompassing 86

species of mammal, 260 different birds and 1500 varieties of plants. If you're here for a couple of days in whale-watching season, chances are you'll be in luck, with occasional reports of a score or more in evidence at one time. July to September is the best time, but you stand a very good chance of a sighting right through June to November.

Inland, rare **Cape mountain zebra**, **bontebok** and other antelope congregate on a plain near the reserve accommodation. Apart from **swimming** and strolling along the length of the white sandy beach, there are **hiking** and **mountain-biking trails**, but you'll need to bring your own bike as there's nowhere here to rent one.

Practicalities

De Hoop is reached along a signposted dirt road that spurs off the R319 as it heads out of Bredasdorp, 50km to the west. **Accommodation** is limited to a **campsite** (①) and **self-catering cottages** (②–③), set on an estuary well back from the sea: the cheaper cottages have views across a plain on which game grazes, and come with a cooker, fridge and electricity (bring your own bedding and kitchen utensils); the more comfortable ones come with linen and towels, and are dramatically sited on the edge of a gorge that overlooks the estuary. **Booking** should be made through the Manager, De Hoop Nature Reserve, Private Bag X16, 7280 Bredasdorp (✆542 1126, fax 542 1679). Overnight visitors must report to the reserve office, about 4km into the reserve, by 4pm. Be sure to stock up on supplies before you come – the nearest shop is 15km north of the De Hoop office, in the hamlet of Ouplaas.

The Winelands

An hour's drive east of Cape Town, the Winelands provide perfect touring country. As well as wine sampling and wonderful scenery, you'll find some of South Africa's best restaurants, both in the towns, and tucked away on estates at the end of oak avenues. Dutch colonial heritage reaches its height here, with impressive gabled homesteads lying dazzling white among vineyards and slatey mountains. The district takes in Cape Town's earliest European satellite settlements, at Stellenbosch, Paarl, Franschhoek and Somerset West, each with its own established wine route. Any of these towns makes an easy daytrip from Cape Town and you can comfortably include visits to three local wineries in your outing. If you want to extend your explorations to two or more of the towns and their wine routes it's advisable to overnight in the region – a thoroughly relaxing way to take in the scenery, sample some great food and meander through the vineyards.

Without private transport, your most sensible option is to head for **Stellenbosch**, which is served by regular trains from Cape Town. The most satisfying of the Winelands towns, it offers beautiful streetscapes, a couple of decent museums and good visitor facilities. Outside Cape Town, it's also the best place to pick up a tour of some of the wineries.

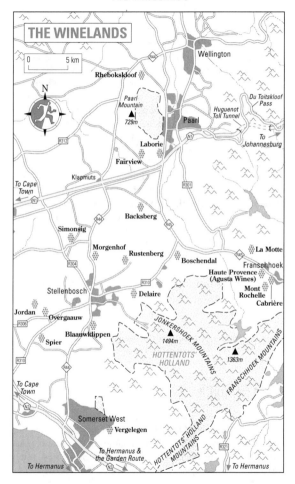

THE WINELANDS

0   5 km

N

Wellington

Rheboksdloof

R44

Du Toitskloof
Pass

Paarl
Mountain

729m

Huguenot
Toll Tunnel

Paarl

R312

To
Johannesburg

Laborie

N1

Fairview

Klapmuts

R301

To Cape
Town

N1

Backsberg

R44

R45

Simonsig

La Motte

R45

Morgenhof

Franschhoek

Rustenberg

Boschendal

R304

Haute Provence
(Agusta Wines)

R310

Mont
Rochelle

Stellenbosch

Delaire

Cabrière

Jordan

JONKERSHOEK MOUNTAINS

Overgaauw

R306

1494m

Blaauwklippen

HOTTENTOTS
HOLLAND

Spier

1363m

R310

FRANSCHHOEK MOUNTAINS

R44

To Cape
Town

N2

Somerset West

Vergelegen

To Hermanus &
the Garden Route

HOTTENTOTS HOLLAND
MOUNTAINS

N2

To Hermanus

R321

To Hermanus

Visiting the Winelands

With over 150 estates in the **Winelands**, the big question is which ones to visit. The selection below covers wineries that feature beautiful architecture or scenery, or do something other than – of course – produce fine wine. **Summer** is the best time to visit: days are longer (as are opening hours), the vines are in leaf and you can enjoy time outdoors. Several estates offer lunch, while some allow picnics in their grounds. Most estates charge between R5 and R10 for a wine-tasting session.

One of the region's scenic highlights is the drive along the R310 through the heady **Helshoogte Pass** between Stellenbosch and **Paarl**, a workaday farming town. Smallest of the Winelands towns, **Franschhoek** has the most magnificent setting, at the head of a narrow valley, and with two dozen or more restaurants, it has established itself as the culinary capital of the Cape. By contrast, the sprawling town of **Somerset West** has a single but outstanding drawcard – **Vergelegen**, the most stunning of all the Wineland estates, which can be easily tacked onto a tour of the Stellenbosch wine route.

....

All phone numbers in the Winelands share Cape Town's ⓣ021 area code.

....

STELLENBOSCH

Dappled avenues of 300-year-old oaks are the defining feature of **STELLENBOSCH**, 46km east of Cape Town – a fact reflected in its Afrikaans nickname, Die Eikestad (Oak City). Seventeenth-century buildings, sidewalk cafés, water furrows and a European town layout centred on the Braak,

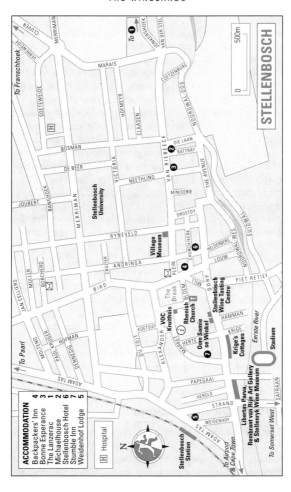

STELLENBOSCH

ACCOMMODATION

Backpackers' Inn	4
Bonne Esperance	3
The Lanzerac	1
Michaelhouse	2
Stellenbosch Hotel	6
Stumble Inn	7
Weidenhof Lodge	5

H Hospital

To Franschhoek

To Paarl

To Airport & Cape Town

To Somerset West

STELLENBOSCH

a large village green, make it a pleasant place to wander around. The city (in name only) is the undisputed heart of the Winelands, having more urban attractions than either Paarl or Franschhoek, while at the same time being at the hub of the largest and oldest of the Cape **wine routes**.

Stellenbosch (Stel's bush) was named in 1679 by **Simon van der Stel**, one of his first actions after arriving at the Cape in November 1679 to take over as VOC commander. It thus became the first of several places dotted around the Cape, including Simonsberg overlooking Stellenbosch, which the governor was to name after himself or members of his family. Soon he settled the area with **free burghers** – company employees freed from their contracts so they could farm independently and supply produce to the VOC. It developed fast, and in 1702 the Danish traveller, Abraham Bogaert, admired how it had "grown with fine dwellings, and how great a treasure of wine and grain is grown here". Eight years on, some of those fine thatch-roofed houses were destroyed by fire, but were soon rebuilt, and by the end of the eighteenth century there were over a thousand houses and some substantial burgher estates in and around Stellenbosch, many of which are still standing.

The authoritative and widely available *John Platter's South African Wine Guide*, updated annually, provides ratings of the produce of every winery in the country, as well as informed commentary on the estates.

Getting there and around

The **drive** to Stellenbosch from Cape Town takes under an hour along either the N1 or N2. Metro Rail **trains** (information ©449 2991) run between Cape Town and Stellenbosch roughly every two hours during the day, and take an hour. The station is about twenty minutes' walk from the centre. **Car rental** can be arranged through Avis (℗883 9103) in Mill Street; it costs from around R220 per day, including 200km free per day, which should comfortably get you around the Winelands.

The Village Museum

Mon–Sat 9.30am–5pm, Sun 2–5pm; R10.

Head north up Ryneveld Street, and at no.18 you'll encounter Stellenbosch's highlight, the enjoyable **Village Museum**, which cuts a cross section through the town's architectural and social heritage by displaying four authentic adjacent dwellings from different periods.

Earliest of the houses is the homely **Shreuderhuis**, a vernacular cottage built in 1709, with a small courtyard garden filled with aromatic herbs, pomegranate bushes and vine-draped pergolas. Across the garden, **Blettermanhuis**, built in 1789 for the last Dutch East India Company-appointed magistrate of Stellenbosch, is an archetypal eighteenth-century Cape Dutch house, built on an H-plan with six gables. **Grosvenor House**, opposite, was altered to its current form in 1803, and reflects the growing influence of English taste after the British occupation of the Cape in 1795. The Neoclassical facade, with fluted pilasters supporting a pedimented entrance, borrows from high fashion then current. The more modest **O.M. Bergh House**, across the road, is a typical Victorianized dwelling that was built in the same period as Blettermanhuis, but was "modernized" in the mid-nineteenth century on a rectangular plan, with a simplified facade without gables.

Dorp Street

From the Village Museum, head back south into **Dorp**

STELLENBOSCH

Street, Stellenbosch's nicely preserved historic axis, well worth a stroll to take in the gabled buildings, oaks and roadside water furrows. Heading west along the street, you'll spot the **Stellenbosch Wine Tasting Centre** on your left, and next door **Oom Samie se Winkel**, a jam-packed Victorian-style general dealer. On your right, look out for **Krige's Cottages**, an unusual terrace of historic town houses at nos. 37–51, between Aan-die-Wagen-Weg and Krige streets. The homes were built as Cape Dutch cottages in the first half of the nineteenth century, and later Victorian features were added, resulting in an interesting hybrid, with gables housing later attic windows and decorative Victorian verandahs with filigree ironwork fronting the elegant simplicity of Cape Dutch facades.

Strand Street

A left turn into Strand Street brings you to **Libertas Parva**, a fine example of an H-plan Cape Dutch manor, and home to the **Rembrandt van Rijn Art Museum** (Mon–Fri 9am–12.45pm & 2–5pm, Sat 10am–1pm & 2–5pm; free); it doesn't actually display any Rembrandts, but is named for its owners, the Rembrandt van Rijn Tobacco company. The gallery, instead, has a small but stimulating collection of South African art, including a wonderful 360-degree panorama of Cape Town rendered in pen, ink and watercolour by Josephus Jones in 1808; *The Conservationists Ball*, an acerbic tryptich by William Kentridge, a leading light among the current generation of South African artists; and a number of Irma Stern paintings and drawings (see p.93). Adjacent in the same courtyard, the Libertas Parva Cellar houses the **Stellenryck Wine Museum** (Mon–Fri 9am–12.45pm & 2–5pm, Sat 10am–1pm & 2–5pm; free), which has some moderately interesting ancient amphorae, winepresses, wineglasses and old bottles.

Stellenbosch wineries

Stellenbosch was the first locality in the country to wake up to the marketing potential of a **wine route**, which it launched in 1971. The tactic has been hugely successful and now draws tens of thousands of visitors from all over the world. This is the most extensive wine route in South Africa, offering some of the Cape's best reds and, overall, the greatest diversity of wines. The wineries are along a series of roads that radiate out from Stellenbosch, all signalled by wine-route signposts along the main road.

Blaauwklippen

4km south of Stellenbosch along the Strand Road (R44) ©880 0133, *mail@blaauwklippen.com*
Tasting and sales Mon–Fri 9am–5pm, Sat 9am–1pm; R10.

Although big enough to take tour buses, Blaauwklippen isn't overly commercialized. Apart from the usual Cape Dutch buildings at the foot of the Simonsberg, there are inexpensive carriage rides through the vineyards (Oct–Easter Mon–Fri 10am–noon & 2–3.45pm), a horse-carriage museum and a little shop selling soft drinks and knick-knacks. A ploughman's-style "coachman's lunch" is served (Mon–Sat) on the verandah. It's one of a handful of South African wineries producing Zinfandel, a flagship red wine.

Delaire

6km east of Stellenbosch along the R310 ©885 1756, *delaire@iafrica.com*
Tasting and sales Mon–Sat 10am–5pm, Sun 10am–4pm; R10.

For the Winelands' best views, head for Delaire on the **Helshoogte Pass**. The drive up from the pass through the slopes of the vineyard-covered hillside brings you to the tasting room and excellent *Green Door* restaurant, with views through oaks across the Groot Drakenstein and Simonsig mountains and down into craggy valleys. After a number of pedestrian years, the output of this winery in the sky is starting to soar: its Chardonnay '97 was rated the New World's best white by the UK's *Decanter* magazine.

Jordan

4km west of Overgaauw along Polkadraai Road (the R306) ©881 3441, *jordanw@cybertrade.co.za*
Tasting & sales May–Oct Mon–Fri 10am–4.30pm, Sat 9.30am–12.30pm; Nov–April Mon–Fri 10am–4.30pm, Sat 9.30am–2.30pm; R7.50 (refundable against purchases).

Part of the new wave of Cape wineries, with a high-tech cellar, modern tasting room and friendly service. The drive there is half the fun, taking you into a *kloof* bounded by vineyards; the vines get a whiff of the seas from both False Bay and Table Bay, which has obviously done something for their outstanding Cabernet Sauvignon, Sauvignon Blanc and Blanc Fumé.

Moddergat Road (the R310) heads southwest out of Stellenbosch parallel to the train tracks, branching off 5.5km later onto Polkadraai Road (the R306).

Morgenhof

Turn off 4km north of Stellenbosch, along the Klapmuts Road (R44 north) ©889 5510, *info@morgenhof.com*
Tasting & sales May–Oct Mon–Fri 9am–4.30pm, Sat & Sun 10am–3pm; Nov–April Mon–Thurs 9am–5.30pm, Fri 9am–5pm, Sat & Sun 10am–5pm; tasting R10.

French-owned chateau-style complex overlooked by the vine-covered Simonsberg, with a light and airy tasting room. Delicious light lunches are served outside, rounded off, when available, by berries and ice cream. All their wines, but particularly the Merlot and Bordeaux-style Premiere Selection, are top notch.

Overgaauw

1km after the Polkadraai turn-off along Polkadraai Road (the R306) ©881 3815.
Tasting & sales Mon–Fri 9am–12.30pm & 2–5pm, Sat 10am–12.30pm; free.

Notable for having the only Victorian tasting room in the Winelands, with an atmosphere that's elegant and under-stated but convivial. A pioneering estate that turns out reds and ports of excellent quality, Overgaauw was the first in the country to produce Merlots and is the only one to make Sylvaner, a well-priced dry white.

Rustenberg

Ida's Valley, 4.5km north of Stellenbosch along the R310 ©887 3153, wine@rustenberg.co.za
Tasting & sales daily 9am–4.30pm, Sat 9am–12.30pm; free.

One of the closest estates to central Stellenbosch, this isn't a member of the official Stellenbosch wine route but is one of the most alluring vineyards. To get there, join the R310 from the R44 to Paarl, just north of town. Just under 2km along the R310 to Franschhoek, turn into Ida's Valley for a further 2km, which, after a drive through orchards, sheep pastures and tree-lined avenues, brings you to the estate. An unassuming working farm, Rustenberg hangs on to a romantic pastoral atmosphere, with a complex of seventeenth-century buildings including two National Monuments, and a gabled Cape Dutch milking shed. No meals are laid on, so you should bring your own picnic to savour under the oaks. The wines themselves are high flyers – the Rustenberg '97 took gold at the 1999 International Wine Challenge in London. Also look out for highly drinkable and less expensive reds and whites under the Brampton brand – their second label.

Simonsig

Turn off to left, 4km north of Morgenhof along the Klapmuts Road (R44 north), then 2km down Kromme Rhee Road ℗888 4900, wine@simonsig.co.za
Tasting & sales Mon–Fri 8.30am–5pm, Sat 8.30am–4.30pm; R3.50; cellar tours Mon–Fri 10am & 3pm, Sat 10am; R10.

The outdoor tasting area under vine-woven pergolas gives majestic views back towards Stellenbosch, of hazy blue mountains and vineyards. There's no restaurant, but you can picnic at tables in a courtyard area, cooled by a fountain. There's huge choice of reds and whites, but among the stars are the Pinotage "Red Hill", Tiara claret and Chardonnay.

Spier

7km southwest of Stellenbosch along the R310 ℗881 3351, info@spier.co.za
Tasting & sales daily 9am–5pm, R6; cellar tours & tasting Mon–Fri 10am, noon & 3pm; R17.50.

A great family outing in a beautiful spot, with the requisite Cape Dutch buildings set around an ornamental lake, edged with lawns and picnic tables. Note that you can't bring your own food: you'll find Portuguese rolls and picnic foods in their Farmstall deli, and cheetahs roaming around in pens nearby. Pony rides for kids and much more besides: the amphitheatre is a major venue for opera, pop and classical music concerts, the *Taphuis Grill* and *Jonkershuis Restaurant* dish up good fare and the wines under the IV Spears label aren't bad either, especially the Chardonnay.

For more on cheetah encounters and pony rides at Spier, see p.235.

Accommodation

Backpackers' Inn, De Wet Centre, corner of Bird and Church streets ✆887 2020, *bacpac1@global.co.za*
Central, squeaky clean and family-friendly hostel. Dorms and doubles ②.

Bonne Esperance, 17 Van Riebeeck St ✆887 0225, fax 887 8328.
Colonial elegance in a terrific two-storey Victorian villa with a lovely front garden and swimming pool and standard or luxury rooms. ④–⑤.

The Lanzerac, Jonkershoek Road, 1km east of town ✆887 1132, fax 887 2310, *info@lanzerac.co.za*
Pure Winelands luxury, with elegant whitewashed buildings surrounded by vineyards and mountains. ⑨.

Michaelhouse, 29 Van Riebeeck St ✆886 6343.
B&B with cast-iron decor, a hint of the ethnic and a garden terrace with trellised vines. ④.

Stellenbosch Hotel, corner of Dorp and Andringa streets ✆887 3644, fax 887 3673, *stb-hotel@mweb.co.za*
Smart town-centre hotel housed in an atmospheric nineteenth-century National Monument. ⑤.

Stumble Inn, 12 Market St ✆ & fax 887 4049, *stumble@iafrica.com*.
Old established hostel in two Victorian houses, with friendly staff. Dorms and camping ①, doubles ②.

Weidenhof Lodge, 24 Weidenhof St ✆886 4679 or mobile 083/653 7225, *weidenhoflodge@hotmail.com*
Good-value and popular self-catering mini-apartments with showers, kitchens and TVs. ③.

Eating and drinking

De Akker, 90 Dorp St.
Pub lunches and late nights (it hots up after 11pm), in a buzzing

joint enjoyed by students.

Green Door, Delaire Wine Farm, Helshoogte Pass ©885 1756.
Worth patronizing just for the view, and the small eclectic menu is
  one of the best around. Booking essential. Lunch Tues–Sun &
  dinner Thurs–Sat.

Mama Roma, Stelmark Centre, Merriman Avenue, central
  Stellenbosch ©886 6064.
Good-value Italian standards including pizza and excellent seafood.
  Closed Sat lunchtime and Sun evening.

San Francisco Coffee Roastery, Drostdy Craft Market, Alexander
  Street, central Stellenbosch.
A dead cert for a fine cup of coffee, with muffins and light snacks.

The Terrace, Shop 12, Drostdy Centre, central Stellenbosch
  ©887 1942.
Centrally located bar-restaurant favoured by backpackers,
  overlooking the Braak. Daily mid-morning till late.

VERGELEGEN

> **Vergelegen is open daily 9.30am–4pm. It costs R7.50,**
> **including wine tasting and cellar tours.**

Vergelegen, on the Lourensford Road, off the N2 in
Somerset West (©847 1334), was the estate visited by the
British queen during her 1995 state visit to South Africa –
a good choice, as there's enough to occupy an easy couple
of hours. Although it's not on the official Stellenbosch wine
route, a trip here can easily be combined with one to
Stellenbosch, just 14km to the north. The **interpretive
centre**, across the courtyard from the shop at the building
entrance, provides a useful history and background to the

Vergelegen's chintzy Lady Phillips Tea Garden (booking essential ©847 1346) serves quiches and homemade pies accompanied by vegetables from the estate's gardens. The less formal Rose Terrace offers outdoor light lunches and wine by the glass.

estate, which you can absorb in about ten minutes. Next door, the **wine-tasting centre** offers a professionally run sampling with a brief talk through each label.

The seventeenth-century **homestead**, which was restored in 1917 by Lady Florence Phillips, wife of a Johannesburg mining magnate, can also be visited. Its pale facade with a classical triangular gable and pilaster-decorated doorways is reached through an octagonal garden that dances with butterflies in summer. Massive grounds planted with chestnuts and camphor trees and ponds around every corner make this one of the most serene places in the Cape.

Vergelegen is synonymous with a notorious episode of corruption and the arbitrary abuse of power at the Cape in the early years of Dutch East India Company rule. It was built by **Willem Adriaan van der Stel**, who became governor in 1699 after the retirement of his father Simon. Willem Adriaan got hold of the land by illegally using his position and VOC slaves to build Vergelegen, and he appropriated Company resources to farm vast tracts of land in the surrounding areas. When this was brought to the notice of the VOC in the Netherlands, Willem Adriaan was sacked and Vergelegen was ordered to be destroyed to discourage future miscreant governors. It appears that the destruction was never fully carried out and only a section at the back was razed, the front remaining intact till the first rethatching, when the house was given its first rudimentary gables. The heavily moulded central gable was probably added in the 1770s and the end gables towards the close of the eighteenth

VERGELEGEN

century. The bold Neoclassical wine cellar gable dates from 1816.

Getting there

Vergelegen is best reached **by car** – in fact, this is the only real option, unless you are taking a **tour** (see p.38). From Cape Town, take the N2 east past the International Airport, and leave the freeway at exit 43, signposted to Somerset West. This will bring you onto the R44, which you should follow into town. Once in Main Street, you'll see the turn-off to Lourensford Road (if you hit the town centre you've missed the turn-off), which you should follow for just over 3km to Vergelegen, off to the right.

PAARL

Although **Paarl** is attractively sited in a fertile valley brimming with historical houses and churches, at heart it's a parochial *dorp*, lacking either the sophistication of Stellenbosch or the new-found trendiness of Franschhoek. A prosperous farming centre, it earns its keep from agricultural light industry – grain silos, canneries and flour mills – on the north side of town, and the cornucopia of grapes, guavas, olives, oranges and maize grown on the surrounding farms. Metro Rail and Spoornet **trains** from Cape Town pull in at Paarl's Huguenot Station in Lady Grey Street at the north end of town, near to the central shops.

Paarl was founded in 1657, just five years after the establishment of the VOC refreshment station on the Cape Peninsula, when a party under **Abraham Gabbema** pitched up in the Berg River Valley in search of the legendary gold of Monomotapa. They obviously had treasure in mind: waking after a rainy night to the sight of the silvery dome of granite that dominates the valley, they dubbed

The history of Afrikaans

Afrikaans is South Africa's third language after Zulu and Xhosa, spoken by fifteen percent of the population. English is the mother tongue of only nine percent of South Africans, and ranks fifth in the league of the eleven official languages.

Signs of the emergence of a new Southern African dialect of Dutch appeared as early as 1685, when H.A. van Rheede, a Dutch East India Company official from the Netherlands, complained about a "distorted and incomprehensible" Dutch being spoken in the Drakenstein Valley around modern-day Paarl. By absorbing English, French, German, Malay and indigenous words and expressions, the language continued to diverge from mainstream Dutch, and by the nineteenth century was widely used in the Cape by both whites and coloureds, although regarded by the elite as unsuitable for literary or official communication. The first attempts by Dominee Stephanus du Toit and the Genootskap van Regte Afrikaners (League of True Afrikaners) to have Afrikaans recognized as a separate language made little impact outside Paarl, but pressure grew, and in 1925 it was recognized with English as one of South Africa's two official languages.

When the National Party took power in 1948, its apartheid policy went hand in hand with promoting the interests of its Afrikaans-speaking supporters. Afrikaners were installed throughout the civil service and filled most posts in the public utilities. Despite the fact that there were more coloured than white Afrikaans speakers, the language quickly became associated with the **apartheid** establishment. This had electrifying consequences in the 1970s, when the government attempted to enforce Afrikaans as the medium of instruction in African schools. The policy lead directly to the **Soweto uprising** in 1976, which ironically marked the beginning of the end for Afrikaner hegemony in South Africa.

it Peerlbergh (pearl mountain), which in its modified form, **Paarl**, became the name of the town.

Thirty years later, Cape governor Simon van der Stel granted strips of lands on the slopes of Paarl Mountain to French Huguenot and Dutch settlers. In the twentieth century the town became significant for the two competing political forces that forged modern South Africa. **Afrikanerdom** regards Paarl as the hallowed ground on which their language movement (see box, p.289) was born in 1875, with the launching of *Die Patriot*, the first white Afrikaans newspaper; it has a missable museum and monument to honour the fact. For the **ANC**, Paarl will be remembered as the place from which Nelson Mandela made the final steps of his long walk to freedom, when he walked out of **Victor Verster Prison** in 1990.

Paarl Museum

Mon–Fri 10am–5pm, Sat 10am–noon, R2.

Paarl Museum, 303 Main St, is housed in a handsome thatched Cape Dutch building with one of the earliest surviving gables (1787) in the "new style", characterized by triangular caps. The contents don't quite match up to the exterior, but include some reasonably enlightening panels on the architecture of the town, and several eccentric glass display cases of Victorian bric-a-brac. A token "Road to Reconciliation" display features press cuttings covering Paarl during the apartheid years. Among these you'll find passing mention that Nelson Mandela spent time here as a "guest" – his last years in jail, in fact (see below).

Victor Verster Prison

9km south of the N1 as it cuts through Paarl, along the R303, the southern extension of Jan van Riebeeck Street.

Victor Verster Prison was **Nelson Mandela**'s last place of incarceration. It was through the gates at Victor Verster (not Robben Island or Pollsmoor as many people suppose) that Mandela walked to freedom on February 11, 1990, and it was from here that the first images of him in 27 years were broadcast around the world. Under the draconian apartheid Prisons Act, he couldn't be quoted and no pictures of him (and other members of the banned anti-apartheid opposition) could be published until 1990. This meant that until he stepped out of Victor Verster, few South Africans had any idea of Mandela's appearance.

Mandela was moved here in 1988 when the apartheid government realized that he had to be part of the solution to the massive crisis facing the country, yet couldn't be seen by its supporters to be going soft on the ANC leader. A pretext arrived in August 1988, after Mandela was rushed to Tygerberg Hospital suffering from tuberculosis. When he was released three months later he was quietly moved under guard to a warder's cottage at Victor Verster, rather than back to a prison cell. He developed an affection for this temporary accommodation and later used its layout as the basis for his new house in his home town of Qunu.

The jail looks like a rather upmarket boys' school, fronted by rugby fields beneath hazy mountains, but there's still something bizarre about seeing a prison sign nonchalantly slipped in among all the vineyard and wine-route pointers. Since it's still a prison and you can't go inside, the usual tourist thing is to have yourself snapped standing in front of the gates.

Paarl wineries

Paarl was historically known as a region producing **fortified wines**, but as the demand for these diminished it established itself as a significant producer of fine **table wines**. There are over three dozen wineries on the Paarl wine route, including the three listed here, which are all photogenic and fun places to spend time.

Fairview

Take the R101 (the southwest extension of Main Road) out of town, turning right at the Fairview sign and continuing for about 2.5km.
Wine and cheese tasting & sales Mon–Fri 8.30am–5pm, Sat 8.30am–1pm; R5 ℗863 2450, fax 863 2591, *fairwine@mweb.co.za*

On the southern fringes of town, **Fairview** is a real crowd-pleaser, with much more than just wine tasting on offer. Your arrival is marked by a spiral tower for the goats to climb, the emblem of the estate. Fairview is an innovative family-run place with interesting tastings, public milking of its exotic goats and a deli that sells picnic fodder – cold meats as well as goat, sheep and cow cheeses made on the estate. It can get a bit hectic when the tour buses roll in, so try to phone ahead to find out when they're expected. Their extensive range of wines includes a couple of top-ranking reds (try the Pinotage) and whites as well as their great value Gamay Noir – a big success in the UK.

Laborie

Taillefert Street, town centre.
Tasting & sales April–Sept Mon–Fri 9am–5pm, Sat 9am–1pm; Oct–March daily 9am–5pm; R5 ℗807 3095, *therongi@kwv.co.za*

This is one of the most impressive **Paarl wineries**, made all the more remarkable for being right in town. The beautiful manor is fronted by a rose garden, acres of close-cropped lawns, historic buildings and oak trees – all towered over by the Taal Monument. There's a truly wonderful tasting-room balcony, jutting out over the vineyards trailing up Paarl Mountain. Try the Cabernet Sauvignon,

Sauvignon Blanc and the Pineau de Laborie, the world's first pot-stilled eau de vie made entirely from Pinotage grapes.

Rheboksloof

Take a left turn from Jan Philips, and continue for 2km.
Tasting & sales Mon–Fri 9am–5pm, free; formal tasting and cellar tour (book in advance) R7 ©863 8386, fax 863 8906, *rhebok@iafrica.com*

A highly photogenic wine estate, overlooking a shallow *kloof* that borders on a mountain nature reserve, Rheboksloof has a growing reputation for its **restaurant**. Although wine tasting is free, for a small charge you can book a formal tasting (24hr in advance) that includes a talk on wine, a video and a cellar tour. Among their good buys are the blended Dry Red and Requiem white.

....

Rheboksloof is a good choice if you find yourself at loose end over a public holiday: it's one of the very few estates open every day of the year.

....

Accommodation

Lemoenkloof, 396a Main St ©872 3782 or 872 7520, fax 872 3782, *lemkloof@adept.co.za*
Well-run guesthouse in an 1820s National Monument, with a TV and fridge in each room. ⑤.

Nantes Vue, 56 Mill St ©872 7311, fax 872 7311.
Good-value doubles decorated with artistic flair in a Cape Dutch National Monument. ③.

Roggeland Country House, Roggeland Road, Dal Jospehat Valley ©868 2501, fax 868 2113, *rog@iafrica.com.za*
Good service, outstanding food and informality at a family-run inn in

PAARL

a wonderful eighteenth-century Cape Dutch homestead. Half-board. ⑧–⑨.

Eating and drinking

Bosman's Restaurant, *Grande Roche Hotel*, Plantasie Street ©863 2727.
One of the best and priciest restaurants in the country, offering superb European cuisine with elaborate service. Lunch & dinner daily.

Gabi's Coffee Shop, 57 Lady Grey St ©872 5265.
Bistro-bar handy for light meals. Lunch Tues–Fri, dinner Tues–Sat.

Laborie Restaurant & Wine House, Taillefert Street ©808 7429.
Seasonal *à la carte* and traditional Cape Cuisine set-menu lunches every day, and dinners. Closed Mon & Sun.

Roggeland Country House, Roggeland Road, Dal Jospehat Valley ©868 2501.
Imaginative set menu that changes frequently, inspired by the regional produce of Paarl and accompanied by a selected wine. Daily lunch & dinner.

Wagon Wheels Steakhouse, 57 Lady Grey St ©872 5265.
Better than average steakhouse with surprisingly tasty sauces, and seafood alternatives. Lunch Tues–Fri, dinner Tues–Sat.

FRANSCHHOEK

It's only relatively recently that **Franschhoek** (79km from Cape Town, 33km from Stellenbosch and 29km from Paarl), has emerged from being the dowdy *dorp* of the Winelands to become the culinary capital of the Western Cape. Its late Victorian architecture, combined with bland modern bungalows, can't match the elegance of Stellenbosch,

A corner that is forever France

Between 1688 and 1700, about two hundred **French Huguenots**, desperate to escape religious persecution in France, accepted a VOC offer of passage to the Cape and the grant of lands. Conflict between the French newcomers and the indigenous **Khoi** followed familiar lines, with the white settlers gradually dispossessing the herdsmen, and forcing them either further into the hinterland or into servitude on their farms. The establishment of white dominance was swift, and by 1713 the area was known as *de france hoek* (French corner). Because of explicit Company policy, French speaking died out within a generation, but many of the estates are still known by their French names. The town Franschhoek itself occupies parts of the original farms of La Cotte and Cabrière and is relatively young, having been established around a church built in 1833.

but the terrific setting, hemmed in on three sides by mountains and with vineyards down every other backstreet, has created a place people from the capital drive out to just for lunch.

Since eating and drinking is what Franschhoek is all about, there's little point in making the effort to get here without trying at least one or two of its excellent **restaurants**. In town, restaurants are concentrated along Huguenot Road, but there are a number of excellent alternatives in the more rustic environment of the surrounding wine estates; booking is essential. Franschhoek's cuisine tends to be French-inspired, but not exclusively so, and salmon trout is a local speciality.

There's no public **transport** to Franschhoek or in the town itself. The only way to get here is by car; head east out of Cape Town along the N1 and take the northbound

FRANSCHHOEK

turn-off onto the R45 or R301, which lead to Paarl.

**Restaurants are listed on p.299. For coffee or a
sandwich, head for one of the many cafés in town,
or book a picnic hamper at one of the wineries.**

The Town

Away from the wining and dining, Franschhoek's attractions
are limited to hiking, horse-riding or cycling in the valley,
or visiting the Huguenot Monument and adjacent museum,
which together occupy a prime position at the head of
Huguenot Road, where it forms a T-junction with
Lambrecht Street. The **Huguenot Monument** consists of
three skinny interlocking arches symbolizing the Holy
Trinity, while the rather unexciting **Huguenot Museum**
(Mon–Fri 9am–5pm, Sat 9am–1pm & 2–5pm, Sun 2–5pm;
R4) covers Huguenot history, culture and their contribution to modern South Africa.

Franschhoek wineries

Franschhoek's **wineries** are small enough and sufficiently
close together to make it a breeze to visit two or three on
foot, by mountain bike or even on horseback. Heading
north through town from the Huguenot Monument, you'll
find virtually all the wineries signposted off Huguenot
Road and its extension, Main Road.

Agusta (Haute Provence)

1km west of the centre of town.
Daily 9am–4pm; R10 refundable against purchases ℗876 3195,
orders@agustawines.co.za
One of the most casual and friendly estates, where you can

sit in comfy armchairs in a tasting room with a traditional *rietdak* (cane-and-mud ceiling), surrounded by original oil paintings. The estate is best known for its Angels' Tears, a fruity white blend whose name derives from the legend of a French village where angels came at night to taste the new vintage, and wept for joy at its brilliance. They also produce a couple of good Chardonnays.

Boschendal

16km west of Franschhoek and almost equidistant from Stellenbosch at the junction of the R45 and R310.
Tasting & sales: April–Sept Mon–Fri 8.30am–4.30pm & Sat 8.30am–12.30pm; Oct–March Mon–Sat 8.30am–4.30pm & Sun 9.30am–12.30pm; R5 ©870 4000.

If you have time for only one estate around here, **Boschendal** is the obvious choice. It's geared to absorbing busloads of tourists, who lap up its impressive Cape Dutch buildings, tree-lined avenues, choice of restaurants and cafés (see p.299) and – of course – its wines. Now owned by the massive Anglo-American Corporation, one of the huge multinationals which has moved from mining to dominate the South African economy, Boschendal is one of the world's longest-established New World wine estates, dating back to 1685, when its lands were granted to Huguenot settler Jean Le Long. The Cape Dutch manor was built in 1812 by Paul de Villiers and his wife, whose initials appear on the front gable. Wine tasting takes place at the Taphuis, where you can sit indoors or sip under shady trees. The range of wines is extensive and generally of an impressive standard.

Cabrière

Berg Road, close to the Huguenot Memorial.
Sales Mon–Fri 8.30am–4.30pm, Sat 10.30am–1pm; tasting Mon–Fri 11am & 3pm; R15, Sat 11am; R20; cellar tours Sat 11am or by arrangement; R20 ©876 2630, *cabriere@iafrica.com*

FRANSCHHOEK

Cabrière Estate is reached through groves of fruit trees that lead up to the homestead and tasting room. The winery is notable for its Pinot Noir, and the colourful presence on Saturdays of winegrower Achim von Arnim, guarantees an eventful visit; his speciality is slicing off the neck of a bottle of bubbly with a sabre.

La Motte

6km west of town along the R45.
Tasting & sales Mon–Fri 9am–4.30pm, Sat 9am–noon; free ©876 3119, *cellar@la-motte.co.za*

La Motte presents a supremely cool front, with a superb designer tasting room that looks onto the cellar through a sheer wall of glass. This was the estate that put to rest once and for all the long-held notion that Franschhoek was a poor region for producing red wines. Their wines are almost all uniformly excellent and the stunning Millennium red blend sells out quickly.

Mont Rochelle

Daniel Hugo Road, next door to Cabrière.
Tasting & sales Mon–Sat 11am–4pm, plus Sept–April Sun 11am–1pm; R5; cellar tours daily 11am, 12.30pm & 3pm; R10 including tasting ©876 3000, *montrochelle@wine.co.za*

Next door to Cabrière, **Mont Rochelle** has one of the most stunning settings in Franschhoek and an unusual cellar in a converted nineteenth-century fruit-packing shed, edged by eaves decorated with fretwork, stained-glass windows and chandeliers.

> **Horseback tours of Franschhoek's wineries can be arranged through Mont Rochelle Equestrian Centre (around R50 an hour ©876 2635, fax 876 2362 or mobile 083/300 4368).**

Accommodation

Le Ballon Rouge Guest House, 12 Reservoir Rd ©876 2651, fax 876 3743, info@ballon-rouge.co.za
Small B&B in a Victorian town house with brass bedsteads and floral fabrics. Rooms lead onto a verandah overlooking a side street. ④.

Chamonix Guest Cottages, Uitkyk Street ©876 2498, fax 876 3237, chamfarm@icon.co.za
Fully equipped, self-catering cottages surrounded by vineyards on a wine farm. ③.

Paradise Cottages, Roberstsvlei Road © & fax 876 2160.
Among the most inexpensive rooms in the valley, in old basic accommodation on a farm. ②.

Le Quartier Français, corner of Berg and Wilhelmina streets ©876 2151, fax 876 3105, lqf@icon.co.za
The most luxurious place in Franschhoek, with two suites (one with its own pool) and fifteen huge rooms arranged around herb and flower gardens. ⑦.

Reeden Lodge, off Cabrière Street © & fax 876 3174.
Three lovely self-catering cottages on a farm, set along a river near Cabrière Estate. Minimum charge R300 per cottage. ③.

Eating and drinking

Boschendal, junction of the R45 and R310 to Stellenbosch ©874 1252.
Three choices for lunch: pricey but substantial daily buffet lunch in the main restaurant, which will set you up for rest of day; light sit-down lunches at *Le Café*; or deluxe picnic hampers daily under the shady pines from *Le Pique Nique*. Booking essential. Daily.

Bread & Wine, Môreson Farm, Happy Valley Road, off the R45 ©876 3692.

FRANSCHHOEK

Enjoy a *meze*-style lunch spread accompanied by the estate's own wines in a courtyard surrounded by orchards and vineyards. Closed Mon.

Chez Michel, Huguenot Road, just north of Le Quartier Francais and opposite the post office ℡876 2671.
Congenial bistro patronized by locals, in a Victorian house. Lunch Tues–Sun, dinner Tues–Sat.

Frandeli, Co-op Building, Huguenot Road.
Licensed deli that serves delicious filled focaccias and bagels accompanied by beer or wine to eat in or take away. Daily for breakfast & lunch.

Haute Cabriére Cellar Restaurant, Franschhoek Pass ℡876 3688.
Bunker-like venue with interesting mix-and-match menu – no starters or main courses – planned around Cabrière wines. There's a helipad on the roof should you wish to fly in. Lunch daily, dinner Fri–Mon.

La Petite Ferme, Franschhoek Pass ℡876 3016.
Justifiably one of the most popular Franschhoek lunch venues with superb views across the valley and great food, which fuses Cape Cuisine influences with local ingredients. Daily.

Le Quartier Francais, 16 Huguenot Rd ℡876 2151.
No-holds-barred formal meals with a local flavour and an imaginative edge at the place that made Franschhoek synonymous with Cape-Provencal food. Their party piece is salmon trout poached in olive oil served with a salmon fritter, cucumber and seaweed.

CONTEXTS

A brief history of Cape Town

Hunters and herders

Rock art provides evidence of human culture in the Western Cape dating back nearly 30,000 years. The artists were hunter-gathers, sometimes called bushmen but more commonly **San**, a relatively modern term from the Nama language with roots in the concept of "inhabiting or dwelling" to reflect the fact these were South Africa's aboriginals. San people still maintain a tenuous survival in tiny pockets, mostly in Namibia and Botswana, making theirs the longest-spanning culture in the subcontinent. At one time they probably spread throughout sub-Saharan Africa, having pretty well perfected their **nomadic lifestyle** – the men hunting and the women gathering. This left considerable time for artistic and religious pursuits. People lived in small, loosely connected bands comprising family units and were free to leave and join up with other groups.

About two thousand years ago, this changed when some groups in territory north of South Africa laid their hands on fat-tailed sheep and cattle from northern Africa, thus transforming themselves into **herding communities**. The introduction of livestock had a revolutionary effect on social organization and introduced the idea of ownership and accumulation. Animals became a symbol of both wealth and social status and those who were better at acquiring and holding onto their herds gradually became wealthier. Social divisions developed, and political units became larger, centring around a chief, who had important powers, such as the allocation of pasturage.

The Cape goes Dutch

Portuguese mariners, under the command of **Bartholomeu Dias**, first rounded the Cape in the 1480s, and named it Cabo de Boa Esperanza, the **Cape of Good Hope**. Marking their progress, they left an unpleasant set of calling cards all along the coast – slaves they had captured in West Africa and had cast ashore to trumpet the power and glory of Portugal with the aim of intimidating the locals. Little wonder then, that the first encounter of the Portuguese with the indigenous Khoi along the Garden Route coast was not a happy one. It began with a group of Khoi stoning the Portuguese for taking water from a spring without asking permission, and ended with a Khoi man lying dead with a crossbow bolt through his chest. It was another 170 years before any European settlement was established in South Africa.

In 1652, a group of white employees of the **Dutch East India Company** (VOC or Verenigde Oostindische Compagnie), which was engaged in trade between the Netherlands and the East Indies, pulled into Table Bay to set up a refreshment station to revictual Company ships trading between Europe and the East. There were no plans at this time to set up a colony; in fact, the Cape post was given to the station commander **Jan van Riebeeck** because he had been caught with his hand in the till. Van Riebeeck dreamed up a number of schemes to keep "dark-est Africa" at bay, including the very Dutch solution of building a canal that would cut the Cape Peninsula adrift. In the end he had to satisfy himself with planting a **bitter almond hedge** (still growing in Cape Town's Kirstenbosch Gardens) to keep the natives at arm's length.

Despite van Riebeeck's view that the indigenous **Khoi** were "a savage set, living without conscience", from the start the Dutch were dependent on them to provide live-stock, which were traded for trinkets. As the settlement developed, van Riebeeck needed more **labour** to keep the show going, and bemoaned the fact that he was unsuccessful in persuading the Khoi to discard the freedom of their herding life for the toil of ploughing furrows for him. Much to his annoyance, the bosses back in Holland had forbidden van Riebeeck from enslaving the locals, and refused his request for slaves from elsewhere in the Company's empire.

Creeping colonization

Everyone at the Cape at this time was under stringent contract to the VOC, which effectively had total control over their activities and movements – a form of indentureship. But a number of Dutch men were released from their contracts in 1657 to farm as **free burghers** on land granted by the Company; they were now at liberty to pursue their own economic activities, although the VOC still controlled the market and set prices for produce. This annexation of the lands around the mud fort, which preceded the construction of the more solid Castle of Good Hope, ultimately led to the inexorable process of **colonization**.

The only snag was the land granted didn't belong to the Company in the first place, and the move sparked the first of a series of **Khoikhoi–Dutch wars**. Although the first campaign ended in stalemate, the Khoikhoi were ultimately no match for the Dutch, who had the tactical mobility of horses and the superior killing power of firearms. Campaigns continued through the 1660s and 1670s and proved rather profitable for Dutch raiders, who on one outing in 1674 rounded up eight hundred Khoi cattle and four thousand sheep.

Meanwhile, in 1658, van Riebeeck had managed successfully to purloin a shipload of **slaves** from West Africa, whetting an insatiable appetite for this form of labour. The VOC itself became the biggest slave owner at the Cape and continued importing slaves, mostly from the East Indies, at such a pace that by 1711 there were more slaves than burghers in the colony. With the help of this ready workforce, the embryonic Cape colony expanded outwards and trampled the peninsula's Khoikhoi, who by 1713 had lost everything. Most of their livestock (nearly 50,000 animals) and most of their land west of the Hottentots Holland Mountains had been gobbled up by the VOC. Dispossession, and diseases like smallpox, previously unknown in South Africa, decimated their numbers and shattered their social system. By the middle of the eighteenth century, those who remained had been reduced to a condition of miserable servitude to the colonists.

Kaapstad

During the early eighteenth century, Western Cape Khoikhoi society disintegrated and **slavery** became the economic backbone of the colony, which was now a rude colonial village of low, whitewashed, flat-roofed houses. Passing through in 1710, Jan van Riebeeck's granddaughter, Johanna, commented contemptuously that the settlement was "a miserable place. There is nothing pretty along the shoreline, the Castle is peculiar, the houses resemble prisons" and "one sees here peculiar people who live in strange ways".

Dutch global influence began to wane in the early 1700s, but by mid-century the Cape settlement had developed an independent identity and some little prosperity based on its pivotal position on the European–Far East trade route. People now began referring to it as "**Kaapstad**" (Cape Town) rather than "the Cape settlement" and by 1750 it had a thousand buildings, with over 3000 **diverse inhabitants**. Some of these were indigenous Khoikhoi people, but the largest number were VOC employees, dominated by an elite of high-ranking Dutch-born officials. The lower rungs were filled by the poor from all over Europe, including Scandinavia, Germany, France, England, Scotland and Russia, while slaves came from East Africa, Madagascar, India and Indonesia. There was also a transient population from passing ships, which by the second half of the century were largely manned by Indian, Javanese and Chinese crews. If nothing else, the constant **maritime traffic** injected some life into this intellectual doldrum, which couldn't boast a single printing press let alone a newspaper. Entertainment consisted mainly of carousing, whoring and gambling.

Britain takes the Cape

By the 1790s the VOC was virtually bankrupt, and its control over the restive Cape burghers had become decidedly tenuous. As Dutch maritime influence declined, Britain and France were tussling for domination of the Indian Ocean. The outbreak of the French Revolution in 1789 and the establishment of a Francophile republic in the Netherlands a few years later made the **British** distinctly jittery about their strategic access to Cape Town. In August 1795, Rear-Admiral George Keith Elphinstone was sent in haste with four British sloops of war to secure Cape Town; by mid-September the ragtag Dutch garrison had capitulated. The British occupation heralded a period of **free trade** in which exports from the Cape lifted off as tariffs were slashed, with the result that Cape wines, the largest Cape export, were meeting ten percent of British wine consumption by 1822. The tightly controlled and highly restrictive Dutch regime was replaced with a more tolerant government, which brought immediate **freedom of religion**, the abolition of the slave trade in 1808, and the **emancipation** of slaves in 1834.

Although British-born residents were a minority during the first half of the nineteenth century, their influence was huge, and Cape Town began to take on a British character through a process of cultural, economic and political dominance. **English** became the language of status and officialdom and, as the century progressed, Victorian values began to take root. By 1860 there were eight newspapers, six of them in English. A vibrant press fed a culture of **liberalism** which led Capetonians to stop British attempts to transport convicts to the Cape (see p.45) – the first time since the American Revolution that an outpost of empire had successfully defied Whitehall. This gave the colonists the confidence to demand **self-government** and, in 1854, males regardless of race who owned property worth £25 or more won the right to vote for a lower house of parliament, which was based in Cape Town. A significant development of the second half of the nineteenth century was the rapid growth of **communications**, both within Cape Town, but also into the interior, which reinforced the city's status as the principal centre of a Cape Colony that by now extended 1000km to the east. The road from Cape Town to Camps Bay across Kloof Nek was started in 1848, a telegraph line between Cape Town and Simon's Town was laid in 1860, but most significant of all was the introduction of steam. The first **railway line** from central Cape Town to Wynberg was completed in 1864, opening up the southern peninsula to the development of a **middle-class suburbia**.

From backwater to breakwater

The development of an urban infrastructure wasn't enough to lift Cape Town from its backwater provinciality – that required the discovery in 1867 of the world's largest deposit of **diamonds** around modern-day Kimberley. Coinciding with this, the city's breakwater was started and the **harbour** was completed just in time to accommodate the massive influx of fortune-hunters, immigrants and capital into Cape Town en route to the diggings. More significant still was the **discovery of gold** around Johannesburg in the Boer-controlled South African Republic in the 1880s, which gave Cape Town a new significance as the gateway to the world's richest mineral deposits.

From the 1870s, growing middle-class self-confidence was reflected in the erection of grand **Victorian frontages** in the city centre's shops, banks and offices. Echoing Victorian London, this prosperous public facade hid a growing world of poverty, inhabited by immigrants, Africans and coloureds who made up a cheap labour force. The degradation and vice that thrived in Cape Town's growing slums were disquieting to the Anglocentric middle class, which would have preferred Cape Town to be like a respectably homogenous Home Counties town, rather than a cultural melting pot.

As the twentieth century dawned, the authorities attempted to achieve a closer approximation to the white middle-class ideal by introducing laws to stem **immigration**, other than from Western Europe, while other statutes sought to protect "European traders" against competition from other ethnic groups. Racial segregation wasn't far behind, and an outbreak of bubonic plague in 1901 gave the town council an excuse to establish **Ndabeni**, Cape Town's first black location, near present-day Pinelands.

Industrialization and segregation

Apart from contributing to Cape Town's development as a trading port, the discovery of gold had more significant consequences for the city. By the end of the nineteenth century, a number of influential capitalists, among them **Cecil John Rhodes** (prime minister of the Cape from 1890 to 1897), were convinced that it would be a good idea to annex the two Boer republics to the north to create a unified South Africa under British influence. In 1899 Britain marched on the Boer Republics, in what was rashly described by Lord Kitchener as a "teatime war", but became known internationally as the **Anglo-Boer War**, which became Britain's most expensive campaign since the Napoleonic Wars. Eventually, three years later, the Anglo-Boer War ended with the Boers' surrender. After nearly a decade of discussions, the two Boer republics (the South African Republic and the Orange Free State) and two British colonies (the Cape and Natal) were federated in 1910 to become the **Union of South Africa**, Cape Town gaining a pivotal position as the **legislative capital** of the country.

Africans and coloureds, excluded from the cosy deal between Boers and Brits, had to find expression in the workplace, flexing their collective muscle on the docks in 1919, where they formed the mighty **Industrial and Commercial Union**, which boasted 200,000 members in its heyday. Cape Town began the process of becoming a modern industrial city and, with the building of the South African National Gallery, promoted itself as the urbane cultural capital of the country. Accelerated **industrialization** brought an influx of Africans from the rural areas and soon Ndabeni was overcrowded and overflowing. Alarmed that Africans were living close to the city centre in District Six and were also spilling out into the Cape Flats, the authorities passed the **Urban Areas Act**, which compelled Africans to live in locations and empowered the city council to expel jobless Africans – measures that preceded apartheid by 25 years. In 1927, the new location of **Langa** (which ironically means "sun") was opened next to the sewage works. Laid out along military lines, with barrack-style dormitories for the residents, it was surrounded by a security fence.

World War II

During the 1930s, Cape Town saw the growth of several fascist movements, the largest of which was the **Greyshirts**, whose favourite meeting place was the Koffiehuis (coffee house) next to the Groote Kerk in Adderley Street. Its members included Hendrik Verwoerd, a Dutch-born intellectual who became a fanatical Afrikaner Nationalist and

South African prime minister from 1958 to 1966. When **World War II** broke out there was a heated debate in parliament, which narrowly voted for South Africa to side with Britain against Germany. Members of all South African communities volunteered for service, the ANC arguing that their support should be linked to full citizenship for blacks. Afrikanderdom was deeply divided and **Nazi sympathizers**, among them John Vorster (Verwoerd's successor as prime minister), were jailed for actively attempting to sabotage the war effort. *Die Burger*, Cape Town's Afrikaans-language newspaper, backed Germany throughout the war.

The war brought hardship, particularly to those at the bottom of the heap, leading to an increased influx of Africans and poor white Afrikaners from the countryside to the cities. This changed the demography of the city of Cape Town, which lost its British colonial flavour and, for the first time in 150 years, had more black (mostly coloured) than white residents. To accommodate the burgeoning African population, Langa was extended and new townships were built during and after the war at **Nyanga** and **Guguletu**.

By the end of hostilities, Cape Town was a mixed bag of ad hoc official **segregation** in some areas of life while in others, such as on buses and trains, there was none. Coloureds in the Cape, in contrast with residents of the former Boer republics, still had the franchise provided they qualified on the grounds of property ownership.

Apartheid and defiance

In post-war South Africa, ideological tensions grew between those pushing for universal civil rights and those whites who feared black advancement. In 1948 the **National Party** came to power, promising its fearful white supporters that it would reverse the flow of Africans to the cities. In Cape Town it introduced a policy favouring coloureds for certain

APARTHEID AND DEFIANCE

unskilled and semi-skilled jobs, admitting only African men who already had work and forbidding the construction of family accommodation for Africans – hence turning the townships into predominantly male preserves.

During the 1950s, the National Party began putting in place a barrage of laws that would eventually constitute the structure of apartheid. Early **onslaughts on civil rights** included: the Coloured Voters Act, which stripped coloureds of the vote; the Bantu Authorities Act, which set up puppet authorities to govern Africans in rural reserves; the Population Registration Act, which classified every South African at birth as "white, Native or coloured" (see p.317); the Group Areas Act, which divided South Africa into ethnically distinct areas; and the Suppression of Communism Act, which made anti-apartheid opposition (communist or not) a criminal offence. Africans, now regarded as foreigners in their own country, had at all times to carry **passes** – one of the most hated symbols of apartheid.

The ANC responded in 1952 with the **Defiance Campaign**, whose aim was the granting of full civil rights to blacks. A radical young firebrand called **Nelson Mandela** was appointed "volunteer-in-chief" of the campaign, which had a crucial influence on his politics. Up to that point he had rejected political association with non-Africans, but the campaign's interracial solidarity brought him round to the conciliatory inclusive approach for which he is now famous. The government swooped on the homes of the ANC leadership, resulting in the detention and then banning of over a hundred ANC organizers. Unbowed, the ANC pressed ahead with the **Congress of the People**, held near Johannesburg in 1955. At a mass meeting of nearly three thousand delegates, four organizations – representing Africans, coloureds, whites and Indians – formed a strategic partnership.

From within the organization, a group of Africanists criticized co-operation with white activists, leading to the formation in 1958 of the breakaway **Pan Africanist Congress** (PAC) under the leadership of the charismatic **Robert Mangaliso Sobukwe** (see p.86). Langa township became a stronghold of the PAC, which organized peaceful **anti-pass demonstrations** in Gauteng and Cape Town on March 21, 1960. Over a period of days, work stayaways spread to all Cape Town's locations, achieving a temporary nationwide suspension of the pass laws – the calm before the storm. As the protests gathered strength, the government declared a **State of Emergency**, sent the army in to crush the strike, restored the pass laws and banned the ANC and PAC. Nelson Mandela continued to operate clandestinely for a year until he was finally captured in 1962, tried and imprisoned – together with most of the ANC leadership – on **Robben Island**.

Soweto and the Total Strategy

With resistance stifled, the state grew more powerful, and for the majority of white South Africans, business people and foreign investors, life seemed perfect. The panic caused by the 1960 uprising soon became a dim memory and confidence returned. For black South Africans, poverty deepened – a state of affairs enforced by apartheid legislation.

In 1966 the notorious **Group Areas Act** was used to uproot whole coloured communities from many areas including District Six and to move them to the soulless **Cape Flats** where, in the wake of social disintegration, gangsterism took root. It remains one of Cape Town's most pressing problems (see p.106). Compounding the injury, the National Party stripped away coloured representation on Cape Town city council in 1972.

The **Soweto Revolt** of June 16, 1976, signalled the start of a new wave of anti-apartheid protest, when black youths took to the streets against the imposition of Afrikaans as a medium of instruction in their schools. The protests spread to Cape Town where, as in Gauteng, the government responded ruthlessly by sending in armed police, who killed 128 and injured 400 Capetonians.

Despite naked violence, protest spread to all sections of the community. The government was forced to rely increasingly on armed police to impose order. Even this was unable to stop the mushrooming of new liberation organizations, many of them part of the broadly based **Black Consciousness movement**. As the unrest rumbled on into 1977, the government responded by banning all the new black organizations and detaining their leadership.

From the mid-1960s to the mid-1970s, prime minister **John Vorster** had relied on the police to maintain the apartheid status quo, but it became obvious that this wasn't working. In 1978 he was deposed in a palace coup by his minister of defence, **P.W. Botha**, who conceived a complex military style approach he called the **Total Strategy**. The strategy was a two-handed one of reforming peripheral aspects of apartheid, while deploying the armed forces in unprecedented acts of repression. In 1981, as resistance grew, Botha began contemplating change and moved Nelson Mandela and other ANC leaders from Robben Island to Pollsmoor Prison in mainland Cape Town. At the same time he poured ever-increasing numbers of troops into the townships.

In 1983, Botha concocted what he believed was a master plan for a so-called **New Constitution** in which coloureds and Indians would be granted the vote – in racially segregated chambers with no executive power. The only constructive outcome of this project was the extension of the Houses of Parliament to their current size.

Apartheid suffers a stroke

As President Botha was punting his ramshackle scheme in

1983, 15,000 anti-apartheid delegates met at Mitchell's Plain on the Cape Flats, to form the **United Democratic Front (UDF)**, the largest opposition gathering in South Africa since the Congress of the People in 1955. The UDF became a proxy for the banned ANC, and two years of strikes, boycotts and protest followed. As the government resorted to increasingly extreme measures, internal resistance grew and the international community turned up the heat on the apartheid regime. The Commonwealth passed a resolution condemning apartheid, the US and Australia severed air links, Congress passed disinvestment legislation and finally, in 1985, the Chase Manhattan Bank called in its massive loan to South Africa.

Botha declared his umpteenth **state of emergency** and unleashed a last-ditch storm of tyranny. There were bannings, mass arrests, detentions, treason trials, torture, as well as assassinations of UDF leaders by sinister hit squads. At the beginning of 1989, **Mandela** wrote to Botha from prison describing his fear of a polarized South Africa and calling for negotiations. An intransigent character, Botha found himself paralyzed by his inability to reconcile the need for radical change with his fear of a right-wing backlash. When he suffered a stroke later that year, his party colleagues moved swiftly to oust him and replaced him with **F.W. De Klerk**.

Faced with the worst crisis in South Africa's history, President De Klerk realised that repression had failed. Even South Africa's friends were losing patience, and in September 1989 US President George Bush told De Klerk that if Mandela wasn't released within six months he would extend US sanctions. Five months later, De Klerk announced the unbanning of the ANC, PAC, the Communist Party and 33 other organizations, as well as the release of Mandela.

On February 11, 1990, Cape Town's history took a neat

twist when, just hours after being released from prison, **Nelson Mandela** made his first public speech from the balcony of City Hall to a jubilant crowd spilling across the Grand Parade, the very site of the first Dutch fort.

Democracy

Four protracted years of negotiations followed, leading eventually to South Africa's current constitution. Following the country's first-ever democratic elections in 1994, Mandela became South Africa's first democratically elected president. One of the anomalies of the 1994 election was that while the most of South Africa delivered an **ANC landslide**, the Western Cape, supposedly the most liberal region of the country, returned the **National Party** as its provincial government. This indicated that politics in South Africa were not divided along racial lines as many had assumed; the majority of coloureds had voted for the very party that had once stripped them of the vote, regarding it with less suspicion than the ANC.

During the ANC's first term, affirmative action policies and a racial shift in the economy led to the rise of a **black middle class**, but even so it represents a tiny fraction of the African and coloured population, and many people feel that transformation hasn't gone far enough. Despite over six years of non-racial democracy, Cape Town largely remains a divided city, with whites and a few middle-class blacks enjoying a leafy existence in the suburbs along the two coasts and the slopes of Table Mountain, while most blacks live in deprived townships. On the **Cape Flats**, some progress has been made in bringing electricity to the shanty towns, but the shacks are still there – and spreading. Despite white fears about **crime**, it is still blacks and coloureds who are overwhelmingly and disproportionately the victims of violence, much of it gang-related.

The language of colour

It's very striking just how un-African Cape Town looks – and sounds. The dominant language of the city is **Afrikaans** (a close relative of Dutch), the only "European" language to evolve outside Europe. Although English is universally spoken and understood, Afrikaans is the mother tongue of a large proportion of the city's **coloured** residents, as well as a good number of whites. The term "coloured" is fraught with confusion, but in South Africa doesn't have the connotations and meaning it does in Britain and the US. It refers to South Africans of mixed race, as opposed to indigenous Africans or whites of European ancestry. This comes as a surprise to most visitors, who assume that it's all black and white in South Africa, when in fact issues of ethnicity and language are extremely complex.

Slavery and the coloureds

Most brown-skinned people in Cape Town (over fifty percent of the population), and many others throughout the country, are coloureds, with origins in the **slave society** of the seventeenth to early nineteenth centuries. Halfway between East and West, Cape Town drew its population from Africa, Asia and Europe, and traces of all three continents are in the genes, language, culture, religion and cuisine of South Africa's coloured population.

Because Cape slave society was predominantly domestic (distinct from the plantation slavery of the Americas), there was always close contact between masters and slaves. Proximity and uneven power relations made sex between masters and female slaves common, and the offspring of these unions were usually themselves slaves – the first coloureds. Proximity also meant a huge degree of convergence between owners' and slaves' culture, one result of which was the Creolized version of Dutch that became Afrikaans.

Afrikaans and apartheid

In the late nineteenth century, Afrikaans-speaking whites, fighting for an identity, sought to create a "racially pure" culture by driving a wedge between themselves and coloured Afrikaans-speakers. They reinvented Afrikaans as a "white man's language", eradicating the supposed stigma of its coloured ties by substituting Dutch words for those with Asian or African roots. In 1925, the white dialect of Afrikaans became an official language alongside English, and the dialects spoken by coloureds were treated as comical deviations from correct usage.

For Afrikaner nationalists this wasn't enough, and after the introduction of apartheid in 1948, they attempted to codify perceived racial differences. Under the **Population Registration Act**, all South Africans were classified as white, coloured or Bantu (the apartheid term for Africans). The underlying assumption was that these distinctions were based on objective criteria. For apartheid it seemed fairly clear who was "Bantu" and who was white, but the coloureds posed particular problems. Firstly, they weren't homogenous so, to accommodate this, the **Coloured Proclamation Act** of 1959 defined eight categories of coloured: Cape Coloured; Malay (Muslim); Griqua; Chinese; Indian; Other Indian; Other Asiatic; and Other Coloured. For reasons of expediency related to trade, Japanese people were defined as "honorary white".

The second difficulty surrounding coloureds was the fact that their appearance spans the entire range, from those who are indistinguishable from whites to those who look like Africans. A number of coloureds managed successfully to reinvent themselves as whites, and apartheid legislation made provision for the racial reclassification of individuals. Between 1983 and 1990, nearly five thousand "Cape Coloureds" were reclassified as "White" and over two thousand Africans were reclassified as "Cape Coloured". Notorious tests were employed – one, for example, where a pencil would be placed in a person's hair and twirled; if the hair sprang back they would be regarded as coloured, but if it stayed twirled they were white.

This wasn't simply a matter of semantics, it was fundamental to what kind of life you could have. There are numerous cases of families in which one sibling was classified coloured, while another was termed white and then could live in salubrious white areas, enjoy good employment opportunities (a lot of jobs were closed to coloureds), and have the right to send their children to better schools and universities. Many coloured professionals, on the other hand, were evicted from houses they owned in comfortable suburbs such as Claremont, which were overnight declared white.

One city, many cultures

With apartheid ended, residential boundaries are shifting and so is the thinking on ethnic terminology. Some people now reject the term coloured because of its apartheid associations, and refuse any racial definitions, while others are proudly reclaiming the term and acknowledging their distinct culture, with its slave roots.

Formal attempts have been made to foster cultural interaction and to forge a more integrated city. In 1999, the *Cape Times* launched a highly popular "**One City, Many Cultures**" campaign, which featured regular articles highlighting the richness of Cape Town's different ethnic and religious groups. To the same end, the city's local government has been restructured, and its 69 racially segregated bodies rationalized into six councils, deliberately linking the wealthy and disadvantaged and bringing black, white and coloured areas under common administrations for the first time ever.

Architecture and urban planning

Cape Dutch style, which developed in the countryside from the seventeenth to the early nineteenth century, is so distinctively rooted in the Winelands that it has become an integral element of the landscape: the dazzling limewashed walls look stunning in the midst of glowing green vineyards, while the thatched roofs and elaborate curvilinear gables seem to echo the undulations of the surrounding mountains. The style was embraced in the twentieth century as part of white South African identity, and elements appear on the facades of many **suburban homes**.

A less attractive twentieth-century development was the attempt to replan Cape Town as a segregated city, one result being the growth of a new architectural vernacular of tin and cardboard shanties that began to appear on the edges of the Cape Town under apartheid, and have proliferated rapidly in the post-apartheid era.

The Cape Dutch vernacular (1652–1850)

The **Posthuys** (1673) in Main Road, Muizenberg, is thought to be the oldest colonial dwelling in South Africa. A rude thatch-roofed cottage consisting of a single rectangular space, its tiny windows served as a defence against feared attacks by the Khoisan, as well as protection from the fierce winds that lash the peninsula. One of the few surviving examples of the so-called "**longhouse**", it represents the primitive language from which a rich vernacular **Cape Dutch** architecture evolved during the first two hundred years of colonial settlement.

Although there were important developments in the internal organization of Cape houses during this period, their most obvious element is the **gable**. End-gables were a common device of medieval northern European and particularly Dutch buildings, but central gables set into the long

Cape Dutch architects

Many of the Cape's nineteenth- and twentieth-century buildings were anonymously designed and built but between 1750 and 1850 – the golden century of Cape architecture – three men were associated with some of the most highly regarded buildings in the colony. So elevated is their status that numerous apocryphal attributions exist, claiming their hand in various projects.

Anton Anreith (1754–1822) was born near Freiburg in Germany, where it is believed he was apprenticed to a Rococo master-sculptor. He joined the Dutch East India Company's army as a private in 1776, but quickly gained employment as a carpenter, later earning the commission to reconstruct the facade of the Lutheran Church in Strand Street. In 1786, he became the VOC's master-sculptor and was probably responsible for the Kat balcony at the castle.

Hermann Schutte (1761–1844), born in Bremen, was apprenticed to an architect in Germany for seven years. After joining the Dutch East India Company as a stone mason, he came to the Cape in 1790 and worked on the Robben Island quarries, where he lost an eye and a hand in a blasting accident. He was discharged from the VOC and became a private building contractor, benefiting from numerous commissions from the influential Louis Michel Thibault. Schutte designed the Groote Kerk in Adderley Street and is also believed to have been responsible for the Green Point Lighthouse, the first lighthouse erected along the South African coast.

Louis Michel Thibault (1750–1815), a highly trained architect, was born near Amiens in France. Having held the honour of premier student at l'Academie Royale d'Architecture in Paris, he joined the Dutch East India Company as Lieutenant of Engineers, effectively making him the colony's principle military engineer and government architect, in which capacity he

Continues overleaf

Cape Dutch architects (continued)

side of roofs were more exceptional. They were to become
the quintessential feature of the Cape Dutch style. Large
numbers of buildings in central Cape Town had gables during the eighteenth century, but they had disappeared from
the urban streetscape by the 1830s to be replaced by buildings with flush facades and flat roofs.

Arson appears to be a major reason for these developments. There was a succession of town fires believed to
have been started by slaves, including one that razed
Stellenbosch in 1710 and Cape Town's **great fires** of 1736
and 1798; this led to a series of measures that shaped the
layout of central Cape Town as well as the design of its
houses. Flat roofs, clad in fireproof materials, became compulsory on all VOC buildings, as exemplified by the **Town
House** (1755) off Greenmarket Square. After the 1798
conflagration, alarmed officials studied reports from
London's Great Fire of 1666 and introduced legislation
based on lessons learned from there. To retard the spread of
flames, narrow alleys were provided between houses, there
was a total ban on thatched roofs, and any protrusions on
building exteriors – including shutters – were banned. This
led to the flush facades and internal shutters that typify early
nineteenth-century Cape townhouses. With the disappear-
ance of pitched roofs, the urban gable withered away,
surviving symbolically in some instances as minimal roof
decoration, one example being the **Bo-Kaap Museum**

(1763–1768) in Wale Street, which sports a wavy parapet.

In an inverse evolution, **rural homesteads** developed from the plain longhouse to become increasingly elaborate over time. As landowners became more wealthy, the size of homesteads grew and the house plan became more complex. The spread of fire from one building to another wasn't a major consideration in the countryside, nor were VOC building regulations. Consequently the pitched roof survived here, and with it gables, which became the hallmark of country manors. Gables were an important element of the facade, positioned above the front door to provide a window that would let light into the loft. Because they were just above the front door, they could also provide protection for the entrance against burning thatch. From these functional origins, gables evolved into important symbols of wealth, with landowners vying to erect the biggest, most elaborate and most fashionable examples.

The British century (1800–1900)

The Cape Town the British occupied at the turn of the nineteenth century was a tightly gridded urban space reflecting the Dutch obsession with control. As the century progressed, Britain's growing global dominance and the development of an indigenous middle class became increasingly associated with a **laissez-faire** philosophy. By the late nineteenth century, this had contributed to Cape Town's rapid and unruly expansion.

Under the governorship of **Lord Charles Somerset** (1814–1826), an official process of Anglicization included the enforcement of English as the sole language in the courts, but as important was his private obsession with architecture, which saw the demolition of the two Dutch wings of **Tuynhuys** in Government Avenue. Imposing contemporary English taste, Somerset reinvented the entire garden frontage with a **Colonial Regency** facade, characterized by a verandah sheltering under an elegantly curving canopy, supported on slender iron columns.

During the second half of **Queen Victoria**'s reign, British influence made its greatest and most lasting impact on the shape and appearance of Cape Town. After the 1870s, as the city expanded on an unprecedented scale, the whole gamut of Victorian building types was erected across the peninsula, from town halls, post offices and dwellings to government buildings, shops and banks. In the city centre, the **Standard Bank** (1880) in Adderley Street, a hefty masonry structure with a central dome topped by a jingoistic statue of Britannia, expressed the pre-eminence of Empire and the solidity of capital, while the **Houses of Parliament** (1884) in Government Avenue were the ultimate statement of Cape Town's status as a colonial centre, using the language of a pedimented portico supported on a series of three-storey Corinthian columns – elements drawn from Imperial Roman architecture. Less monumental but no less typically Victorian was the transformation of **Long Street** from a thoroughfare dominated by plain flat-roofed one- and two-storey Georgian dwellings to a street of elaborately articulated roofscapes and intricately textured **wrought-iron** balconies.

In the 1880s and 1890s, Cape Town experienced an explosion of **speculative building**. While the town houses of Observatory, Woodstock, Sea Point and Green Point have a uniquely local flavour, they are still recognizably Victorian, with local adaptations that include verandahs and balconies, edged with intricate ironwork to shelter their facades from the elements.

Imperial architecture and identity (1892–1910)

The process of defining Cape Town's architectural identity as British Imperial but still distinctly African reached its climax at the turn of the century. Closely associated with the figure of **Cecil John Rhodes**, the megalomaniac diamond magnate who became prime minister of the Cape in 1890, this architecture projected a feudal vision of a British landed gentry in Africa, lording over the landscape from their stately homes. Rhodes, as a director of the British South Africa Company, had overseen the privatized colonization of Southern and Northern Rhodesia (now Zimbabwe and Zambia), and in his personal capacity owned vast tracts of land in the Rhodesias as well as in Cape Town.

In the Mother City, he is connected with numerous architectural projects and monuments. He commissioned **Herbert Baker**, a young English architect schooled in the **British Arts and Crafts Movement**, to build **Groote Schuur** (1898), his home on Klipper Road in Rondebosch. Baker used recognizable Cape elements such as gables, curving multipaned windows and steeply pitched roofs, while other aspects relate to quite different traditions, for example the barley-sugar chimneys suggest Tudor prototypes and the gargoyles are replicas of totem bird figures pillaged by Rhodes from Great Zimbabwe.

The style synthesized by Baker became known as the **Cape Dutch Revival**, and was again used by the architect at **Rust en Vrede** (1902), Rhodes' seaside residence in Main Road, Muizenberg. The Cape Dutch Revival has become well established in South African architectural parlance: it became popular in the twentieth century to use Cape Dutch elements, particularly gables in suburban houses, no matter how inappropriate their scale or context.

Monuments from the same period are also concerned with European domination of Africa. The **Van Riebeeck Statue** (1899), commissioned by Rhodes, stands in a prominent position at the bottom of Adderley Street, brazenly proclaiming colonial conquest. Rhodes himself, after his death in 1902, became a symbol of Britain's imperial destiny in Africa and the **Cecil John Rhodes statue**

(1908) in the Gardens has the entrepreneur pointing north with the inscription: "Your hinterland is there", a reference to his dream of an Africa from Cape to Cairo under the Union Jack.

Although that particular dream was never realized, Cape Town had established itself as a recognizably British city by the start of the twentieth century. Its coming of age was embodied in the **City Hall** (1905) in Darling Street – the first building that represented the city as a whole, as opposed to the municipal halls that existed in each suburb.

Modernism and modernization (1910–1948)

The search for a new kind of architectural identity was prompted by the unification of South Africa in 1910, which brought together the white communities (predominantly Afrikaners and those of British extraction) while excluding blacks. During the 1920s and 1930s, architects briefly flirted with the **Art Deco** style, which was used for a number of office blocks in the city centre such as **Shell House** (1929), now the *Holiday Inn*, on Greenmarket Square.

But issues of design were frivolities compared with Cape Town's real planning crisis. This centred around what to do with the rapidly growing urban population, the accompanying **slums** and the lingering desire of many whites for Cape Town to be a modern European-style city.

Under the guise of slum clearance, Africans were compelled in the 1920s to live in segregated **locations**, which owed more in concept to the Anglo-Boer War **concentration camps** than they did to the Modern Movement. **Langa** (1927), for instance, used industrial-style organization to create a rationally gridded area, divided into quarters by a pair of wide crossroads that permitted easy access to troops. African locations were sited adjacent to factories, leaving little doubt that their real purpose was to serve the needs of industry. In contrast, whites were served up

American-style suburbs, such as **Pinelands** (1923), which aimed to create a leafy environment close to the city centre. Spaciously laid out, it consisted of detached houses set in large gardens. Although coloureds didn't do quite so well, they usually fared better than Africans; after the removals of the 1960s and 1970s better-off families were accommodated in free-standing houses such as the ones you pass as you drive south to Muizenberg on the M4, through areas like Heathfield. However, closer to the coast alongside the M5, the dispiriting and decaying ranks of low-rise tenements in the ironically unfragrant suburb of Lavender Hill are far more typical of Cape Flats mass housing.

Pressures on housing were paralleled by pressures on Cape Town's harbour, with the **Victoria and Alfred basins** unable to cope with increased shipping during the first half of the twentieth century. Just before World War II, work was begun on the **Duncan Dock** (1938–1943), which literally transformed Cape Town's **Foreshore** – 2km of land north of the Castle of Good Hope were reclaimed from the sea. The huge empty space between the city centre and the docks opened up a golden opportunity to define physically the role of Cape Town as a busy international port, the "**gateway to Africa**". The French architect E.E. Beaudouin was commissioned for the job and drew up plans in 1947 for an area of parks and grand boulevards, with an axis leading directly from the harbour up to the Gardens and the Houses of Parliament. Implementation of the plan took place under the National Party, which came to power in 1948 but, unfortunately, the resulting development is monumental and dehumanizing.

Grand apartheid, grand plans (1948–1994)

The government's "**grand apartheid**" scheme literally entailed redrawing the map of South Africa. While implementing unprecedented levels of ethnic segregation, the regime attempted to gain international acceptance through the construction of what appeared to be a modern and efficient capitalist country. At the Foreshore, a landscape of teeming roads and vast car parks was created, desolate spaces being punctuated by bland glass, concrete towers and monumental buildings. Among them was the hugely expensive government-financed **Nico Malan Theatre** (1971), named after a local National Party administrator. The docks were enclosed by a security fence, denying free flow between it and the city, and a pair of flyover freeways erected in the 1950s and 1970s cast a gloomy shadow over it all.

Freeways were part of the modernization of Cape Town, providing rapid access to the heart of the city, but they could also – as in the case of the **M5** – be used as a concrete instrument of apartheid. A potent physical barrier, the motorway roughly marked Cape Town's racial divide, with the whites-only southern suburbs to the west, and the Cape Flats, to which coloureds and Africans were removed during the 1960s and 1970s, to the east. Apartheid's contribution to low-cost housing was the so-called "**matchbox house**", a bland facebrick cube with basic cooking and sleeping facilities and no internal running water. Lacking parks, public buildings and places of entertainment, the townships they occupied were featureless and Orwellian.

The townships reflected the fact that under apartheid Africans were regarded as foreign guest workers in Cape Town, their "real" place of residence being in one of the supposedly independent Bantustans, 1000km or more from the city. But, ultimately, laws proved unable to withstand the demographic pressures that were bringing people from impoverished rural areas throughout the country. In Cape Town, **Crossroads** squatter camp, adjacent to the airport along the N2, was first settled by "illegal" African families in the 1970s. By the mid-1980s it was estimated that between forty and eighty thousand people were living on this 2.5 square kilometre plot in corrugated-iron and timber shacks. Despite waves of pass arrests and brutal police raids in which shanties were flattened and their contents torched, the squatter population continued to grow. Realizing that it faced an immovable force, the government attempted to control the urbanization process, and in 1983 announced the creation of a new mega-township called **Khayelitsha**, close to Crossroads; the following year it scrapped the faltering influx-control laws. Far from eradicating Crossroads, which was its intention, Khayelitsha existed beside it, dwarfing its predecessor with a population that swelled to around half a million by the 1990s; fourteen percent of the population lived in brick houses and the remainder in shacks, making corrugated iron, timber and plastic the evolving vernacular style of the Cape Peninsula.

As the squatter camps lining the road from the airport to the city became Cape Town's real "gateway to Africa", the authorities revived the idea of a public face for the city that would link the central business district to the harbour. In 1988, work began on revitalizing the derelict Victoria and Alfred basins, which were turned into the **V&A Waterfront**, a development that sought to bring about a kind of Victorian Disneyland, incorporating the working harbour. Authentic examples of Victorian heritage such as the **Clock Tower** (1883) stand alongside modern buildings that pay homage to Victorian styles. The **Victoria Wharf** draws its inspiration from innovative nineteenth-century steel-ribbed structures, but here amounts to an oversized shell providing cover for a massive shopping mall. The Waterfront Development drew fire from the ANC, which saw it as a sanitized preserve, cut off from the realities of Cape Town life. Nevertheless, the development has been hugely successful and pulls in around twenty million local and foreign visitors each year.

Books

For a country with a relatively small reading public, South Africa generates a huge number of **books**, particularly politics and history titles. Some of the South African published books may be tricky to find outside the country, but almost all those listed below are in print and should be available from the larger bookshops listed on pp.198–199. Publishers of each book are given, where available, in the United Kingdom (UK), the United States (US) and South Africa (SA). University Press is abbreviated as UP.

Fiction

Andre Brink, *A Chain of Voices* (Vintage UK). Superbly evocative tale of Cape eighteenth-century life, exploring the impact of slavery on one farming family, right up to its dramatic and murderous end.

J.M. Coetzee, *Disgrace* (Vintage UK; Viking Penguin US). A subtle, strange novel set in a Cape Town university and on a remote Eastern Cape farm, where the lives of a literature professor and his farmer daughter are violently transformed. Bleak but totally engrossing, this won the Booker Prize in 1999. See opposite for more on Coetzee.

Rayda Jacobs, *The Slave Book* (Kwela SA). A carefully researched historical novel dealing with love and survival in a slave household in 1830s Cape Town, on the eve of the abolition of slavery.

Ashraf Jamal, *Love Themes For The Wilderness* (Kwela SA). The inhabitants of a bohemian subculture are lovingly observed in this funny and free-spirited novel set in mid-nineties Observatory.

Pamela Jooste, *Dance With A Poor Man's Daughter* (Black Swan UK). The fragile world of a young coloured girl during the early apartheid years is sensitively imagined in this hugely successful first novel.

J.M. Coetzee: Cape Town's most famous novelist

To read a **J.M. Coetzee** novel is to walk an emotional tightrope – at certain points you're exhilarated, at others overcome with a strange, brittle sadness. Throughout, you cannot but sense that you're under the guidance of a strong creative intellect and an exceptionally careful observer of human experience.

Coetzee's taut, measured style strikes some readers as cold and bloodless; he is relentlessly unsentimental and his plots tend to end on an unsettling note. But despite his reputation as a "difficult" writer, Coetzee never fails to be arresting, to involve us absolutely in the fates of his characters. And there is a deep undertow of compassion to his writing; in the words of Nadine Gordimer, J.M. Coetzee "goes to the nerve-centre of being".

Born in Cape Town in 1940, Coetzee trained as a linguist and computer scientist in South Africa and the US. In the early 1970s he began to write fiction. *Dusklands* and *In The Heart Of The Country*, his first two novels, were dense and often over-wrought dissections of settler psychology. But Coetzee's prose reached a soaring maturity with *Waiting For The Barbarians* (1980), in which an imaginary desert landscape is the setting for a chilling exploration of the dynamics of imperial power.

In 1983, *The Life and Times of Michael K* won the Booker Prize. *Michael K* follows the wanderings of a reclusive refugee across a future South Africa ravaged by civil war – moving from a flaming, Beirut-like Sea Point beachfront to a Great Karoo roamed by guerilla bands. The novel ends with a passage of extraordinary beauty and subtlety, and stands as a postmodern masterpiece that now bears ironic testimony to South Africa's actual future. After *Michael K* came the novels *Foe*, *Age of Iron* and *The Master of Petersburg*. Coetzee has

Continues overleaf

J.M. Coetzee: Cape Town's most famous novelist (continued)

also written an anthology of criticism, *White Writing*, and a moving childhood memoir, *Boyhood*.

When Coetzee won an unprecedented second Booker Prize for *Disgrace* in 1999, he became famous beyond literary circles for the first time. This has meant exasperation for soundbite-hungry media hounds, since Coetzee abhors publicity – he chose not to attend the Booker Prize award ceremony and is notoriously cagey in social interactions. Gossip has it that he is liable not to utter a single word at a dinner party, preferring instead to monitor proceedings with a steely, absorbing gaze.

Sindiwe Magona, *Mother to Mother* (Beacon US; David Philip SA). Magona adopts the narrative voice of the mother of the killer of Amy Biehl, an American student murdered in a Cape Town township in 1993. The novel is addressed to Biehl's mother, and is a trenchant and lyrical meditation on the traumas of the past.

Mike Nicol, *Horseman* (Vintage UK; Alfred Knopf US). A dark and surreal allegory that investigates contemporary South Africa in mythic terms. Nicol is one of the country's most inventive novelists.

Richard Rive, *Buckingham Palace, District Six* (David Philip SA). The unique urban culture of District Six is movingly remembered in this short novel about the life of a now-desolate street and its inhabitants.

Jann Turner, *Heartland* (Orion UK). A white farmer's daughter and a black labourer's son are childhood companions on a Boland fruit farm; a betrayal occurs, and years later the boy returns from political exile, ready to stake his claim to the land. A hefty and ambitious popular novel.

Guides and reference books

David Biggs, *The South African Plonk Buyer's Guide* (Ampersand Press SA). Updated annually, this pocket guide seeks out great wines that won't break the bank.

Duncan Butchart, *Wild About Cape Town* (Southern Books SA). Compact, well-illustrated pocket guide to common animals and plants of the Cape peninsula. Covers mountain, seashore and garden environments.

Richard Cowling and Dave Richardson, *Fynbos: South Africa's Unique Floral Kingdom* (Fernwood Press SA). Lavishly illustrated coffee-table book. A fascinating layman's portrait of the fynbos ecosystem.

Tony Jackman, *Cape On A Plate* (Guides for Africa SA). Snazzy and comprehensive annually updated pictorial guide to restaurants in the Cape Town area.

Trish Lane *Playing: More Than 101 Things To Do With Little People In The Cape* (International Motoring Productions SA). Not a goblin-spotting handbook, but a very handy compilation of kiddie activities and destinations.

Mike Lundy, *Easy Walks In The Cape Peninsula* (Struik SA). An invaluable, not-too-bulky book for casual walkers, offering plenty of possibilities for an afternoon's stroll.

Mike Lundy, *Weekend Trails In The Western Cape* (Struik SA). The best guide to outings in the Cape. Good maps, good advice, and notes on flora and fauna.

John Platter, *John Platter's South African Wine Guide* (The John Platter South African Wine Guide SA). One of the best-selling titles in South Africa – an annually updated pocket book that rates virtually every wine produced in the country. No aspiring connoisseur of Cape wines should venture forth without it.

History, politics and society

Vivian Bickford-Smith, Elizabeth van Heyningen and Nigel Worden *Cape Town: The Making Of A City* (David Philip SA). Richly illustrated and exhaustively researched, this book recounts the growth of Cape Town, from early Khoisan societies to the end of the nineteenth century.

Vivian Bickford-Smith, Elizabeth van Heyningen and Nigel Worden, *Cape Town In The Twentieth Century* (David Philip SA). A thorough and elegant account of modern Cape Town, which interweaves rich local history with international events.

Antjie Krog, *Country of My Skull* (Vintage UK; Random House US). An unflinching and harrowing account of the Truth and Reconciliation Commission's investigations. Krog, a respected radio journalist and poet, covered the entire process, and skilfully merges private identity with national catharsis.

Nigel Penn, *Rogues, Rebels and Runaways* (David Philip SA). A hugely entertaining collection of essays on deviant types in the eighteenth-century Cape. Tragi-comic and written in a wry, engaging style.

Robert C-H Shell, *Children of Bondage* (Wesleyan UP US; Witwatersrand UP SA). Definitive social history of Cape slavery in the eighteenth century – a compelling academic text that is accessible to the lay reader.

Allister Sparks, *The Mind of South Africa* (Random House US). An authoritative journalist and historian traces the rise and fall of the apartheid state; a lively, economical and serious work.

Desmond Tutu, *No Future Without Forgiveness* (Rider UK; Doubleday US; Random House SA). Tutu's gracious and honest assessment of the Truth Commission he guided. An important testimony from one of the country's most influential thinkers and leaders.

Frank Welsh, *A History of South Africa* (HarperCollins UK; Kodansha US; Jonathan Ball SA). Solid scholarship and a strong sense of overall narrative mark this recent publication as a much-needed addition to South African historiography.

Biography and autobiography

J.M. Coetzee, *Boyhood* (Minerva UK). A moving and courageous childhood memoir by South Africa's greatest novelist. Written in the third person, it depicts the thoughts of a young boy with profound attentiveness.

Adrian Hadland and Jovial Rantao, *The Life And Times Of Thabo Mbeki* (Zebra SA). The definitive biography of an enigmatic and powerful man. Much lies ahead for South Africa's president; this book is a solid account of what went before.

Nelson Mandela, *Long Walk To Freedom* (Abacus UK; Little Brown US). Superb best-selling autobiography of the former president and national icon, which is wonderfully evocative of his early years and intensely moving about his long years in prison. A little too diplomatic, perhaps, on his love life and on the inside story behind the negotiated settlement that spelt the end of apartheid.

Art

Marion Arnold, *Women and Art in South Africa* (David Philip SA). Comprehensive, pioneering study of women artists from the early twentieth century to the present.

Sue Williamson and Ashraf Jamal, *Art in South Africa: The Future Present* (David Philip SA). Stylish and beautifully designed appraisal of contemporary South African art, profiling an enormous range of innovative artists.

Music

Despite the slow pace of the Cape Town **music** scene, which is a lot less lively that Jo'burg's, a steady stream of quality records have been produced, particularly by jazz artists (see p.211). A handful of adventurous independent recording studios for jazz, kwaito and hip hop music have sprung up in recent years, and the industry is expanding; see pp.210–220 for the lowdown on individual acts and live-music venues. Of the established labels, Melt 2000 is the most innovative and intelligent. All the titles listed here should be available at one of the music shops listed on p.199 or can be ordered through them.

Essential Cape Town sounds

Basil Coetzee, *Monwabisi*. Smoky, intensely energetic jazz record from the greatest of Cape Jazz saxophonists.

Dantai, *Operation Lahlela*. R'n'B-flavoured *kwaito* from one of Cape Town's up-and-coming dance acts.

Jimmy Dludlu, *Echoes From The Past*. Slick Capetonian jazz with some truly infectious licks and tunes.

Brenda Fassie, *Nomakanjani*. The tempestuous queen of township pop produces a string of ballsy post-kwaito tunes on this winning album.

Paul Hanmer, *Windows To Elsewhere*. A subtle, invigorating jazz album from a gifted pianist who extends the tradition of Abdullah Ibrahim.

Abdullah Ibrahim, *African Marketplace*. Pianist-composer Ibrahim's best album – a wistful, nostalgic, other-worldly journey.

Winston Mankunku, *Crossroads*. Sinuous, upbeat township jazz from the veteran Cape Town saxman.

Tim Parr, *Still Standing*. Simplicity, emotion and melodic power make for a beautiful rock-reggae record by one of South Africa's greatest songwriters.

Prophets Of Da City, *The Struggle Continues*. Unflinching political rhymes from one of the finest hip-hop outfits to emerge from the Cape Flats.

Springbok Nude Girls, *Surpass The Powers.* Brave anthemic rock from a charismatic band that merits international acclaim.

Essential South African sounds

Bayete, *Mmalo We*. Smooth, mellow, joyous African pop: Bayete are the Rolls-Royces of South African music.

Gloria Bosman, *Tranquillity*. A young and compelling jazz vocalist, Bosman juggles African and American styles with consummate ease. Paul Hanmer arranges and tickles the ivories.

Juluka, *Universal Men*. Seminal late-seventies album in which traditional Zulu folk music collides with Celtic-flavoured rock: the results are spine-tinglingly brilliant.

Ladysmith Black Mambazo, *In Harmony*. The evergreen maestros of *isicatamiya* fuse their rich voices to exhilarating effect.

Vusi Mahlasela, *Silang Mabele*. Known as "The Voice", Mahlasela is a singer-guitarist whose songs are timeless and affecting.

Pops Mohamed, *How Far Have We Come?* An exciting celebration of traditional African instruments: mbiras, koras, mouthbows and various percussion instruments are supplemented by bass and brass in this ethereal but funky album.

Moses Molelekwa, *Genes And Spirits*. Pianist-arranger Molelekwa's second album is a tour de force of progressive African jazz – mobile, imaginative and atmospheric.

Tananas, *Seed*. Enchanting instrumental grooves that fuse African, Oriental and Middle Eastern idioms.

Glossary

ablutions Communal washing facilities found at campsites

African Indigenous South African, who speaks a Bantu language – in Cape Town usually Xhosa (see also "black")

Afrikaner Literally "African": a white person who speaks Afrikaans

apartheid National Party's discriminatory policy of "racial segregation"

arvie Afternoon

baai Afrikaans suffix meaning "bay", used in place names such as Smitswinkelbaai

bakkie Light truck or van

bergie A vagrant in Cape Town, often living on the slopes of Table Mountain

biltong Sun-dried salted strips of meat, chewed as a snack

black Collective term for Africans, Indians and coloureds

boerewors Spicy lengths of sausage that are *de rigueur* at braais

Boland Southern part of the Western Cape

bottle store Off-licence or liquor store

braai Barbecue

bredie Vegetable and meat stew

BSAC British South Africa Company; Cecil Rhodes' private company, which colonized Zimbabwe and Zambia in the 1890s

Cape Doctor The southeaster that brings cool winds during the summer months

Cape Dutch Eighteenth- and nineteenth-century style of architecture, the buildings being whitewashed and featuring gables

Cape Dutch Revival Twentieth-century style based on Cape Dutch architecture

coloured Person of mixed race

dagga Marijuana

dassie Hyrax

Dominee Minister of the Dutch Reformed Church

dorp Country town or village

free burgher VOC employee released from his/her contract to farm independently on the Cape Peninsula and surrounding areas

frikkadel Fried onion and meat balls

fynbos Term used for vast range of fine-leafed species that predominate in the southern part of the Western Cape (see p.98)

gogga Creepy crawly or insect

Group Areas Act Now defunct law passed in 1950 that provided for the establishment of separate areas for each "racial group"

Hottentot Outmoded term for indigenous Khoisan herders encountered by the first settlers at the Cape

is it? Really?

jislaaik! Exclamation equivalent to geez or crikey

jol Party

just now In a while

Kaapstad Afrikaans name for Cape Town

Khoikhoi Self-styled name of South Africa's original herding inhabitants

kloof Ravine or gorge

koeksister Deep-fried plaited doughnut, dripping with syrup

kopje Hillock

kramat Shrine of a Muslim holy man

krans Sheer cliff face

lekker Nice

location Old-fashioned term for African township

Madiba Mandela's clan name, used affectionately

Malay Misnomer for Cape Muslims of Asian descent

mealie Maize

melktert Traditional Cape custard pie

mielie *see* mealie

MK Umkhonto we Sizwe (Spear of the Nation), the armed wing of the ANC, now demobbed or incorporated into the national army

Mother City Nickname for Cape Town

naartjie Tangerine or mandarin

nek Saddle between two mountains

Nkosi Sikilel 'i Afrika "God Bless Africa" the anthem of the ANC and now of South Africa

pawpaw Papaya

protea National flower of South Africa and part of the fynbos kingdom

robot Traffic light

rondavel Thatched cottage, circular in plan

rooibos tea Indigenous herbal tea

shebeen Unlicensed tavern

skelm Villain

skollie Gangster, usually on the Cape Flats

snoek Large fish that features in many traditional Cape recipes

sosatie Spicy skewered mince

stoep Verandah

Strandloper Name given by the Dutch settlers to the indigenous people they encountered at the Cape (literally: "beachcomber")

tackies Sneakers or plimsolls

township Urban areas set aside for Africans under apartheid

trekboer Itinerant Afrikaans farmer during the nineteenth century – particularly one leaving the Cape to escape British rule

tsotsi Villain
vlei Marsh
VOC Verenigde Oostindische Compagnie, the Dutch
   East India Company

Afrikaans street signs

derde third
doeane customs
drankwinkel liquor shop
eerste first
geen ingang no entry
gevaar danger
hoof main
hoog high
ingang entrance
inligting information
kantoor office
kerk church
kort short
links left
lughawe airport
mans men
mark market
ompad detour
pad road
padwerke voor road works ahead
perron station platform
polisie police
poskantoor post office
regs right
ry go
sentrum centre
singel crescent
stad city
stad sentrum city centre

stadig slow
stasie station
strand beach
swembad swimming pool
verbode prohibited
verkeer traffic
versigtig carefully
vierde fourth
vrouens women
vyfde fifth

INDEX

Rough Guides
on the Web

www.travel.roughguides.com

We keep getting bigger and better! The Rough Guide to Travel Online now covers more than 14,000 searchable locations. You're just a click away from access to the most in-depth travel content, weekly destination features, online reservation services, and an outspoken community of fellow travelers. Whether you're looking for ideas for your next holiday or you know exactly where you're going, join us online.

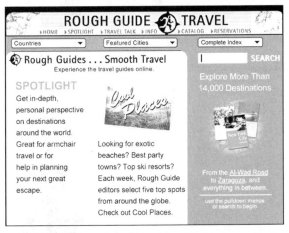

You can also find us on Yahoo!® Travel (http://travel.yahoo.com) and Microsoft Expedia® UK (http://www.expediauk.com).

ROUGH GUIDES: Travel

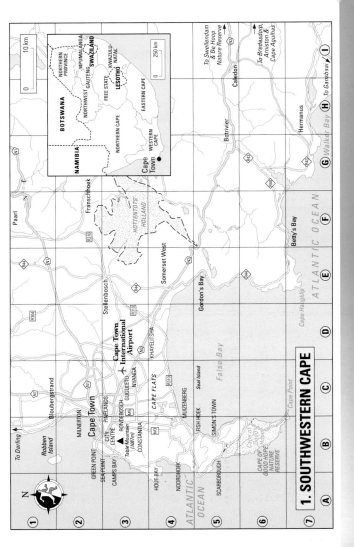

1. SOUTHWESTERN CAPE

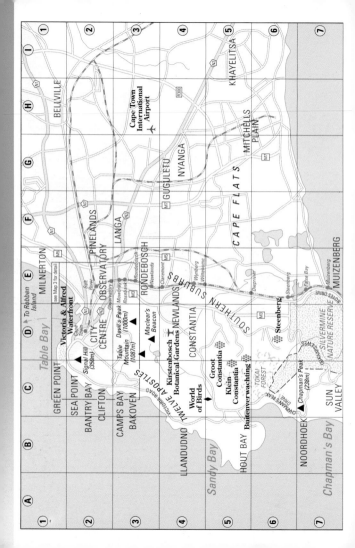

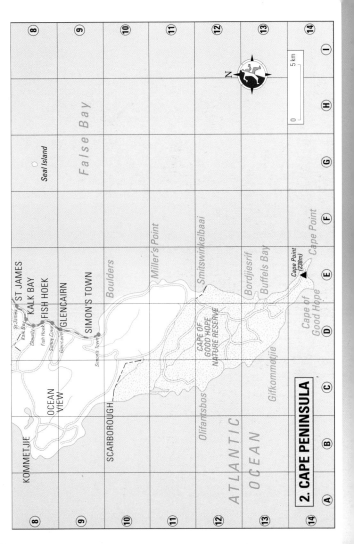

2. CAPE PENINSULA

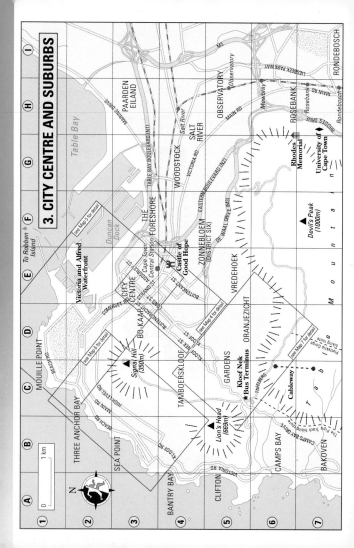

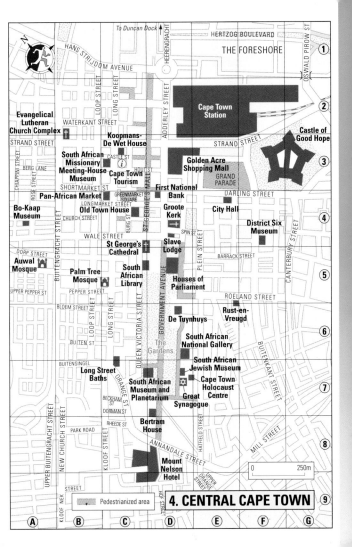

To Duncan Dock

HANS STRIJDOM AVENUE

HERTZOG BOULEVARD

THE FORESHORE

OSWALD PIROW ST

HEERENGRACHT

Cape Town Station

WATERKANT STREET

Evangelical Lutheran Church Complex ✝

STRAND STREET

Koopmans-De Wet House

STRAND STREET

Castle of Good Hope

CHIPPINI STREET

BERG LANE

ROSE STREET

South African Missionary Meeting-House Museum

CASTLE ST *i*

Cape Town Tourism

HOUTSI

Golden Acre Shopping Mall

GRAND PARADE

Pan-African Market

GREENMARKET SQUARE

First National Bank

DARLING STREET

Bo-Kaap Museum

Old Town House

LONGMARKET STREET

BURG ST

Groote Kerk

City Hall

CHURCH STREET

SPIN ST

District Six Museum

WALE STREET

St George's Cathedral ✝

Slave Lodge

BARRACK STREET

CANTERBURY STREET

DORP STREET

Auwal Mosque

South African Library

UPPER PEPPER ST

Palm Tree Mosque

South African Library

Houses of Parliament

PEPPER STREET

ROELAND STREET

BLOEM STREET

De Tuynhuys

Rust-en-Vreugd

BUITEN ST

The Gardens

South African National Gallery

BUITENKANT STREET

BUITENSINGEL

Long Street Baths

South African Jewish Museum

BECKHAM ST

South African Museum and Planetarium

Cape Town Holocaust Centre

DORMAN ST

Great Synagogue

PARK ROAD

RHEEDE ST

Bertram House

MILL STREET

UPPER BUITENGRACHT STREET

NEW CHURCH STREET

ANNANDALE STREET

HATFIELD STREET

Mount Nelson Hotel

0   250m

KLOOF NEK

KLOOF STREET

JOH ST

UPPER ORANGE STREET

Pedestrianized area

4. CENTRAL CAPE TOWN

A   **B**   **C**   **D**   **E**   **F**   **G**

①②③④⑤⑥⑦⑧⑨

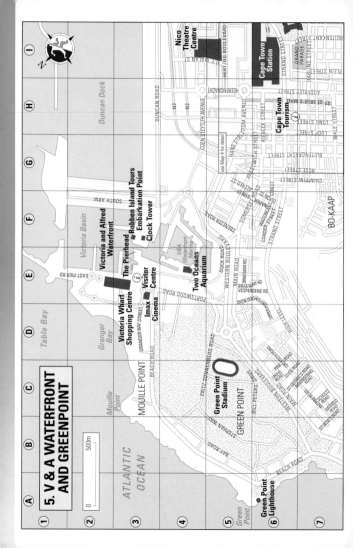

5. V & A WATERFRONT AND GREENPOINT

0   500m

ATLANTIC OCEAN

Table Bay

Granger Bay

Mouille Point

Green Point

Duncan Dock

Victoria Basin

SOUTH ARM

EAST PIER RD

Victoria and Alfred Waterfront

The Pierhead

Robben Island Tours
Embarkation Point

Clock Tower

Victoria Wharf Shopping Centre

Imax Cinema

Visitor Centre

Two Oceans Aquarium

V&A Waterfront Marina

MOUILLE POINT

BEACH ROAD

PORTSWOOD ROAD

DOCK ROAD

WESTERN BOULEVARD

DOCK ROAD

BRAEMAR RD

BRAEMAR RD

VESPERDENE RD

VESPERDENE RD

HIGH LEVEL ROAD

MAIN ROAD

EBENEZER ROAD

Green Point Stadium

GREEN POINT

FRITZ SONNENBERG ROAD

STEPHAN WAY

BAY ROAD

BILL PETERS

BEACH ROAD

WESTERN BOULEVARD

MAIN ROAD

Green Point Lighthouse

Nico Theatre Centre

HERTZOG BOULEVARD

MECHAU ST

RHINE RD

OSWALD PIROW ST

HERTZOG BOULEVARD

DUNCAN ROAD

N2

N2

OOEN STEYTLER AVENUE

HANS STRIJDOM AVENUE

Cape Town Station

Cape Town Tourism

ST GEORGE'S MALL

BUITENKANT STREET

GRAND PARADE

DARLING STREET

STRAND STREET

ADDERLEY STREET

PLEIN STREET

LONG STREET

LOOP STREET

WALE STREET

BURG STREET

RIEBEEK STREET

BREE STREET

WATERKANT STREET

LOADER STREET

STRAND STREET

SOMERSET ROAD

PRESTWICH STREET

CHIAPPINI STREET

ROSE STREET

BUITENGRACHT STREET

GREENMARKET

HOUT STREET

CASTLE STREET

SHORTMARKET STREET

LONGMARKET STREET

CHURCH STREET

DORP ST

LEEUWEN ST

BLOEM ST

PEPPER ST

KEEROM STREET

BO-KAAP

see Map 4 for detail

N

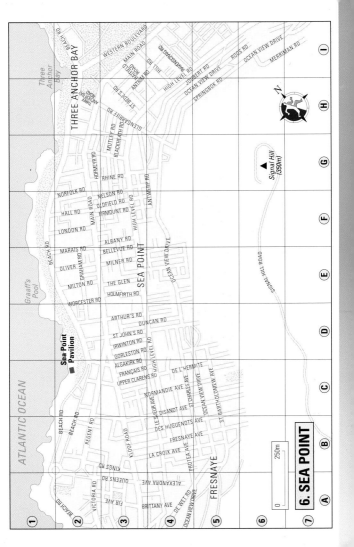

6. SEA POINT

0   250m

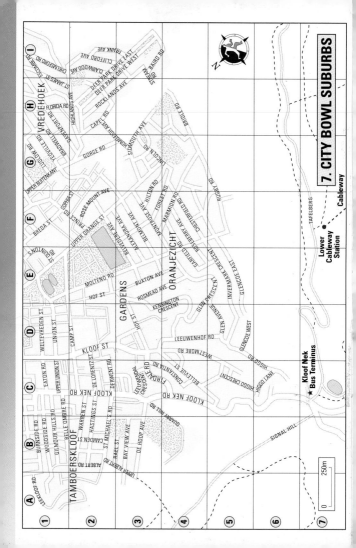

7. CITY BOWL SUBURBS

TAMBOERSKLOOF

VREDEHOEK

GARDENS

ORANJEZICHT

Lower Cableway Station

Cableway

TAFELBERG

★ Kloof Nek Bus Terminus

SIGNAL HILL

N

0   250m